New:

Nursing and the Art of Being Human

New:

Nursing and the Art of Being Human

By Tenley Force
RN, BSN

New: Nursing and the Art of Being Human

Written by Tenley Force

Copyright 2023

All rights reserved. No part of this publication may be reproduced or used in any manner without the written permission of the copyright owner or licensed representative.

ISBN 978-1-959111-0-0-9
hardcover

First Edition, 2023
Published by Polyverse Publications
www.polyversepublishing.com

Printed in the USA

*For my dad who taught me how to be kind
&
my mom who taught me how to be brave.*

Artist's Bio:

The cover art for *New* was done by artist Black Light King. BLK is a painter with a background in Graffiti Art and the Los Angeles underground music scene, where he began painting large, guerrilla style murals in the inner city.

His work taps into the psychedelic and surrealistic style of the 60s, combined with modern light and painting technology, merging neon fluorescent colors with the cultural symbolism of ancient cultures like Maya, Mexica, and Egypt. Inspired by Shamanism, nature, time, space, and music, he bends the viewers' experience through a technique he calls 'carving with light,' blending modern and ancient aesthetics to reveal his worlds.

His work communicates a message of rhythm, vibration, passion, love, and sound. But most of all it acts as an inspiration to others to create and attain 'symbolic freedom through personal expression.'

Black Light King was born and raised in Long Beach, and moved to greater LA in his late teens. He has been living and working in Downtown Los Angeles ever since.

His work can be found at:
WWW.BLACKLIGHTKING.COM

Intro Poem

I Am Your Nurse.

All of life can be summed up between the sounds of lub and dub
The beat of which turns the body into a masterpiece with the soul as its essence and musical hub
Meanwhile, the work of the heart can be measured on a six second strip
With definable waves and predictable dips
And the effort of the lungs can be equated to a rate of twelve to twenty
A symphony of breath so peaceful and constant that it goes unnoticed by many
But who will care for the sum of a soul?
Not just as categorical numbers, but as parts of a whole?
For heart beats and heart rhythms do not go without error
The mechanisms of the body will one day break down, leaving a wake of uncertain terror
For though it is beautiful, the body does fail
The calm tide of the lungs and steady rate of our breaths will not always prevail
Where once our bodies were host to strength and tenacity
We weaken as sickness brings pain with each inhale as our clear lungs fill with ground glass opacities
So who will catch you when your body falls?
For sickness and death will eventually be promised to all
When normal life is torn apart and ripped wide open
Who will step up and help mend what's been shattered and broken?
We will, the nurses, the strong and illustrious
Your nurses, who are intricately woven with a blend of parts both compassionate and industrious
Where others waiver, we run
We go towards not away, into the fire and the blaze of the sun
We are warriors on the front lines of life where death is the enemy and sickness its weapon
We fight armed with a countenance made of strength that nothing can threaten
Each day we put on our scopes and our scrubs, willingly stepping into environments that are uncertain

NEW

But we put on brave faces so that you won't see the truth behind the curtain
The truth of which is this, we can't save you all
But we will do our best to come alongside you so that in the shadow of the mountain of disease you won't feel alone or small
We will sacrifice for you, our sleep, our backs, our hearts, our minds
But we do it gladly so that you will find peace and comfort no matter what ailment holds your body in a bind
We will wear your tears, we will carry your weight
We will hold you tightly with loving embrace, no matter your story, no matter your fate
To the nurses out there, to you, the illustrious, thank you for your kindness and bright burning souls
Thank you for your wisdom and your willingness to step into the difficulties that come with each of your roles
To the patients out there, to you the weary and the downtrodden, thank you for letting us into the worst moments of your lives
For allowing us to walk with you in the most vulnerable situations that circumstance can contrive
For together we live, together we fight
Whether it be within the shadow of darkness or beneath the gleam of the light
So from the first cry of life to the last sigh of death, who will journey with you no matter what life pulls from the folds of its purse?
I will. Because I am your nurse.

For the nurses,
Nurses' Week 2019

Table of Contents:

Dedication: V
Artist's Bio: VII
Intro Poem: IX

1. Welcome to the Family 1
2. Small Love 19
3. Great Expectations 39
4. Pride, Humility, and Dancing   62
5. Waiting Under Weight...89
6. I Wish, If Only, My Fault 113
7. When It Is Actually Your Fault..140
8. The Lock and Key: Resilience and Joy............................168
9. One Day at a Time 193
10. The Burn of Burnout 221
11. The Moment You Know You're Going to Make............243
12. Epilogue:..278

Acknowledgments: 284
References: 286
Glossary: 296
Author's Bio: 297

Chapter One:
Welcome to the Family

If you were my patient and I were your nurse, I would say to you, "Hi. I'm Tenley. I'm going to be your nurse tonight." But since I am clearly not your nurse, and you are clearly not my patient, let's be a little less formal. We are in this together. No matter what new job or unknown situation you are facing, we are partners in being new. There are no rules, no having to be professional, no having to be strong, and no having to fake it till we make it—there is only honesty, real life, and true stories from here on out.

So, let's cut to the chase. If you are opening up your heart and mind to me by picking this book up and reading it, then it is only fair for me to be open and candid with you as well. That being said, allow me to let you in on three areas of my life that you should know about going into this so that there won't be any surprises along the way.

1. I never intended on being a nurse.

This might come as a shock, considering I wrote an entire book about being new predominantly through the lens of nursing. This book, which is largely inspired by nursing, is written by someone who somehow unwittingly fell into the profession. I wasn't playing with a toy stethoscope as a kid. I didn't grow up with any nurses in my family. Yet here we are. Maybe you feel like you don't trust me at this point. Who does this baby nurse think she is? That would be a fair question to ask, but I am a nurse all the same. I survived nursing school. I have earned my license. As I write this I have a little over a year of acute care bedside nursing experience under my belt. It's not much in the large scheme of things, but it still counts. It hasn't been easy for me either. But do you want to know something? It is because it wasn't an easy transition for me that I am equipped to write a book such as this.

2. This is a book that I never intended to write.

If I wasn't playing with toy stethoscopes as a kid, then what was I doing? In all actuality, I was writing. If you had asked me back then what I wanted to be when I grew up, I would have told you without hesitation that I wanted to be a writer, an author of adventure and epic fantasy. Never in my wildest imagination would I have thought that my first book would revolve around nursing.

Yes, I am just as confused as you are. You are reading a book that I never planned to write about a profession that I never planned on going into. One of my biggest motivators in making it through my first year as a nurse was writing this book. I let an old passion fuel a new passion. While writing may not be a passion typical of your traditional medical professional, it is mine. It is my passion to empower people who are new, who are in the middle of the unknown, and who are out of their minds with anxiety to reclaim their time, life, and personhood.

3. This is a way that I never imagined loving my neighbor.

Nurses are trained to be champions for our patients' holistic health. This picture of complete wellness touches not only on a patient's physical health but also on their emotional, mental, and spiritual health. Nurses must address each of these four areas in order to care for a patient as a whole being. Holistic care is what allows us to give—and preserve—each of our patient's dignity. Beyond that, holistic care is what gives us all dignity. The biggest lesson that I learned from my first year as a nurse had nothing to do with the

Chapter 1

profession of nursing itself. Instead, it had everything to do with what it means to be human.

I went into nursing thinking that I knew what it meant to love others, but in reality, it was nursing itself that truly taught me how to love. It taught me to love without judgment, to love amidst the difficult, and to love fiercely without wavering. There is an abundance of ways that one can demonstrate love as a nurse. But as a writer? I wasn't so sure what that would look like.

I never intended to pair writing and nursing together in order to perpetuate beauty in the world, but here we are. Nursing has given me a great capacity to love, while writing has given me a unique medium to channel that love through. As for whom I love? All you need to know about me and how I view others is that loving my neighbor is the proverbial hill I choose to die on. I don't care what my neighbor looks like, where my neighbor comes from, whom my neighbor loves, or what my neighbor believes in. I love my neighbor. Full stop. As far as I am concerned, you, reader, are my neighbor. I love you so much that I wrote this book for you, so that in your own journey of being new, you wouldn't feel so alone.

Maybe you are thinking to yourself, You don't know me. How could you love me? You're right. I don't know you, but chances are if you picked up this book, it's because you're new and you're hurting. If you are hurting, my heart goes out to you because not only do I remember the heaviness and hurt that being new brings, but I still feel it. So, hi again. With more context this time—I'm Tenley. I am honored to meet you, and I am humbled that you have decided to read my book.

Perhaps you are a new nurse reading this fresh out of school, equal parts excited and terrified of your first steps in the world as a Registered Nurse. Or, maybe you are not a new nurse at all and have no affiliation with the medical profession whatsoever but still find yourself wondering what it means to be a holistically healthy human being in the midst of new situations. Whoever you are and

NEW

whatever new circumstance you find yourself to be in: hello and welcome.

If you are, in fact, a new nurse, I want to take a moment to say welcome to the nursing family. That is what nursing is: a family made up of the toughest, most compassionate, most hardworking, most sleep-deprived people you'll ever meet. You're in the club now. Wherever you go, if you run into a nurse, you've found someone who gets it. Birthday party? Coffee shop? Out on a hike? There is nothing more comforting than the words, "You're a nurse? Me too." It is an extraordinary relief to find nurses who can walk with you in solidarity because no one else will understand all that you are going through.

As for all of you non-nurses, while you are not part of the nursing family per se, you are still part of the family of those who are new. This book is nursing-heavy, for that is my most acutely lived experience, but it is called *New* for a reason and not *New Nurse*. While my heart is largely for nurses, it is also for all of you out there who have ever cried yourself to sleep at night because you were so afraid to face the next day.

So, to all of you reading this, nurse or otherwise, in new jobs or new life circumstances, answer me this: have you ever felt alone? And I mean really alone? I have. Have you ever felt inadequate? And I mean deeply inadequate? I have. Have you ever had the weight of responsibility thrust so heavily upon you that you thought it might kill you? And I mean actually kill you? I have, and for a very bleak moment in time at the beginning of my nursing career, I thought that I was the only one who felt that way. That is, until I asked for help.

Author's Note: *To allow for better clarity and insight into the medical terminology and nursing language used throughout this narrative, a QR code is provided in the back of the book. This code links to a complete glossary of terms on my author website for your convenience.*

Chapter 1

It is now my mission to help all of you new people out there not to feel so alone as you embark on the vulnerable and polarizing experience that is being new. For when we feel incredibly alone, it is easy to let those other pieces—the inadequacy and the weight of it all—strip us of our humanity.

At the end of the day, this isn't a book about how to be a new nurse or new professional well—it is a book about how to be a holistically healthy human being in the midst of new situations. The truth is, we will all be new at some point or another. That's just part of life. It is how we respond to being new that shapes us as humans. So how can we best take care of ourselves in the midst of the unknown and remember our own humanity as we transition into new jobs, new roles, and new worlds? Well, truly, there is no one better to learn about life with than someone who brings life into the world and ushers it out. Who better to learn about life with than a nurse?

Because not everyone will have the opportunity to work within the healthcare setting, when a nurse shares their narrative, they give others a unique insight into areas of life that those not in the field would have never gotten to see otherwise. Even so, I am just one nurse. Beyond that, I am just one person. While I do believe in the power of one's own personal story, I also believe that what is even more powerful are our collective shared stories. No one person could possibly know everything about life, but when we can come together and share the aggregate of our experiences, we can get a little bit of a better handle on it.

In light of this idea, this book is told from three perspectives:

1. My own. This perspective is perhaps the rawest because it is based on my own experiences as a new nurse working nights on a respiratory floor. The entirety of this book was written during my first year as a nurse or very shortly thereafter. It comes from the heart of yours truly, a human who fully lived out the experience of being new: I was new and proud, new and terrified, and new and humbled, but I didn't let the grueling process of being new strip me of my humanity.

2. Other new nurses. Since I myself can only offer one perspective, I included the experiences of twenty-five other new nurses who, as I did, battled through the trial-by-fire that is the brutal first year of nursing. In doing so, I aimed to illustrate all the unfiltered emotions that come with being new in one of the most demanding professions in existence.

3. Experienced nurses.* One of the most important parts about being new is being able to learn from those who have gone before us. Therefore, I included the rich wisdom, resilience, and grace of twenty-five experienced nurses who each demonstrate what it takes to make it in the world of professional nursing. This perspective is the experienced nurse's calm, "You can do it," responding to the new nurse's frantic, "I can't do this!"

One of the nurses that I had the chance to interview surmised this very sentiment:

"Everyone should experience a little bit of what it is like to be a nurse and see what it means to witness life and death and to love and cry the way a nurse does."
—*AP, renal telemetry nurse, eight months of experience*

Author's Note: *All interview quotes are cited using the nurses' initials, the specialty they practiced in at the time of the interview or had most recently practiced in, and the length of time for which they had been a practicing nurse. All nurses with one year or less of experience are categorized as new nurses, while nurses with over one year of experience are categorized as experienced nurses. In the nursing world, it is a tremendous accomplishment when a nurse reaches their one-year mark and transitions from being what is called a "new graduate" nurse to an "experienced nurse."*

Chapter 1

This book is also both a love letter to, and an inside look at, one of the nation's most trusted professions: nursing. Being new in the field of nursing is quite possibly one of the hardest professional journeys anyone could ever embark on. Personally, I did not make the transition into the nursing world well. I was hurting for a long time, but I wasn't just struggling with the question of, *How do I become a nurse?* It came down to the question and the struggle of, How do I stay a person while becoming a nurse? *How do I stay human, preserve my dignity, and keep my mental faculties healthy in the midst of such a sacrificial profession?*

You are taught about holistic health and self-care in nursing school, but once you get out there as a nurse and are actually caring for other people—giving your job your all while feeling like you are never fully measuring up—it is easy to lose perspective of your humanity. In the medical community, people often say, "There is a person in that bed." That sentiment isn't just the battle cry of nurses—it is a call to remember the dignity of the patients we work with. But do you want to know something else? There is a person inside of those scrubs too— a person who also needs to be taken care of, because that person is you.

Just as it is important to remember the dignity of the patient, client, or customer, it is essential to remember our own dignity and humanity. So, how do we do that? This is where this book comes in. What differentiates this book from traditional how-to books is that it does not prescribe, instruct, or command. Instead, without judgment, the book shows how other nurses and I made it through to the other side with our holistic health intact. Ultimately, your situation will look starkly different than mine, and your journey will be your own.

When I sat down with former classmates, coworkers, professors, and nursing friends that I have made along the way, one thing I found we all had in common was that our nursing journeys looked exceedingly different from one another's. To me, the fact that all of our stories were so different was refreshing

NEW

and beautiful. Some people's paths may have looked cleaner and straighter than others, but I can promise you this: no one was just strolling around. At one point or another, we all had to climb, scramble over rocks, and work for it.

One experienced nurse I interviewed described this idea best:

"We have this whole subconscious expectation that 'I need to be this kind of nurse on this floor for five years in order to set up my career well,' but that's not the case for everyone. Not everyone's journey looks like that, and that's ok. It doesn't mean that you failed. All of our paths look different."

—AB, *women's oncology breast clinic nurse, four years of experience*

Three new nurses that I interviewed said this when asked, "What did you wish someone had told you before you started?"

"I wish that in nursing there were more clear landmarks. With babies, there are developmental milestones, but as a new nurse, there is such a sense of insecurity, and you ask yourself, 'Am I where I need to be?' There are no clear milestones, like, 'You should be here at six months.'"

—NM, *cardiovascular nurse, ten months of experience*

"I wish someone told me that there is a lot to figure out on your own. You would think that someone would guide you through the process of becoming a nurse, but there is a huge gap between being a student and being an actual nurse. That process isn't really clearly explained or defined. Even being part of a new graduate nurse program, there are still a lot of things to figure out. I wish someone had talked more about that process because it can get very lonely when you are practicing on your own as a nurse, but whatever experiences you go through are what build you up into the nurse that you are today. Everyone goes through something different."

—DY, *bone marrow transplant oncology nurse, nine months of experience*

Chapter 1

> "In school, they kept telling us that they were preparing us for what was to come, but I don't think they ever actually gave us any indication as to what it was really going to be like. They would tell us that it was hard, but they wouldn't necessarily say why. They had high expectations for us, and I thought that I was the only incompetent one not meeting those expectations, but then when I talked to people and found out that they felt the same way, I felt better. I wish they told us why it was going to be hard and that I wasn't alone. It was hard for other people, too."
>
> —JW, *high risk labor and delivery nurse, ten months of experience*

Naively, when I started writing this book back in my seventh month as a new nurse, I thought that I would be able to create a clear-cut, easy-to-navigate path for you. But as time went on, I realized that is something I would never be able to fully do. Being new is an individual process that each of us must go through in our own way and on our own time.

Dr. Judy Boychuk Duchscher—nurse researcher, founder of *Nursing the Future,* and advocate for new graduate nurses—describes the process that all new nurses go through during their first year of nursing in an article she wrote for the *Journal of Continuing Education in Nursing* entitled "A Process of Becoming: The Stages of New Graduate Professional Role Transition," quoted here:

> "The initial 12 months of transition to professional acute care practice for the graduates in this research was a process of becoming [...] Although this journey was by no means linear or prescriptive nor always strictly progressive, it was evolutionary and ultimately transformative for all participants."

Being new is a "process of becoming." While that process is not something that I could ever tell you specifically how to do, it is a process that I can at least do *with* you within the pages of this book. You don't have to do this alone. We are a family now, remember?

NEW

Whether your first year as a new nurse or as a new person in any profession is exceptionally wonderful or abysmally terrible, don't forget that there are people out there who understand what you are going through. You just have to know where to look.

While we will be delving deeply into what being new looks like within the profession of nursing specifically, no one reading this should be made to feel excluded. Why? If I, as well as fifty other nurses, learned how to be holistically healthy human beings in the midst of the chaos that is being new within the field of professional nursing, then anyone can take those same life-altering lessons and apply them to any context. If nurses can learn these lessons in the face of death, then anyone can learn these lessons in the face of life. There is both beauty and pain within these pages. Beyond that, there is life between these pages as well, a whole year of my own life, interwoven with the lives and stories of some of the strongest and bravest people that I have ever known.

Within the nursing community, we are extremely fortunate in that we promote a unique mentality that I like to call the *You're My Baby Now* phenomenon. I personally become intensely protective whenever I see a nurse newer to the profession than I am. I just want to squeeze and assure them that it will all be ok because *they are my baby now.*

To better explain, let's jump into an excerpt that I wrote during my eighth month as a new nurse.

*****

As I write this, I am about to conclude my eighth month as an RN, and I have caught onto something that is spectacular about nurses. We are unequivocally united in the war against sickness and death as well as in the war against our own fatigue. I noticed this particular phenomenon when I was a few weeks into the start of my first year as a nurse. Then, even more recently, I noticed myself participating in it, too. When I first started, I reached out to all the

Chapter 1

nurses that I could think of because I was struggling to come to terms with it all. Do you know what happened? They wanted to help me.

It was like I was falling down a dark hole, spiraling down and down with no end in sight. Then, when I reached out an arm to try and grab onto something to stop my fall, hands caught me and pulled me back into the land of the living. It was the more experienced members of my nursing family who stopped my fall. They showed me kindness, bought me coffee, took time out of their days, and imparted their invaluable wisdom upon me in small yet significant ways. They saved me from disaster.

They did it because they remembered what it was like to be new and scared. They remembered that it is treacherous and tumultuous when one first starts out. One of the first people who I reached out to was one of my previous nursing professors. I told her, through quite a lot of tears, that I was absolutely terrified of everything regarding nursing. I was shaking-in-my-scrubs scared, feeling very isolated, and thinking to myself, *There is no way that other people can possibly feel this inadequate.*

But do you know what she said? She told me that I wasn't alone. When she first started she cried on the way to work, on the way home from work, and in the bathroom on her lunch break at work. I was shocked, because in my head she was my professor, a knows-what-she's-doing professional nurse. I realized that while she is that now, she wasn't back then—no one is when they first start out.

She told me that she wished there was something she could say to make it better, but the simple truth was that there wasn't. She said that it was just something that I was going to have to get through, but that she would be right there for me if I needed to talk.

Since then, almost anytime I have run into a more experienced nurse—whether they be one year more advanced or twenty—and I say that I am having a hard time, they immediately give me their phone number and tell me to call them if I need to. They don't just remember the pain of being new—they feel it.

Now, as some time has passed, I have found myself doing the exact same thing to the people I meet who are even newer to nursing than I am because I still freshly feel that aching heart full of fear and inadequacy, that crushing weight of responsibility, and that tremor of anxiety that loudly blares in your mind when you are trying to enjoy a day off.

Back in my seventh month as a nurse, I met a new nurse in my CPR recertification class who was just about to get off precepting.* She asked me, "Does it get better?" to which I replied, "Honestly? Yes. Slowly, but I'm not going to lie—it's still hard." Then, I gave her my phone number and invited her to coffee because I know intimately how important encouragement is in making it through your first year, especially at the beginning.

Similarly, one of my dearest friends from nursing school who became a practicing nurse a few months after I did texted me one night telling me how anxious she was for her shift the next morning. She had just started out on her own independent practice, and she was feeling the pressure. I told her to call me immediately. No

Author's Note: *When a nurse who is completely new to the profession first starts out, they have to go through a process called 'precepting.' This is a period of time lasting weeks to months during which the new nurse works under the direct instruction of an experienced nurse called a 'preceptor.' While precepting, nurses learn not only how to be a nurse but also how to be a nurse in that specific unit or department. Once the new nurse has met all of their evaluation requirements during that time and been deemed safe to practice on their own by both their preceptors and their management, they are then released to take care of patients on their own. This transition into 'autonomous practice' is inexplicably weighty in the responsibilities that it brings with it. The first time becoming independent is the most intimidating and challenging, but experienced nurses also have to go through the same process when switching specialties, jobs, etc.*

Chapter 1

one knows what it's like to be there, sobbing your soul out because of the stress of it all, like another nurse.

While I was overjoyed to have the privilege of walking with her through her pain, it also hurt my heart to hear her cry. She is one of my strongest friends. She watched me cry hundreds of times during the course of our five years in nursing school, but throughout all the time I had known her, I had never seen her waver for a minute. But over the phone, I could hear her hurt, and I could feel it. It got me wondering, *What is it about this job that makes us feel so small?* My nursing friends are the toughest, most determined people that I know, yet this job makes us feel about two centimeters tall in the face of a club-swinging giant.

Maybe at the end of my first year I will know the answer to this. Maybe I never will. But I do know that nurses need other nurses. Humans need other humans. We are family, and in this family, we take care of one another.

*****

My point in sharing these stories isn't just to brag about how amazing the community of nursing is. My point is that we are all going to feel extremely inadequate in this life, especially when we are in new situations, but we can't let those feelings of inadequacy stop us from living our lives in a way that is healthy. I have found that the best way to live life is not to live it alone, hence my asking for help, hence my trying to adopt all the new nurses that I come across, hence my trying to adopt all of you.

My challenge for you, my readers, is this: show up for one another. Help each other. Encourage each other. Stick together. How do we best combat the club-swinging giant of inadequacy? By not fighting it alone. Life tends to hurt and not a single one of us is making it out alive. I know that is morbid, but cut me some slack—I'm a nurse. Morbidity is an occupational hazard.

NEW

We have one shot at this life. One. That can be tremendously intimidating to think about, especially in nursing where lives are on the line. Not only do we get one chance at life, more specifically, we only get one chance at being new in a specific job or circumstance. For nurses, we only get that first year of our career once, brutal though it may be. People always say that the first year of any job is the hardest. Maybe it is just a year or a season, but it is our year, and beyond that, it is part of our precious and momentary time on Earth. No matter how hard it is, no matter what it is, or what it looks like, we only get that time once. So, we need to ask ourselves, how do we want to spend our time? Do we want to spend it well?

When I was faced with a choice about how I wanted to live out my first year as a nurse, I knew that I really only had two options: I could either lean into it, learn from it, and seek beauty in the midst of it, or I could let it make me feel small, wreck me, strip me down, and break me as a human being. Maybe the second option sounds dramatic to some of you, but I know that the other new nurses out there reading this feel the ice-cold, truthful weight of what I just said in their bones. For those of us learning how to stare into the depths of death every day, the reality that we might break down is striking and altogether too real.

During my first six months as a nurse, as I was being slammed relentlessly by feelings of inadequacy, I thought to myself over and over again, *There has to be a better way.* I didn't want to spend my time being a new nurse cowering in fear, but I wasn't sure what else I could do. You see, no one had ever really told me what being a new nurse was truly going to be like. In the past, when I would ask older nurses for the inside details, I was always met with, "Nursing is really wonderful! You get to help people, make a difference in the world, make good money, have career stability, and have flexible hours. The first year is going to be the worst year of your life, but after that, you really will have an amazing career!"

This would then leave me bewildered and wondering, *Excuse me, what? What was that part about my first year as a nurse being the worst*

Chapter 1

year of my life? Then, when I would ask more about that, they would say, "Don't worry, you'll be fine! Don't take yourself too seriously when you want to quit for your whole first year!"

Again, excuse me, *what?* We can't pass off what is clearly not fine as fine, bury the harsh realities, and never discuss them again. I knew deep down that there had to be a better way to both practice as a nurse and live as a human, so I became determined to figure out what that way looked like.

As I was simultaneously navigating all of the harsh realities that were thrust upon me during my first year as a nurse, I became engrossed in the ancient wisdom book of Ecclesiastes. Initially, I was simply looking for encouragement. Instead, I found a robust ideology that completely reshaped everything about my life and person. When I was on the precipice of writing this book, I was specifically studying Ecclesiastes 3: 1-11, a paraphrase of which reads as follows:

"There is a time for everything, and a season for every activity under the heavens:
a time to be born and a time to die; [...]
a time to weep and a time to laugh,
a time to mourn and a time to dance [...].
What do workers gain from their toil?
I have seen the burden God has laid on the human race.
He has made everything beautiful in its time.
He has also set eternity in the human heart;
yet no one can fathom what God has done from beginning to end."

During the initial stages of considering writing a book such as this, I was in that time of mourning. I was breaking down and weeping. That brought me specifically to Ecclesiastes 3:11a, which states, "He has made everything beautiful in its time." I was desperate, wondering to myself, *How is this pain ever possibly going to be made beautiful? How is what is not ok going to become ok? How will my mourning ever be turned into dancing?* Then, after almost seven months of practicing as a nurse, wrestling with depression and anxiety, and wondering how those questions would be answered, I found out.

While I was in that seventh month, things completely changed for me when I had a chance encounter with a brilliant artist* who had recently gone through a hospitalization himself. This artist shared with me that he had taken his sketchbook with him to the hospital, so that he could continue to actively create art from within the confines of his hospital bed. The art that he created during that time was profoundly striking; for the sketches that he had been working on were intricate and vivid depictions of lungs.

He told me that in the midst of being hospitalized, through all the uncertainty and discomfort, he was determined to create something beautiful out of his situation. Beauty out of pain. Life out of ash. Light out of darkness. Sensing that we were kindred spirits, I shared with him that I had recently resumed writing, which was an old passion of mine, and that I wanted to somehow tie my life as a nurse and life as a writer together, but that I didn't really know how to do it. When I shared with him that becoming a nurse had been a very difficult transition for me, he suggested I write about that. That I make something beautiful out of something painful, so the pain wouldn't have been all for nothing.

That was it: the catalyst and founding inspiration for this entire book. The tangible way that I was able to understand how Ecclesiastes 3:11a, "He has made everything beautiful in its time," was going to be realized in my life as a writer, as a nurse, and as a human.

***Author's Note:** Not only did this artist change my life back then, but over a year after our initial meeting I reached out to him and asked if he'd be interested in designing the cover artwork for this book in order to continue the theme of creating beauty out of pain. He said yes. For more information, please see the 'About the Art' note at the front of the book.*

Chapter 1

Ever since that defining moment, I have been bound and determined to turn all my times of pain into beauty, mourning into dancing. Now, looking back, I have come to realize that learning how to turn mourning into dancing is quite possibly one of the biggest lessons that we can ever hope to learn in this life. If we can do that well, then we have learned how to claim our time well, and if we have learned how to claim our time well, then we have learned how to live our lives well. For when we make peace with time, we make peace with ourselves.

Perhaps you haven't always been good at this. I haven't been, but there is grace in that. To reiterate what Dr. Judy Boychuk Duchscher said, it is all a "process of becoming." As long as we have breath left in our lungs, it is not too late to start stewarding our time well. But, we all do need to *start*.

A perfect example of this comes from "The Explosive Origins of the Nobel Prizes," an article written by Juan José Sánchez Arreseigor and published in 2017 in *National Geographic:*

"Alfred Nobel, creator of the famous Nobel Prizes, was a paradox: An arms dealer in life, Nobel decided in death to use his dynamite fortune to fund a peaceful foundation. [...] What was it that prompted Alfred Nobel to create the endowment and the prestigious prizes? The answer may lie in a case of mistaken identity. In 1888 his brother Ludvig died. A French journalist mistakenly believed that it was Alfred who had died and wrote the headline: *'Le marchand de la mort est mort'*—The merchant of death is dead. It has been suggested that Nobel was deeply affected by this incident, and it caused him to reflect on his legacy."

Mr. Nobel himself realized that he wasn't using his time to perpetuate beauty, so he chose to do something about it. The impact that he has left on the world, which could have been solely one of actual death and destruction, instead became one of great peace.

NEW

He reclaimed his time on Earth and created peaceable beauty from what would have otherwise been a legacy of ash and ruin.

Simply identifying beauty in the midst of difficult situations isn't enough. Once we have found that beauty, that light within the darkness, we need to perpetuate it. You might be wondering what I personally did to seek beauty in the midst of what was the hardest year of my life, just like all the nurses who have gone before me said it would be? More importantly, what lessons did I learn from it all? And how am I using those lessons to perpetuate beauty in this world? Well, I wrote this book, a book filled with all the lessons that have taught me how to mourn well, dance well, and live well in the middle of the very difficult season that is being new.

So, let's mourn together. Let's dance together. Let's be human beings together in the midst of new situations and let's do it well. That isn't just what being new is about—it is what life is about. Therefore, let's seek and perpetuate beauty within the context of being new. You. Me. Together. Welcome to the family.

Chapter Two:
Small Love

While we will be talking about a multitude of weighty subjects in this book, the content in this particular chapter is by far some of the heaviest. At first, I thought to myself, *Don't do this to your readers. Ease them into this process.* But then I realized that in life we are rarely eased into things, especially when you are new, and especially when you are a nurse. We have to deal with things as they come, and some of those things are simply heavy.

You are probably wondering to yourself, *How bad can it possibly be?* Allow me to start by saying that the content in this chapter is the key to unlocking all the rest of the lessons in this book. If we can come to terms with what is presented in this chapter, then we can come to terms with anything else in our seasons of being new. Actually, scratch that. If we can come to terms with this content, then we can come to terms with anything else in this *life*.

Let's start off with a statement that we all will probably be familiar with: "Another day, another dollar." Have you ever said that exact phrase to another coworker as you walked into work? Nurses say that. As selfless as we are, we say it a lot. When you work twelve-hour night shifts, it truly feels like you live at the hospital. I would often joke around with my coworkers by saying it was like we were at a really un-fun slumber party together. Our un-fun sleepovers always did have the best food, however. Nurses know how to do a midnight potluck the right way.

But back to the idea of *another day another dollar*. That's what a lot of us would say when we would come back into work, because nurses get exponentially fatigued. To us, being at the hospital is just another day, and at the end of that day, it is just another way to make another dollar.

I have let this expression come out of my mouth more than once. In fact, I was the worst perpetrator of using this phrase. During my first year of nursing, I was tired. I was tired and stressed out of my mind. The days—or the nights, in my case—and the shifts blurred together. But it was not just the shifts that blurred together—the people did, too.

Another day, another dollar, another *person*. A lot of the time, I missed the person who was right in front of me because I was exhausted, anxious, and over all of it. Yes, I am a nurse, but I am also human. In the general experience of being a human being, those are very normal feelings to have. We'll talk about that more specifically in chapter ten. But for now, I will say this: I broke my own heart when I realized that I had begun to equate human beings with dollars, and I thought about all of the people whom I had missed due to being blinded by my own anxieties and fears.

You might be wondering, *What were you afraid of?* Well, a whole mess of things. Making mistakes. Missing details I should have been aware of. Getting in trouble. Lawsuits. Plummeting into a cycle of depression that I wouldn't be able to get out of because of something that I had done. Accidentally killing someone. The list could go on. But after doing a lot of self-examination, I realized that my fears could be boiled down to two things: death and inadequacy.

If you are a nurse reading this, you are probably not afraid of entering into this space with me because you live and operate in a territory where you are either constantly dealing with those feelings yourself or you are having to walk someone else through them.

If you are not a nurse, let me encourage you to keep reading. As we mentioned in the previous chapter, I can assure you that whatever inadequacy you feel, if nurses can overcome the fear

Chapter 2

of inadequacy in the face of death, then you can overcome your feelings of inadequacy as well in the face of life, no matter where you are. By no means am I trivializing the weight of what you feel, whoever you are, wherever you are, whatever you are doing. Not at all. What I am trying to offer you within the context of this chapter, however, is the lesson of how both myself and other nurses faced this particularly stark inadequacy and were able to successfully come to terms with it. That being said, here is the whole of it, the very heavy whole of it. Once we can face this, we can face anything. Let me tell you the story of how I came to this conclusion.

*****

I am writing this to you at the beginning of my eleventh month as a nurse. I finally bought myself new work shoes today. After ten full months of practicing as a registered nurse, my white leather nursing school shoes are no more. I had been putting off getting new work shoes for the longest time because I was convinced that I was either going to quit or get fired.

Today, however, I realized that I was being absurd. My old work shoes were disgusting. At this point, I have stepped in every bodily fluid that could possibly come out of a human being while wearing them. Every. Fluid.

Needless to say, I needed new shoes, but I refused to get them for ten whole months because of the fear that I was not going to measure up and that I would then be stuck with new shoes for a job that I lost.

When I go to work in my nasty shoes and my thin, hospital issued scrubs, I feel timid. I feel scared. I feel incredibly small. Almost two months ago, at the start of my ninth month, I wrote an excerpt in which I posed the question, *What is it about this job that makes us feel so small?* Then, I wondered if I would ever be able to answer that question. At the time when I wrote that, the

NEW

bewilderment was still fresh. The wild feelings of inadequacies were barely—just barely—starting to fade. In reality, the answer I arrived at in response to that question was actually pretty simple, and it is one that surprised me.

If you look at the beginning of this book, you will see that I included a poem that I wrote for Nurses' Week 2019 in honor of the nurses who stood alongside me during my first year as a nurse. There are a few lines in it that read as follows:

> *Each day we put on our scopes and our scrubs, willingly stepping into environments that are uncertain,*
> *But we put on brave faces so that you won't see the truth behind the curtain,*
> *The truth of which is this: we can't save you all,*
> *But we will do our best to come alongside you so that in the shadow of the mountain of disease you won't feel alone or small.*

I wrote that poem about two months ago and didn't fully realize what I was saying until today. Remember how I said that this job makes us feel about two centimeters tall in the face of a club-swinging giant? Well, that club swinging giant isn't nursing. It isn't any career or profession. It isn't a hard unit, long hours, or demanding patients. It isn't even our own inadequacies, imperfections, or anxieties. It is simply disease, and beyond that, death. And death? Death is not something that any of us ultimately stand a chance against.

We cannot save them all, no matter how hard we fight or how much medicine progresses. We are pebbles at the foot of the tremendously tall mountain that is life and death. We can fight against death. We can keep it at bay. Sometimes, we are able to give people the chance at lifetimes. Sometimes, we can give them years. Sometimes, we can only give them months. Even more pressingly still, sometimes, we are only able to give people days, hours, or mere minutes. But at the end of the day, death is the one summit

Chapter 2

that we will never be able to overcome, because it will eventually come for all of us.

That is why we feel so small deep down: we know that if death is going to come for one of our patients, there is absolutely nothing that we can do to stop it. No amount of CPR, medications, or treatments are going to help. That is the cold reality of the situation that we all face as nurses. Beyond nursing, that is the cold reality that we all face as humans.

So, yes, when I think about that club-swinging giant being death itself, then I feel incredibly small. For what am I—in my paper-thin hospital issued scrubs, old shoes, and stethoscope that I borrowed from a friend because I lost mine—going to be able to do to thwart the giant of death and disease? Even the code team, with all their shared knowledge and skills, isn't going to be able to do much for the patient who has death coming for them. We can buy them time sometimes, that is true, but that's it. Sometimes we can't even do that.

If present me were having this conversation with past me, I would have never bought those new shoes. Past me would have promptly gone to my manager and quit out of sheer terror. But do you know what? That thing that would have once imprisoned my mind in fear has now given me a new sense of freedom and empowerment.

As nurses, we are never going to be ultimately victorious over the adversary of death. So, then what? Should we just give up? Believe me, I want to. The patient population I work with is predominately people for whom we can only buy more time, but not a better quality of life, and that is very difficult.

But even though I have desperately wanted to give up in the past, right now, at this particular moment, I don't want to. I realize something now that I didn't before. We will never measure up to death. We will never be enough.

It doesn't matter if we are the best, the smartest, the quickest, or the sharpest nurse in the world—we will always be inadequate because we cannot possibly be everything to all of our patients. We cannot save them all, but we can come alongside them in the shadow of the mountain of disease so that they won't feel alone or small. We do not have to do it perfectly either. If the only thing that we can do is buy our patients more time, then we need to come alongside them and make that time count by showing up to work, working our hardest, and trying our best. In life, that is really all that you can do. No matter how much we want to fix a person or a situation, in reality, we won't always be able to do that.

In that same poem, I wrote the following:

Where others waiver, we run
We go towards not away, into the fire and the blaze of the sun
We are warriors on the front lines of life where death is the enemy and sickness its weapon
We fight armed with a countenance made of strength that nothing can threaten

It was never about being perfect or providing perfect care. Instead it is about loving, fighting for, and coming alongside complete strangers so that they do not have to go through the uncertainty of illness and death alone. Even if death is looming imminently on the horizon, in that shift, you are making that limited time the patient has with you, count.

So, let go of everything else. Let go of the anxiety and feelings of inadequacy. Remember that you are a warrior. Buy yourself the nicer set of scrubs if you need to. If that is your armor, by all means put it on. Do not forget that even if the final battle of life and death is one that we cannot ultimately win for all of our patients, each day we step into life with them we are winning the battle against their loneliness and fear. We are supplying them with the weapons of support and encouragement so that their time, no matter how short, is spent as well as it possibly can be, even if that is within the cold walls of a hospital room and the confines of a bed.

Chapter 2

In an article published in *International Journal for Human Caring* entitled "Healing the Healer: A Caring Science Approach to Moral Distress in New Graduate Nurses," nurse researcher Jacqueline van Wijlen writes, "The nurse is not simply in the environment, the nurse is the environment." If we go into work thinking to ourselves, *What can I do to provide a better environment for the people whom I am working with?* instead of, *What can I do to not make mistakes?* then we will be able to take some of the pressure off of ourselves. Can we be perfect? No. Can we provide someone with a supportive environment even if we are only with them for a short amount of time? Probably. We show up. We do our best. We love our hardest. We chart everything, and that is all that we can do.

I will say, however, that even though death is part of life and part of being a human, that doesn't make it any easier or less painful. I've lost people. We all have. Loss is one of the hardest things that we have to go through as humans. So, I do not want to minimize—in any way, shape or form—the power, pain, and weight of loss. But, death itself is one reality that we all have to face. Death is human. Therefore, we need to talk about it.

*****

Heavy? Yes. Death always is. To summarize what I just threw at you, I will ask you a question. It is the question that we all want to ask ourselves but is also the question that we do not ever truly want to hear the answer to. It is the question, "Am I enough?" In light of what you just read, the answer is no, you are not. You're not enough. I am not enough. We are not enough. We are inadequate, and that is ok. No matter how hard we work or how hard we try, at the end of the day, sometimes we are simply not enough. Instead of holding onto that feeling of inadequacy and making it our own personal burden, we have to wrestle with it, come to terms with it, and let it go.

One of the nurses I interviewed said the following quote. It is this piece of wisdom that not only led me to write this chapter but

NEW

also to reframe my entire understanding of inadequacy and what it means to come to terms with that inadequacy healthfully.

"It is all to make sure that the patient is safe. If I mess up, I mess up, but I know that my integrity is on the right path. I can only do my best. If I fall short, I fall short, but I am doing my best at the end of the day to keep my patients safe, and I can hold onto that."
—*PM, medical-surgical float pool nurse, two months of experience*

Now, if that sentiment alone was the catalyst for my exploration into inadequacy, then this next quote is the conclusion I found regarding how we can respond well to that inadequacy. Another nurse said the following, which spoke to the idea of letting the inadequacy go:

"Relying on God helps me take things not so personally. It is more of a surrender than a giving up. Surrendering reminds us that we cannot always fix everything. It doesn't mean that we don't try—it means that we do all we can and then pray from there."
—*MA, emergency department nurse, ten months of experience*

The mountain of death and disease looms in front of both ourselves and our patients alike, taller and more ominous than ever before, but we can stand in front of it together so that no one has to face it alone. Maybe you feel upset right now. This is not easy. Death is never easy, but at some point, we have to let go of the inadequacies that we feel in the face of it. This begs the question, "How can we possibly endeavor to let go of our inadequacies?" How are we going to claim our time well and perpetuate beauty in the face of death? While doing our best and showing up is incredibly important, we need to do so equipped with the one thing more important and powerful than death itself. We need to do it with *small love*.

Chapter 2

While death and inadequacy take the forms of big mountains and club-swinging giants, *small love* is the key to being victorious over all of those things. *Small love* is the key to surmounting the otherwise insurmountable.

For a moment, let's think about the iconic line, "It's a beautiful day to save lives." We can thank *Grey's Anatomy* creator, writer, and executive producer Shonda Rhimes for that one. This line was something members of my clinical nursing class would often repeat to one another over and over again: in the car on the way to clinicals, in hospital elevators as we set out to start our days. I have to say, it is truly a beautiful and powerful line, but at the end of the day, it is just a line, a poetic sentiment.

I am not for a moment speaking on behalf of surgeons and doctors, because I cannot fathom the pressure that they are under and the decisions that they have to make. I have an inordinate amount of respect for doctors and surgeons alike, mark my words. But, I have to tell you, this particular line doesn't always practically hold up. Why? Well, as I said, I have found that the field of nursing is much less about saving lives and much more about loving people.

Instead of focusing all of our attention solely on our roles as warriors against death and disease, we need to remember that we are first and foremost stewards of time and curators of loving and comforting environments, no matter where we are or what we do. Instead of saying to ourselves, "It's a beautiful day to save lives," we should be saying, "It's a beautiful day to love people." In a world of such great fluctuation, a world where death and loss are guaranteed, the most fulfilling way we can spend our time is by showing one another love and kindness. While we cannot always save the person in front of us, we can always choose to love them.

I don't say this from a saccharine place of rainbows and heart-eyes: I say this from a practical place embedded with grains of salt. In order to not sugar-coat anything, here is an example from my own life that took place during my tenth month as a nurse, right around the time I was first discovering this concept.

NEW

*****

Two nights ago, I was intentionally spat on by a patient. It wasn't just plain spit, either. It was gunky, tan sputum. To make things worse, that sputum got in my eye. There is no naive optimism in this situation, but here is the thing: real love isn't that glistening, cheery nonsense at all. It isn't just blindly believing the best while disregarding what is truly difficult about the situation. Real love is saying to yourself, *This is hard. I don't like this patient, and I really hate my job right now, but I am going to do my best to provide the best care possible for this person—this living, breathing, human being.*

On the topic of such love, Fyodor Dostoevsky writes the following in his novel *The Brothers Karamazov*:

"Love in action is a harsh and dreadful thing compared with love in dreams. Love in dreams is greedy for immediate action, rapidly performed, and in the sight of all. Men will even give their lives if only the ordeal does not last long but is soon over, with all looking on and applauding as though on the stage. But active love is labour and fortitude, and for some people too, perhaps, a complete science."

Active love is hard work. While it might not seem outwardly radical, it is most certainly inwardly radical because of the persistence and self-sacrifice that it takes to love someone truly and actively. In this circumstance with the spitting patient, it was hard work to muster up even the smallest of desires to go into her room to check on her. Now, I don't want you to think that I didn't stand up for myself. I am one tough human being who knows how to fight when it comes down to it, but this particular patient was severely confused. She didn't know what was going on and needed wrist restraints for her own protection. She was spitting, cursing, crying, yelling, and trying to hit and bite me. To top it all off, she yelled for

Chapter 2

almost twelve hours straight. Every time I so much as poked my head in the room, I was met with a shrieking nightmare.

It was such a bad shift that I sobbed the entire way to work the next night because I did not want to work with this patient again. People even told me that they wouldn't blame me if I called off my second night because of her. But, I went back the next night, crying and regretting my decision the whole drive back to work, dreading the thought of having to spend another whole twelve hours taking care of this human being.

In reality, I could have called off, but I knew that I had a job to do. That job wasn't to save this lady's life, because she was stable enough. She was a heavy patient, sick but stable. There was no medication that I could give her or intervention that I could possibly perform that was going to magically fix her. I was not returning to work to save her by any means, so was I going back to work just to show her love and kindness? Honestly, no. Not really. I wish I could have said that my heart was that refined. Instead, I went back because I love my coworkers. The poor nurse who I gave report to when I left that morning walked into a hot yelling and fighting mess. I didn't want to leave that nurse hanging. I wanted to show up for *her*.

Often, it isn't about loving our patients, our customers, or our clients—it is about loving our teammates. It was love for my coworkers that got me back into the car that night. It was that small, I-am-doing-this-for-my-coworker kind of love. It was not because I wanted to or because I felt like I was making any sort of difference, and that is ok.

Was my second night just as bad as my first? No, but only by a minuscule fraction and only because, this time, the patient fell asleep for two hours out of the twelve and managed to keep her spit to herself. If I am going to be honest, I did not feel any sort of warm-and-fuzzy love for this patient my second night with her. In fact, I caught myself thinking about how much I didn't like working with her. But, I still spoke to her gently. I still cleaned vomit off of her face. I still showed up and did my job. For on this Earth, it is imperative that we show people love and kindness, even when we do not want to.

*****

I wish that I had prayed for the strength to love the spitting patient, but I didn't. Instead, I selfishly prayed that I would be able to make it through the night. While I did not show that patient great love by any means, I feel as though I did show her at least a little bit of *small love* through my actions. As humans, we are small, and *small love* is the only love that we are capable of showing in most moments. We can't beat ourselves up over it, because *small love* is something. *Small love* is still love, even if it isn't perfect.

The patient in that excerpt was extremely confused, so it was easy to write off her actions in my head as just that—products of confusion. But what about people who are completely oriented? What about the people who know exactly what they are doing, who are just mean? We all encounter those people, no matter where we work.

I had another patient about a month before the spitting incident who was just that: she was completely with it and oriented, but she was really unkind. The day before I worked with this particular patient, she had yelled at a doctor so badly that the doctor had removed herself from the case and refused to work with the patient any longer. The nurse who gave me report that night pulled me aside and gave me a talk before we even went into the room.

He told me that the patient was angry, grumpy, irritable—you name it—and would yell, curse, and grumble, but he urged me to be patient with her because she had just received a very bad diagnosis and was scared out of her mind. Now, that was exceptionally good advice, because it is often easy for us just to write people off as angry, crazy, or bad people. We make up our

Chapter 2

minds, set our attitudes, and harden our hearts towards them for our own protection. In truth, sometimes we need to do this in order to keep ourselves safe, but in this case, the day-shift nurse's words encouraged me not to write off this patient.

So, I tried to be kind to her that night. Did she yell at me? Actually, no, not really. She was snappy, but at the end of the shift, she thanked me for my help. I was so surprised that I'll never forget it. Just as I was about to leave the room, she said in a whisper so faint that I almost missed it, "Thank you for all your help last night."

For that brief moment in which she thanked me, I got to see her fear dissipate and her hard shell come off. I got to see a real human being sitting before me instead of someone completely closed off by fear, and that experience was tremendously special. Again, by no means am I condoning bad or inappropriate behavior. We need to look out for our mental and physical safety in this world. If you are in an unsafe situation, I urge you to tell your charge nurse or manager, call security, or do whatever you need to do to stay safe. But, if you are safe and the person is simply cantankerous and unpleasant, I also urge you to consider this: whether it is a beautiful day to love people or an incredibly terrible day to love people, it is still a day in which we need to love people, even if it is just with a small amount of love.

So, is life really just another day, another dollar? No. Each day is another day to show another human being love. Interestingly, when I was interviewing the fifty nurses quoted in this book, the theme of *small love* stood out. While I did not ask any interview questions specifically about *small love* itself, the topic showed up again and again in multiple contexts.

Small love, while small, is a robust and multifocal entity. Showing *small love* can mean giving our very best effort, our one-hundred percent, even though a positive outcome is not guaranteed. It can mean showing compassion through beautiful actions. It can mean showing compassion even when we don't know that our actions are

NEW

beautiful. But, at the end of the day and at its core, showing *small love* means showing up for one another as fellow human beings.

Let's take a closer look at these four facets of *small love:*

1. Small love is giving our very best effort, even if a positive outcome is not guaranteed.

"One time we had a code and the doctor asked us, 'Who wants to run this code?' then, 'Who's new?' Someone suggested that I should do it, so I ran the code. I hadn't done a code since I'd been practicing on my own—to be the one calling the shots was scary because I didn't remember how to do everything. The doctor was going to call it and have us stop resuscitations, but then he asked me if I wanted to call it. I said, 'Let's do one more round of CPR,' and we ended up getting pulses back and a blood pressure. I want to say that the patient ended up passing away a few days later in the ICU, but I feel like by doing that we at least gave them a chance."

—*CH, emergency department nurse, ten months of experience*

I would like to note that this story was this new nurse's answer to the question, "What is a good memory that you have from your first year?" It is beautiful that this is how he chose to answer the question. For you non-nurses out there—codes are brutal. If ever there were a time when everyone has to give their one-hundred percent, it is in a Code Blue situation. We are talking about fifteen people crammed in a room fighting for a person's life, giving everything they've got for an extended period of time. Codes are terrifying for new nurses. By answering my question with a story about a Code Blue, that new nurse showed that while we don't always know what the final outcome will be, when we try our absolute hardest in that moment, when we give them our one hundred percent, we are able to love the person in front of us well. There is *small love* even in the midst of uncertainty.

Chapter 2

2. Small love is showing compassion through beautiful actions.

"I was sad to skip Father's Day with my dad at church, but I had a lot of downtime at work that day. I remembered that one of my professors had once told me, 'Never stop caring for your patients,' and explained that in her downtime she would get a basin and wash her patients' feet. That memory struck me deeply. I had free time that day, so I told my patient, 'I want to give you a Father's Day gift, the best one that you have ever gotten—I am going to wash your feet!' He was so thankful, and his gratitude gave me so much gratification. I gave him a massage and really cleaned him up, and his response showed me that what I did for him mattered to him. He told me his children lived far away and that he didn't want to call them and burden them, so it was special getting to take that time with him and be the hands and feet of Christ for him. It allowed me to see that this is what I am really meant to do and that what I am doing makes an impact.

"That day sparked a desire in me to serve all my patients in that capacity. In this field, you can either bring yourself to care or not care. Some nurses don't care, so you have to remember to keep caring and keep showing compassion. I could be a person who doesn't care, but I don't want to be. I want to extend compassion and provide for the patient's heart and their emotional needs. I don't want to see them just as tasks."

—*AP, renal telemetry nurse, eight months of experience*

3. Small love is showing compassion even when we don't know that our actions are beautiful.

"I remember having one patient who I didn't have a great time with. They were a tough patient to work with, not because of how sick they were but because it was a really tense environment. They were one of the ones who, when you discharge them, you breathe a sigh of relief because they were so difficult to work with. You love them the best that you can and show them God's love the best that you can, but you are still excited when they leave.

"A few weeks later, I opened up my mailbox at work and saw that I had a positive review sheet in my file from a family member of that difficult patient. They said that they were touched that I did such a good job of being an emotional support for him and that I had been so intentional with him. To me, the situation wasn't that special in my head. I didn't cry with him or pray with him—I just did my best and sent him on his way—but hearing that from the family member really meant a lot to me. I am no stranger to crying with my patients and connecting with them in a way that is emotionally supportive, so it was special to know that even such a small, frustrating interaction with this patient was huge to his family."

—*EP, medical-surgical oncology nurse, one year of experience*

4. Small love is showing up for one another.

"It is a very rare opportunity to be involved in someone's life in such a way, involved with things that change people's lives. People are getting new diagnoses and having financial changes; it's stuff that rocks their world. It makes me grateful for what I have. I feel honored to be part of a person's care team, even if it is only for one or two days. Some people try to go into nursing for money, but that is the wrong reason and you will get burnt out by that. But, if you do it to care for others, to be with a person in the worst moments of their life, and to show them love, then those are the right reasons. If no one else in the world is there for that patient, then at least I am going to be there."

—*AN, medical-surgical respiratory nurse, nine months of experience*

To quote the film *Love Actually,* and more specifically the character of the British prime minister, "If you look for it, I've got a sneaky

Chapter 2

feeling you'll find that love actually is all around." I bring this up because perhaps you are reading this and you are not a nurse and you are thinking to yourself, *This is nice and all, but I work in accounting and offering to wash my client's feet would be weird. I agree with you. That would be weird.* While nurses get to participate in love in ways that many people do not, that doesn't mean that those outside of nursing can't participate in loving others as well.

Like the *Love Actually* quote says, "Love actually is all around." So, we each have to ask ourselves how we can show others *small love* on the day to day, in the midst of the mundane. How can we make one another feel seen, known, and heard in any life situation? Well, I'll tell you: we need to show up and look for small ways to love one another, and then we need to not be afraid to actively do so. The giants of death and inadequacy don't just live at the hospital. Therefore, we need to armor up with *small love* whenever and wherever we have the chance to combat those aforementioned titans.

During the time I was working as a sales associate at a clothing and lifestyle store prior to becoming a nurse, I was exceptionally depressed. One morning around 7:00 a.m., a coworker and I were unloading coffee mugs onto a display. Somehow, we got talking about relationships, and my coworker asked me if I was seeing anyone. I immediately almost started crying and replied that no, I wasn't. In fact, I was going through the tail end of a difficult breakup. She stopped what she was doing, put down the mug she was holding, looked me straight in the eye and said, "I am so sorry to hear that. It sounds like that was very painful experience for you." Then, after a minute or two, we went back to re-shelving the rest of the inventory. But, I have to tell you, I truly felt known and seen at that moment, not in any particularly astounding way, but in a way that made me feel like I wasn't alone.

Small love, anywhere, anytime, even if it is just taking a minute to look someone in the eye and be present with them in between shelving coffee cups. It doesn't have to be anything of high

NEW

significance or great importance—we just have to make the choice to do it. Quite miraculously, it is *small love* that makes us feel less small in the face of the dark and looming worldly giants that we often have to face in this life.

No matter what you believe about God, about the afterlife, about anything, we can all agree that we need to make this life count, for ourselves and for the people that we interact with, whether they be patients, customers, friends, family members, whomever. The best thing that we can do is show up, and love others, even if it is just with a small love in the face of a big mountain. *Go toward not away, into the fire and the blaze of the sun.* We need to step up for each other amidst the hard, amidst the flame, because all human beings need love and support.

While it can be difficult and draining, few get to do life with people like nurses do. We have the unique capacity to fight for people in a way that few others can. We mean the world to our patients, even if they don't thank us, even if they cuss or spit at us, because even if it is just for one shift, we are *carrying* the weight of their world for them. So, if nurses can learn to do this, can learn how to love people well in the midst of actual hellish darkness, then any new person can learn to use small love to perpetuate beauty in the face of any inadequacy anywhere.

In the end, when we look back at a hard work day—no, forget that—when we look back at our lives and see that we have been kind to people, that we have tried our best to love people, then that is a job well done and a life well lived. Even though we don't do things perfectly, even though we can't measure up fully, we will not regret taking the time to love people and be kind, because the best way that we can perpetuate beauty in this world is to love others.

The same nurse I quoted as the catalyst for this chapter, also said this:

"You can't teach compassion, but you can make a choice to be compassionate."

—PM, *medical-surgical float pool nurse, two months of experience*

Chapter 2

To love actively, one has to choose to do so. As Dostoevsky wrote, "Love in action is a harsh and dreadful thing compared with love in dreams." It is hard, and a lot of times it most certainly isn't beautiful, but because of that raw, active, small, unglamorous love, we are able to perpetuate beauty in this world even in the face of death and inadequacy.

As I said at the beginning of this chapter, I feel a little badly for smacking you with such a heavy life lesson so soon out of the gates, but at the end of the day, I don't feel that badly, because that is what this book is about: it is about wading through the heaviness together. Being new is heavy. Being a nurse is heavy. Being a person is heavy. Life is heavy. Don't worry, in Chapter Five we will talk about just how to carry that weight in detail, but for now I'll just say this: we don't have to go through life alone. We don't have to look up at that mountain alone. This sentiment of not going through life alone isn't just for the patients that nurses have to deal with—it is for all of us.

Now that we have made it through the heaviest chapter of this book together, hopefully feeling one step closer in being able to let go of our feelings of inadequacy, the other lessons will come much more easily. Once we learn to let go of the bad, we have a greater capacity to hold onto the good.

One new nurse I interviewed posed the following to the experienced nurses on her floor:

"It's good to talk to experienced nurses and ask them questions. I like to ask, 'How do you still have compassion and do this every day?' They basically just say that you have to learn what is important and then also learn not to let what's not important get to you."

—MK, *medical-surgical telemetry sepsis nurse, eight months of experience*

Let's get to the good stuff, then. Well, love is the good stuff, so let's get to the *rest* of the good stuff. Let's let go of the bad things,

NEW

the things that we cannot change, and instead talk about all the things that we can do to make our traversing of the mountain of life, death, and being new a little bit more manageable and a whole lot more beautiful. Are you ready to climb? I am, and if we can do death together, like we did in this chapter, then we most certainly can do life together in all the chapters to come. So, let's go hiking.

Chapter Three:
Great Expectations

What is the first thing that one has to grapple with when walking into a new situation? It's something that is true of any new area of life that we find ourselves to be in. Jobs? Yes. Friendships? Yes. Living spaces? Yes. So, what is it? It is the meeting or the non-meeting of our own expectations.

We always have some sort of expectations whenever we face new circumstances. Sometimes those expectations are met positively, sometimes they are met negatively, and sometimes we don't even know what our expectations are until we get there.

I will try to ease us into this chapter with an experience that we can probably all relate to on some level. Have you ever been to a wedding? I have been to well over twenty. Why bring up weddings? Well, unless we are actively part of the wedding planning process with the happy couple or are in fact part of the happy couple, we have no idea what the actual wedding is going to be like until we arrive. Yes, we may know the couple as individual people, but how is the celebration of their love for one another going to be visibly displayed for all to see?

When we go to weddings, five things can happen:

1. We can feel pleasantly surprised.

At one wedding I went to, my gorgeous friend was wearing an equally gorgeous gown. She looked elegant and classy, but this girl is also hilarious, so do you know what shoes she had on underneath that glamorous dress? If you guessed hot-pink, cheetah-print high heels then you would be correct. When she laughingly said, "Everyone look at my shoes!" while we were on the dance floor, it was a beautiful moment. When we go to a wedding and we see our friend's personality radiate throughout fun, personal touches on their special day, it is a pleasant surprise.

2. We can feel unpleasantly surprised.

Before nursing, I wanted to be an events coordinator, so I used to watch a myriad of wedding coordination shows. There was always the dreaded question of, *What is going to happen during the cocktail hour?* I've been to some truly exceptional cocktail hours. Then, at other weddings, I have been to some not-so-exceptional cocktail hours. Have you been there? Starving unpleasantly at a cocktail hour that somehow turned into a cocktail three hours? That's not a pleasant surprise.

3. We can feel excited.

I personally love weddings because weddings mean dancing, and if you were ever to see me at a wedding, you would be thinking to yourself, *What is that crazy person doing right now?* When I dance, I *dance*. It is my sole mission and endeavor in life to make sure that whatever wedding I go to, I do my part to keep that dance floor alive. So, to me, weddings are exciting.

4. We can feel scared.

That being said, I respect that some people don't like to dance. So, maybe for all of you non-dancing wedding attendees out there, weddings are scary for you because you don't want to dance because it is outside of your comfort zone.

Chapter 3

5. We can come without any expectations at all. We can just be along for the ride.

After attending so many weddings, I can tell you what a typical Southern Californian wedding looks like. They are pretty formulaic in structure, and there is no shame in that at all. But have you ever been to a wedding outside of the culture that is your own? Those weddings are the best. I have been blessed to be invited into that space by a number of people. In those instances, not only do you have no idea what to expect, but you also get to learn about another culture in the process.

Weddings are all of those five things rolled into one. They are pleasantly surprising, unpleasantly surprising, exciting, scary, and unknown all at the same time. What's more is that we aren't going to know what kind of combination of those things the wedding is going to be until we get there. Do you know what else is like that? Being new. Similarly, we are never going to find out the truth behind how that new job or situation is going to relate to each of those components until we arrive.

If being new in any job is like that, then what is it like to be new in the wild, untamed, circus that is nursing? How are the expectations of new nurses met and how are they not met? Being new in nursing is the hot mess express to end all hot mess expresses. So, let me be our conductor on the journey that is dealing with all of the great expectations that we put on our jobs, whatever they may be.

One nurse made this painfully accurate statement regarding the expectations that she had going into nursing:

"I don't even know what I thought it was going to be like. I really don't. But whatever it was that I thought, it was *not* that."

—HH, *surgical-telemetry step-down nurse, nine months of experience*

NEW

That pretty much encapsulates all the expectations of a new nurse: the good, the bad, and the unknown. I'm not sure how it is with other jobs, trainings, professions, internships, or college majors. Nursing is my only lived experience after all, but in nursing school, we spent the entirety of our clinical programs in hospitals shadowing nurses, in classrooms learning to think like nurses, and in simulation labs practicing to *be* nurses.

To extrapolate, if you go to nursing school, you eat, sleep, and breathe nursing. Even if you are good at balancing your time outside of nursing, your life still ends up being nursing. Yet, somehow, the majority of us get out there into the hospitals, onto the floors, and into our careers, and we come to find that even after all of our schooling, we are still surprised.

If we were to look at being new in nursing as we looked at how we attend weddings, I would equate the two as such:

1. We can feel pleasantly surprised.

"I didn't feel prepared while I was in school. School can't fully prepare you. There are things in nursing that you can only learn if you are on the go as a nurse. It is a culture shock. It is very different from what we were taught in school, but that isn't a bad thing. I thought I would hate nursing, but then after my first week starting on the floor, I couldn't imagine doing anything else. It is such a blessing to have found a career that allows me to say that."

—LC, *medical-surgical respiratory nurse, seven years of experience*

"School was a shadow of what nursing really is. Everything is different. Nursing school was a fake life. It is a necessary step, I get it, but it was a fake life. It is not the same in any way, not at all. As a student, I got bored during day shift. That goes to show you just how different it is. Nurses cannot sit down or pee in real life, but you can pee in school. I felt prepared enough by school, but you are never going to learn how to do the job until you are actually doing it. Even though school is a fake life, I don't think the system is flawed. Nursing school needs to be as hard as it is so that you can have that basic knowledge then build on it based on your specialty. I can't believe I went from hating school so much to enjoying work so much. I felt like I should have had a harder time, but I think it was my coworkers who made it so good. They made it easier."

—MK, *medical-surgical sepsis telemetry nurse, eight months of experience*

2. We can feel unpleasantly surprised.

"I expected it to be difficult, but it has exceeded my expectations. I knew it would be hard because everyone said it would be. I expected the worst, but I didn't expect worse enough. It is just worse."

—RL, *medical-surgical sepsis nurse, three months of experience*

"It isn't talked about how little time you have to do spiritual care with your patients. You were pushed to do it a lot in school, and it is an important part of your job, which is good, but what if you literally don't have time to do it? It has happened to me multiple times where I want to dive in with a patient, but I am too busy to do so because someone is having active chest pain in the next room or something. It feels so impersonal to admit someone and have them tell you that they are a widow, or you do their suicide screen and they tell you that they are depressed, then you just keep working. It feels so impersonal. It is such a weird job because you are being so intimate with a stranger. It is really scary to me that I am actively participating in this person's life. Do they feel like I care about them? They apologize to me for bothering me, but it is a privilege to care about them. That has been burdening me a lot."

—BF, *progressive cardiac nurse, three months of experience*

3. We can feel excited.

"I didn't realize that I was going to have this much responsibility. It is more than I thought we were told that we were going to have. On that same note, I am the go-to person for the patient. I like being the patient's number one advocate, so I do like that responsibility."

—KH, *medical oncology nurse, eleven months of experience*

"My first day while I was precepting, I was so excited to finally be there and do what I thought at that time was the perfect job for me. But, I realized that I had so much responsibility and so much to learn, and seeing my nurse educating patients about medications and defects that I didn't even know about, I felt overwhelmed. I didn't even know what I didn't know. I was so excited to learn and do new things, but I was worried that I would never be able to get to the level of a nurse who does know all those things. It was fun to follow my preceptor everywhere, but I felt overwhelmed for sure."

—MO, *pediatric cardiac intensive care nurse, one year of experience*

4. We can feel scared.

"I wasn't expecting the responsibility and the weight of every decision that you make. Realizing that this is a real person and a real life and that they are counting on you to make the right calls is a scary thing, especially when you don't have all the answers."

—JW, *high risk labor and delivery nurse, ten months of experience*

"People say you won't be ready for your first day on your own, but no one ever believes it. Then suddenly, you get there, and you feel like, 'Oh my God, I'm not ready.' This isn't a profession where you can just be getting by. You feel like you should be doing well, but people tell you, 'Yeah you're just going to be getting by for a while,' and that is a scary thought."

—KR, *medical-surgical respiratory nurse, nine months of experience*

Chapter 3

5. We can come without any expectations at all. We can just be along for the ride.

If you recall, in Chapter One I told you that I never intended on being a nurse. That fact remained to be true starting from day one, when I applied to nursing school, to now, after having been a nurse for an entire year. The truth is, I am simply an along-for-the-ride kind of person. With nursing, it was no different—I was just along for the ride. As I was about to start off my career, I had no set expectations at all. Let me paint a picture of my own no-expectations experience for you.

*****

I am writing this to you in my seventh month of being a registered nurse. Yes, that makes me new. New and proud. New and terrified. People told me in school, "Your first year as an RN will be the hardest year of your life. Then, after that, things get better, and you will have a great life and career as a nurse." To be honest, I shrugged off that notion for a long time. How bad could it be?

Well, as it turns out, it can be pretty bad. For me, it has been a whirlwind of things: tiring, anxiety-exacerbating, tear-producing, chaotic, messy, and all of the above. You could name any feeling, and I would tell you that I've probably felt it. At this point, you might be thinking, *Wow, so being a new nurse must be terrible?* Well, yes and no, all rolled into one, and again, this is coming from my individual perspective. Let's unpack this.

I am a new nurse on the same floor that I worked on as an aid for two years during nursing school. My staff is amazing. They have had my back time and time again, and I love them to bits and pieces, but it is a hard floor. The patients are sick with high acuities. As an aid, I scraped by. I learned the ropes of the unit, the charting system, the people, how to stay alive on a twelve-hour overnight

NEW

shift, etc. It should have been an easy transition into the role of a RN, right?

Wrong. How could I have been so wrong? I was set up for success by my coworkers, my management, even by my own self. So, what happened? Part of me just wants to say that I don't know, that your first year is just hard. But, I think if someone had told me why it was going to be so hard before I started, that would've been helpful. Maybe they did. Maybe I just wasn't listening. New and proud.

A couple months into being a nurse, I was sitting next to one of the experienced nurses while we were charting, and she asked me, "So, what do you think of nursing so far?"

I think I said something about it being hard.

She responded with a laugh, "It's not what you thought it would be, is it?"

I laughed too and said, "No. Not at all."

To which she then replied, "And school didn't prepare you for this at all, did it?"

I laughed again, nervously and knowingly. What she said hit home. That is one of the hardest things about being a new nurse: you have absolutely no idea what being a nurse is really going to be like until you become one. In my case? I genuinely and mistakenly thought that I would just be able to figure it out.

One minute, you're in school watching interesting procedures and taking extra-long lunches in hospital cafeterias with your friends, then a few months later, after the absolute tsunami of stress and confusion that is the NCLEX licensure exam, you are suddenly taking care of multiple extremely sick people who are depending on you. During my first couple of months practicing on my own, I would be constantly yelling in my head, *Who put me in charge?*

At my hospital, the nurse aides wear maroon scrubs and the RNs wear blue. We have the expression, "You got your blues," whenever an aid becomes a nurse. When I came back one day in

Chapter 3

my blues instead of my maroons, people were excited for me. It was a good feeling having the people who I had worked alongside for two years run up to me and give me hugs, exclaiming, "You got your blues!" But, wearing my blues the entire first month I was a nurse brought a lot of mixed feelings. New and proud; *new and terrified*.

When you are in blue, suddenly people look at you like you are in charge. They look to you for help. They look at you with trust. That was a difficult feeling for me to come to terms with. I remember during my first shift precepting, a patient asked me something, and my brain, still in aid mode, almost made me say, "I don't know, let me go ask your nurse." But suddenly, I was the nurse. I couldn't defer the responsibility anymore. If there was a question, an issue, a problem, *anything*, I was now the one who would have to step up and figure things out.

*****

All five of the components of expectations that we talked about are normal. To have all five is healthy. Even fear can be healthy at times, because it means that we are being cautious and thoughtful about the situations that we are walking into. It is ok to be unpleasantly surprised sometimes, too, because that is a natural part of life. Not everything is perfect, and truth be told, sometimes we are disappointed with how things turn out.

The thing about expectations, however, is this: they are great, and are therefore greatly met, or they greatly unravel. If there is an in-between, I have yet to discover it. A fair question to ask would be, "Why are nurses so often blindsided by the profession of nursing?" If I were an outsider looking in at all of this, I would be confused. As an insider looking at all of this, I am still confused, perhaps even more so. But, the answer is this: nurses have great expectations because we are made to have great expectations. Our

NEW

expectations, callings, and dreams have to be great if we are going to stand even remotely close to the mountain of death and disease.

Allow me to take us on another detour. If you have ever been drawn into a corner by illusion then got kicked right back out of it by disillusionment in any aspect of your life, then you will be able to relate to what I am about to say. Here is an excerpt I wrote during my tenth month as a nurse.

*****

Today in the car on the way to therapy, I realized something. I was struck by the idea of disillusionment. First, let me ask you, have you ever been met with one of the following sentiments after telling someone that you are either studying nursing or that you are a nurse? Maybe you've heard something along the lines of, "Wow that's awesome! Nurses are so needed," or maybe, "Good for you! There is so much job security there," or even, "You're a nurse? My so-and-so is a nurse. I love nurses!" My personal favorite is when people sincerely thank me for being a nurse.

Maybe some of you nurses have had this same experience. It is like wherever we go, whenever we tell people what we do, we are met with praise. That is a privilege that I do not take for granted. But, I can't help but feel like when I tell people what I do for a living, I am somehow fooling them.

So, what went wrong? I went to an excellent school where the professors poured into us academically, professionally, and personally. Many other new nurses reported that their schools did the very best that they could in preparing them to be registered nurses. One of the marks of a good nursing program, department, or professor is that they encourage the students. Nursing school is so exceptionally demanding that you need the extra encouragement to survive it.

All that being said, all the positive feedback I got from my professors, from the general public, from older nurses, and from

Chapter 3

the entire world, I built up a very large glittering dream castle in my mind of what nursing was going to be like. I didn't even realize that I was doing it. There I was, subconsciously building up something in my mind for five years, something that was beautiful and glistening, an infinite world of possibilities.

People did say that it would be hard. You would hear older nurses swap war stories and professors reveal their hearts, and you would hear time and time again, "It's going to be hard, but you can do it. You are going to have an amazing career." We are talking working three days a week, tons of time to travel, good pay, and an abounding amount of street credit. That sounds like the dream, right?

Well, I am telling you that is exactly what it is. If we only view nursing in that way, then we are viewing it as an unrealistic dream. That is what no one told me. It wasn't until I was a nurse in the thick of it, crying all the time, that the disillusionment set in. It wasn't until the castle of my illusions, hopes, and dreams broke down around me that I even realized that I had such a castle.

Inversely, two of my dearest non-nursing friends were art majors in college. They never had illusions to begin with. They were constantly met with questions such as, "What are you going to do with that when you graduate?" and, "How are you going to support yourself with that?" Art is a tricky business. Whereas nurses are met with a world of yeses, artists are constantly met with a world of nos.

I am in no way, shape, or form endeavoring to put down artists, not at all. This is something that absolutely breaks my heart, because I deeply love, respect, and appreciate my creative friends and the art that they make. But, the facts remain the same: they were not disillusioned with their field of study, because they never had any illusions to begin with. They knew it would be hard. They knew that they might have to take jobs that they did not like. They knew that they might have to move back in with their families after college. The term "starving artist" is not an unfamiliar concept in our society. The world was already telling them no from the start. As a side note, these two particular women are both very happy and are excelling in both art and life.

Then, there was me with my shiny dream castle of nursing. I was blinded by illusion. I heard it would be hard, but I was a resilient person, so I could handle hard, right?

Again, wrong. One month into precepting, and my dream castle began to show fractures in its gossamer surface. One month on my own, and the whole thing completely crumbled around me. I became disillusioned, and I became disillusioned quickly. Maybe my dreams shattering and falling around me wouldn't have been so bad if that had been the only thing that I was dealing with at the time, but you have to remember that in nursing, you are never the only one who you are dealing with. There is always someone on the receiving end of the care that you are giving.

I was disillusioned and heart-broken, and I still had to take care of multiple very sick human beings a night. The disillusionment didn't just eventually come—it came and devastated. Even though I was well prepared, even though I was well poured into, even though I was encouraged, nothing could have prepared me for what nursing was actually going to be like.

The first two months practicing on my own were brutal. I remember during Thanksgiving 2018, at which point I was in the middle of my first month practicing on my own, I cried through the entire holiday. Thankfully, my brother's mother-in-law is a nurse and a wise and accomplished one at that. Do you know what she told me? She told me that what I was experiencing wasn't uncommon. The first two months of independent nursing practice are excruciatingly difficult. She told me to give myself grace and simply hang in there for those first two months. Just two months. If I was still feeling that badly after that, then I could think more seriously about pursuing other career options.

Two months. I remember thinking that was both doable and impossible, but it was a far more realistic goal than completing an

Chapter 3

entire year of nursing, which is what I had set out to do. In truth, it did get better after those first two months. Not a lot and not all at once, but little by little it got better. People said that by month eight or nine I would start to feel more confident. Things would start to click. As I sit here writing this, I am in my tenth month and have found that people were right. I feel like I have a small handle on what I am doing. I feel like I can keep my patients safe. I feel like I can deliver decent quality care, and that is monumental.

But the disillusionment, oh, the disillusionment. How does one come back from that? How does one get out of that? Well, it takes time.

Who out there feels exceptionally frustrated right now? "Just giving it time" is a nice sentiment, but what are we supposed to do in the meantime? What are we supposed to do while we cry every night and feel like we have chainsaws rumbling in our large intestines? It's true though. With time, some of the things that used to scare you no longer do. You find that the things that used to keep you up at night become something that you know you can handle. But, what about *in the meantime?*

Those are quite possibly the hardest words to have to think about because the hardest parts of our lives happen in between them. Truly, I don't have all the answers for you. But between those words, in the middle of the time that you are in, you are not alone.

*****

Aside from putting myself back into therapy, I decided that I was going to get to the bottom of why I felt as terribly as I did. So, I did some scientific database research, and I discovered two things. Primarily, I found out that I am not the only one who felt overwhelmed when they first started out, just as my brother's mother-in-law had said. Beyond that, I discovered that what I was feeling was not just anxious or even overwhelmed—it was something even more distinct and imperative to address. Before I

NEW

go any further, I want to make it abundantly clear that all that I am about to say stems from research that I stumbled across. It turns out I was in shock. Actual shock.

I have two women to thank for this discovery: Marlene Kramer and Dr. Judy Boychuk Duchscher. I had no idea what I was going through until I read Kramer's Reality Shock: Why Nurses Leave Nursing and Duchscher's *From Surviving to Thriving: Navigating the First Year of Professional Nursing Practice*. Kramer, a leading nurse researcher who conducted her monumental research in the 1960s and '70s, was the original voice for new nurses. She was the very first person to research the process and ramifications of what being new in the field of nursing entails. There had been no formal research done on this topic until Kramer came along. According to her research, new nurses don't just transition into nursing. Oftentimes they experience "reality shock." Kramer describes this term as such in her aforementioned book:

"The phenomenon and the specific shock-like reactions of new workers when they find themselves in a work situation for which they have spent several years preparing and for which they thought they were going to be prepared and then suddenly find that they are not [...] Shock, as used in the construct of reality shock, means the total social, physical, and emotional response of a person to the unexpected, unwanted, or undesired, and in the most severe degree to the intolerable. It is the startling discovery and reaction to the discovery that school-bred values conflict with work-world values."

If Kramer was the original melody of new graduate nurse research, then Dr. Boychuk Duchscher, whom we discussed in Chapter One, is the harmony of this field. She took Kramer's initial research, expanded upon it, and developed her own research, which she put forward in a friendly and applicable way in the 2000s. She

Chapter 3

also came up with the more specific term "transition shock." She describes transitions as the following in her own book:

> "Anytime someone makes a 'change' from what they know to what they don't know or are not completely familiar with, they experience a transition—a journey from what was to what is. It is not so much the actual change (motivating event or 'catalyst') that challenges us, but the process of making the change. Transitions are considered passages or movements from one state of condition to another and they can profoundly influence and alter the lives of the individuals involved as well as their significant others (friends, family, and coworkers). Transitions usually begin with events that create instability and make change necessary—graduating as a nurse and moving forward from being a nursing student to being a fully responsible nurse is such an event […] *Transition Shock* is the term I have coined to embody the elements of the new nurse's initial entry (the first 1–2 months after orientation) into the workplace. I chose this term because it best captures everything related to roles, responsibilities, relationships, and knowledge that both motivate and mediate the intensity and duration of a graduate's earliest experiences as a nurse."

Quite relatedly, Dr. Boychuk Duchscher also notes the following in her investigation of this topic:

> "It was not uncommon in my research, nor is it in my ongoing work with nursing students and new graduates, to hear them using words, phrases or expressions such as 'terrified' and 'scared to death' when referring to their transition experience."

In my own exploration, I, too, came across multiple nurses who voiced similar experiences. From 1960 to 2000 to 2020, it is imperative to point out that none of us are immune to the uncertainties and difficulties of transitions and being new.

NEW

One nurse spoke into the very idea of experiencing shock as a new nurse as such:

"It was a culture shock experience of going from the regular world to the hospital where everyone is really sick and there are a lot of hopeless people. Seeing that and then trying to reconcile that with my normal reality was hard. I would get irritated with my roommates when they would complain about homework and I would think, 'Well you are not sick or dying!' It was a culture shock."
—*GH, radiation oncology nurse, four years of experience*

To build off of that notion and bring us full circle in our discussion of the disillusionment of our own great expectations, two nurses said the following:

"We all start out idealistically thinking that we are going to change the world and save lives, but in reality, it isn't every day you are able to say, 'Yes, I saved that person's life!' Being content with making small differences regularly, one at a time, would have been a better framework for my expectations. Youthful idealism is where we all start, but experience in life helps you see things more realistically and also lets you give yourself some grace."
—*CM, pediatric advice line nurse, thirty-seven years of experience*

"Part of the problem is that in our generation, as millennials, we have such an idealized view of calling and career. The reality is that a job is a job. It is work, so if you walk in thinking that you are going to love all of this, all aspects of the job, then you are going to be surprised, especially in nursing, because you deal with hard things. You are literally cleaning up people's bodily fluids. So, what it really is, is the death of this idyllic picture that we had in our minds of what the job is going to be like, especially as Christians in the medical field."
—*BS, internal medicine hospitalist nurse practitioner, eight years of experience*

Chapter 3

Although the initial shattering and crumbling of our own disillusionments may be devastating, the effects of the loss of our own dreams can be reshaped and rebuilt into actual abounding possibilities. We just have to choose to do the work that it takes to move ourselves from the space of broken idealism into the realm of hopeful realism that is only brought through time, work, and growth. Another nurse explained this idea as such:

> "In nursing school, my classmates and I were so excited about all of the ways that we would change the world. Once we actually became RNs, we had many conversations along the lines of, 'What am I doing?' and processing through the idea that, 'I thought I would be changing people's lives, but really, I am just trying to survive and not mess up.' Especially during that first year, a lot of that idealism faded away. But as I have continued in my career and have more life experience, I feel like I am in a space now where, yes, there are hard times, but there are many ways to make a difference. My hope is to be able to connect with people and make a difference actually happen now, even though it often doesn't look the way that I envisioned it would years ago."
> —KS, *community health nurse, eight years of experience*

Similarly, I myself acutely felt exactly what both Kramer and Duchscher described in their research. I experienced and lived that shock, but I knew that I couldn't simply stay in a state of perpetual shock for long. I had to do something, anything, to get past it. Eventually, I did, but it was one of the most difficult things that I have ever had to work through.

Another nurse remarked on such difficulties with this wise statement:

> "I had to learn to deal with difficult situations, but that is the way of life. There are always difficult situations that come up. We just have to find our own ways of dealing with them."
> —WB, *hospice nurse, thirty years of experience*

NEW

Working through this particular brand of difficult shock wasn't something that I could do on my own. In Chapter One, I mentioned that I felt like I was falling down a dark hole, and when I reached out to stop my fall, my nursing family caught me. Well, Kramer and Duchscher are two of the nurses who helped in that process, because they dedicated their lives and careers to make sure that no new nurse has to feel like they are alone. That poses the question, "How do we go forth and actively live as holistically healthy human beings amidst dealing with our own expectations regarding new situations?"

Well, aside from asking for help, realizing that we are not alone, identifying that we might be in shock, recognizing that that is ok, being gentle with ourselves in the healing process, and working through it all with trusted people in our lives, we need to, after all of that important work, show ourselves some tough love.

When I tell people that I am a nurse, they often say, "Oh, you must be so compassionate and caring." But, the danger of summing up nurses as only compassionate and caring is that this perception gets quickly, and falsely, translated into the idea that nurses are simply nice.

In Chapter Two, we discussed how active love is not the same as the love in dreams. Well, dream love equates to niceness whereas kindness equates to active love. Kindness is saying and doing the right and hard thing whereas niceness is often a false love based solely on trying to not hurt people's feelings.

One nurse I interviewed said the following on that very topic, in response to the question, "How has your perception of yourself changed?"

"I am a lot tougher than I was before. I can handle more than I thought I could. I didn't even know how much I could take on. I am a very soft, gentle, and squishy soul. I get hurt easily, but I also comfort people easily. I learned how to be tough. Being soft all the time and being nice all the time isn't being kind. Being kind

Chapter 3

is tough love, and it is being able to stand up for yourself and for your patients even when it isn't what they want."
—EP, *medical-surgical oncology nurse, one year of experience*

Yes, we need to do the work of being gentle with ourselves, being patient with ourselves, and processing our expectations with both ourselves and others, but we cannot just stop there. There is more work to be done, and that work is tough-loving ourselves. But what does all this have to do with expectations?

I was disillusioned. So, maybe a lot of us are when we graduate from college and enter the working world. But, eventually we need to ask ourselves, "So what?" The question of *why*, while important, needs to eventually take a back seat to the question of *what*.

Why did I feel disillusioned? Because I was shocked. Ok, we worked through that. Now what? What are we going to do about it? In reality, I let myself dwell in the *why* phase for too long. I thought I had moved onto the *what* phase, but it turns out I had not. I came to this conclusion just a few days after I surpassed my one-year mark as a registered nurse. Yes, it took me an entire year to realize what I am about to share in the following excerpt.

*****

I just finished reading Marlene Kramer's *Reality Shock: Why Nurses Leave Nursing* and can I just say, she paved the way for all of us nurses. I am not sure what was happening to new nurses prior to 1974, when this research came out, but I can't imagine that it was a good time to be a new nurse.

I expected to learn a lot from reading this book, which I did. I expected to be surprised by how different nursing was back in the 1970s, which I was. I was *very* surprised, however, to see that the same struggles and feelings that Kramer outlines in her research are the exact same ones that I found myself going through as a new nurse in 2019. I thought that there might be some overlap, but seeing the same concerns I had running through my head written down in a book that is forty-five years old was equal parts shocking and hilarious.

It was hilarious because I remember thinking that I was alone in the way that I felt. To go from first finding out that other new nurses in 2019 felt the same way as I did, to finding out that other experienced nurses felt the same way, to finding out the landmark study on reality shock in new graduate nurses produced the exact same emotions that I myself felt was truly and deeply hilarious. Alone? More like accompanied by decades of nurses who have felt beyond inadequate in their jobs when they first started.

What really surprised me was a quote that Kramer pulled from a popular novel at the time and included towards the end of her own book. In actuality, I was already very familiar with this particular novel. When I initially read it, I wasn't expecting the book to have a lasting impact on me, but let me tell you, it did. It has impacted me in such a way that I have talked about it on numerous occasions in a variety of contexts. So, what was this book? It was *I Never Promised You A Rose Garden* by Joanne Greenberg.

The book's little blurb, if you look it up on Amazon, says this:

"Enveloped in the dark inner kingdom of her schizophrenia, sixteen-year-old Deborah is haunted by private tormentors that isolate her from the outside world. With the reluctant and fearful consent of her parents, she enters a mental hospital where she will spend the next three years battling to regain her sanity with the help of a gifted psychiatrist. As Deborah struggles toward the possibility of the 'normal' life she and her family hope for, the reader is inexorably drawn into her private suffering and deep determination to confront her demons. A modern classic, *I Never Promised You a Rose Garden* remains every bit as poignant, gripping, and relevant today as when it was first published."

The quote that is most often highlighted from this book is as follows (and for context it is Deborah's therapist speaking to her):

Chapter 3

"'Look here,' Furii said, 'I never promised you a rose garden. I never promised you perfect justice... And I never promised you peace and happiness. My help is so that you can be free to fight for these things. The only reality I offer is challenge, and being well is being free to accept it or not at whatever level you are capable. I never promise lies, and the rose garden world of perfection is a lie... and a bore too!'"

Usually, I am the one to bring up this quote to people, and they frequently tell me, "You're right," but not this time. No, this time I was at the receiving end of the *I Never Promised You A Rose Garden* speech. Marlene Kramer smacked me upside the head with that exact same quote toward the end of her *Reality Shock* book and it made me upset in a way that I was not prepared for.

Was I again angry at my disillusionment of nursing? Was I mad because I felt like people hadn't told me the truth about how hard it was going to be? Was I mad at myself because they had told me, and I just hadn't listened? Was I mad because I spent so much time feeling inadequate when really nursing, as well as life, is just really hard, and we all need to cut ourselves some slack? Or, was I mad because even though I was at the end of my first year, I was still terrified of what was to come next?

Truly, as Greenberg writes, life is a series of challenges. Some, we get to say no to. Some, we have no choice but to say yes to. Some, we will become victorious over, and some, we will succumb to. Some challenges we aren't even cut out for to begin with, but if we were fully prepared, equipped, and ready for every challenge that we face, then it wouldn't be much of a challenge, would it? More often than not, we are not capable when we start. In some cases, we become capable. Then, in some other cases, the challenge proves to simply be too much, and we fail.

Another thematic element in Greenberg's book is that the main character, Deborah, sees patients be cleared to be discharged and re-enter normal life only to be brought back in again. But, should that discourage those other characters from trying to get well? Should we let the possibility of failure keep us from rising to meet our next challenge? Will we cower? Or, will we face our fears?

*****

It was Kramer's quoting of *I Never Promised You a Rose Garden* that finally caused me to move from asking myself *why* to asking myself *what*. It was this moment of tough love that made me realize that, at the end of the day, our own great expectations don't really matter. Our expectations are not reality. It doesn't matter how they are met. It doesn't matter how they aren't met. The *whys* of our great expectations are not as important as *what* we are going to do with them. Are we going to cower, or are we going to face our fears?

To close, one of the nurses that I interviewed said this:

"There is a lot of weight in our words but also a lot of validity in our circumstances."
—MK, *medical-surgical sepsis telemetry nurse, eight months of experience*

Our words and expectations carry a certain weight. And because they serve as the pillars that support our hopes and dreams they are burdensome. There is a certain validity that comes along with circumstance. Circumstances are our reality, regardless of what our words and expectations are telling us. To truly see our expectations we must assess and reassess the fine line between our dreams and our realities. Both are important, but what is even more important is discovering how the two merge together, in our jobs and in our lives.

While rose gardens are never promised to us in this life, when we can get a hold of our own great expectations and find that space where dreams and reality meet, then we are well on our way to planting our own roses. Once we have started to do that, we can

Chapter 3

begin to perpetuate the beauty that we have found in our own lives outward to the rest of the world.

We will revisit rose gardens throughout the course of this book, but for now, let's start with step one: how do we get roses to grow?

Chapter Four:
Pride, Humility, and Dancing

We talked about external expectations for most of the last chapter, but we didn't have a chance to talk about the heart of the matter, our expectations for the *internal*. The expectations that we have for *ourselves*. If there is anything that carries a greater significance to us than our external expectations, it is our internal expectations. These are the standards that we have for our very beings. And if we want any roses to grow, we need to figure out how to deal with our inner expectations.

When we have to figure this concept out within the context of a new job or environment, it can be challenging to say the least. We are grappling with the weight of all our expectations, both external and internal, in the midst of learning how to do the job or tackle a new situation while trying not to make any mistakes.

Being new is an exhausting endeavor. As for being new in nursing? It is beyond exhausting, because the consequences of making mistakes can be, well, not great. We will talk about mistakes in depth in both Chapters Six and Seven. Don't worry, those chapters are not exclusively for nurses, because the possibility of making mistakes is a scary part of any new job, and beyond that, it is a scary part of life.

Being a new nurse can be accurately described by the expression, "Out of the frying pan and into the fire." In nursing school, the responsibilities are hot—they are frying-pan hot. But, in the real nursing world, those responsibilities are actually on fire. It is quite like the transition from moving out of your parents'

Chapter 4

house for the first time. You thought you knew what responsibility was, but you really didn't. Or, perhaps it is like becoming a parent for the first time. Again, you thought you knew what responsibility was, but you didn't.

One nurse provided insight into this very topic by saying the following:

"I didn't feel prepared for my first nursing job, that's for sure! I think I was prepared by my schooling to build on things, but school is really just an introduction. It equips you to begin, but it doesn't really equip you for the first job. It gives you theory to base things off of, but I don't think anything can really prepare you for real life. It is like parenting—you can only be prepared so much, but you aren't really going to be ready for it or know what to expect until you do it."

—CM, *pediatric advice line nurse, thirty-seven years of experience*

As we discussed in Chapter Three, we can't ever be fully prepared for the new situations that come our way, because we can never fully know what to expect. Therefore, our internal expectations can take us from the heat of the frying pan into the actual scorching open flames, and they can take us there quickly. Why? Because the internal expectations that we have for ourselves are the native stomping grounds of the giants of shame, self-doubt, and anxiety. While the external new situations that we find ourselves in can be challenging, they are only made more or less challenging based on how we deal with them internally.

But what do our internal expectations have to do with the title of this chapter? Well, there is a direct correlation between our internal expectations and either the pride or the humility with which we approach being new. We'll get to the dancing part a little bit later.

There is a mixture of things that we feel when we start in a new position. We want to excel. We want to do a good job. Part of that stems from the simple fact that we don't want to make any mistakes, because mistakes are embarrassing. Beyond that, depending on one's circumstance, they can actually be dangerous.

This brings us to the interesting intersection of pride and humility. Pride and humility—polar opposites, it's true—are inconveniently intertwined. Where do they collide the most strikingly? That messy mess of wrestling both pride and humility at the same time takes place within our own internal expectations.

This can be observed in any job during the training process of any new employee, but it can be clearly seen when training a new nurse. I turned to one of the interviews I did with an experienced nurse for some wisdom. For context, this particular nurse has trained over twenty new graduate nurses. When asked, "What is a common mistake that you see younger nurses make?" her response was as follows:

"There are two ends of the spectrum. There are new grads who come in thinking that they are going to be fine. They act confidently, and they don't have enough of the fear of God instilled in them for the magnitude of the potential of which they can mess up or the understanding of the breadth of what they don't know. Then, there are the new grads who are so anxious that they can't even think straight. Each one has to be dealt with differently. For the ones who are overly confident, they need to recognize how much they don't know and how much they have to learn. A lot of times, those new grads aren't willing to ask questions.

"My number one flag in a new grad is if they are not asking me a trillion questions. My number one flag! Because there is no way they know! On the other side of the spectrum, with the ones who are hyper-anxious, they take forever to do everything because they are so focused on doing every detail perfectly. They are probably the hardest ones to help, because you don't want to tell them not to be careful, but they have to figure out a way to be faster and to

Chapter 4

find some level of fake-it-till-you-make-it so they are not breaking down every shift."

—BS, *internal medicine hospitalist nurse practitioner, eight years of experience*

This got me thinking. Which one was I when I was first starting out? Was I overly confident? Was I overly anxious? Somehow, I think I was both. Looking back, I think I was overly confident when I started. Then, once I realized the sheer size of the beast that is nursing, I became overly anxious.

I quickly went from feelings of pride to feelings of shame, and that is where many of my issues at the beginning stemmed from. *Shame?* you might be thinking to yourself. *What do pride and shame have to do with each other?* Well, they actually have a lot to do with each other, because shame is the place that fuels our anxieties. Once my pride melted away, the shameful feelings of inadequacy kicked in.

To quote the wise Uncle Iroh from the animated show *Avatar the Last Airbender*, "Pride is not the opposite of shame, but it's source. True humility is the only antidote to shame."

If I had known what I know now about the true power of healthy humility, I would've handled the situation differently. But instead I transitioned from being overly confident to being a crying, anxious mess. Now that I have reflected on my own new experience and have discussed the topic with numerous nurses, both experienced and new, I have found the following to be true: being healthfully confident does not equate with being prideful, and being healthfully humble does not equate with being ashamed.

Let's talk about what being prideful looks like. In his book *Mere Christianity*, C.S. Lewis wrote on the topic of pride, "The essential vice, the utmost evil, is Pride." Being prideful equates with being blind: blind to truth, blind to others, blind to everything. Prideful people are the worst to deal with. When we fall victim to pride, we don't listen—we just act. We don't see others for who they are. We

NEW

just try to get people to pay attention to us, because our opinions of ourselves can truly be that high.

In the film *10 Things I Hate About you,* two teenage sisters, who are polar opposites have a squabble. Bianca, the younger sister says, "Where did you come from? Planet Loser?" and her older sister, Kat, replies, "As opposed to Planet Look-at-Me, Look-at-Me?"

What do C.S. Lewis and a 1990s teen comedy have in common? Pride. Such pride lives on Planet Look-at-Me. Do you want to know who was a resident on Planet Look-at-Me when she first started as a nurse? Me, and for a variety of reasons. Did I think I was the best? No. Did I think I was the worst? Also, no. But, my fault lay in thinking that I didn't have to worry because I would just figure it out as I went along, and I don't mean that in a positive, always-be-learning kind of way.

Thankfully, it was a state of being that only lasted a couple of weeks for me. Looking back, I am actually glad that the pride got kicked out of me as soon as it did, because if I had been proud and practicing on my own, who knows what dangerous things could have happened? The possibilities are both endless and terrifying. Here is an excerpt that I wrote in my ninth month as a nurse on this very topic.

*****

Since I worked for two years as an aid on the same floor that I eventually became a nurse on, I saw a lot of new nurses come through our unit. There were two new graduate nurses that stuck out in my mind—let's call them New Grad X and New Grad Y.

New Grad X. Oh man, did I look up to this new grad. New Grad X was confident, expedient, and always seemed to be in control. If you asked New Grad X a question, New Grad X knew the answer. New Grad X seemed to be dominating the new grad game.

Chapter 4

Then, there was New Grad Y. New Grad Y was slow. New Grad Y took a long time doing anything. New Grad Y didn't seem insecure per se, but New Grad Y did not have the confidence that New Grad X did. Overall, however, New Grad Y was steady, kind, and did a good job.

I remember thinking to my naive nursing-student self, "I hope I am like New Grad X when I am a nurse."

This brings us to the present. I am now a new nurse myself and have seen a thing or two, and do you know what? I am New Grad Y. I am slow. It takes me longer than anyone else on my floor to do pretty much anything. That makes me incessantly frustrated with myself.

Then, the other night, I was talking to a coworker who also knew New Grad X and New Grad Y but through the lens of a more experienced nurse as opposed to me, who knew them as an inexperienced student aid. What he said quite frankly floored me and reframed my perspective at the same time. He said, "Yeah, I remember New Grad X. New Grad X was one of the most confident new grads I have ever seen, but New Grad X was also one of the most reckless nurses I have ever seen. If you have never seen or done something before, you need to ask, but New Grad X would just troubleshoot things. You can't just be doing that. It's not safe."

My bubble burst. All this time, I had the wrong mindset. In my head, someone who was confident and fast, someone who never needed to ask questions, was the ideal. But, being too confident, being too fast, and failing to ask questions is ultimately reckless and unsafe. It dawned on me that maybe I am not like New Grad X at all and maybe that is actually a good thing.

*****

If being prideful is the reckless, fast, one-man-wolf-pack approach to a new setting, then what is the healthily confident approach?

NEW

Well, let's talk about what healthy confidence looks like. Nurse researcher Marlene Kramer wrote this:

> "One of the primary requisites for making a relatively smooth transition from the school to the world setting is self-confidence in one's ability to learn and in one's resources. This does not mean overconfidence, bragging, or a know-it-all attitude, but faith in oneself and in one's ability to think things through under pressure of time, such faith being grounded on at least some experience. New graduates should not be expected to know everything, but it is realistic that they should come to the work scene schooled and practiced in basic interpersonal, organizational, manual, and communication skills. This will not guarantee a smooth transition but, if along with these fundamental learnings the new graduate also has a reasonable self-confidence and the necessary wisdom to seek out support and help at crucial junctures, there is a good chance the road will be smoother."

Healthy confidence can only occur when it is balanced with healthy humility, which we will talk about a little bit later on in this chapter. For now, let's just stick to the topic of healthy confidence. One experienced nurse said this in response to the question, "What is a piece of wisdom that you have for someone in their first year/ what advice would you give your younger self?"

> "Be more confident. Even if you don't know what you are doing, you have to recognize that no one fully knows what they are doing. Even the experienced nurses have to ask questions. So, for the new grads out there, you need to know how to learn, how to ask questions, and how to fake it till you make it. If I was confident in myself, even if it was in limited knowledge, I would have a better day, because the patients would be more confident in me and it would have a ripple effect."
>
> —*GH, radiation oncology nurse, four years of experience*

Chapter 4

I don't know what they say to those of you who are in other professions, but "fake it till you make it" is the oft spoken mantra of nurses. Are nurses excellent providers of customer service? Yes. Are nurses also excellent performers? Also, yes, but I assure you, not in a bad way.

When you are a new nurse, you have a lot of first-time experiences, like in any profession. Except you are performing on people—living, breathing *people*. When you are with the patient, you are on stage. You don't get to be afraid. You don't get to be weak.

You are brave and you are strong. That patient is depending on you in their moment of weakness. You are dealing with someone's life, and the show must go on, regardless of how confident or competent you personally feel. Should you lie to them? Never. But you do have to build their confidence in both you and in the process.

For the nurses reading this, what is the most intimidating nursing skill you had to learn in school? The one you were so nervous to do on the mannequin and even more nervous to do on a person? What I am talking about is a nursing student's first IV start. I remember mine clearly. I was in my critical care rotation and the census was low, so there were not enough nurses in critical care to take on students that day. I begged my instructor to let me go to the emergency department, and she kindly obliged.

Starting an IV is probably the scariest skill that nursing students have to learn. Sticking needles in veins and getting the little catheter to stay patent and in place is anxiety-inducing. I wanted to wait. In my earlier rotations, I refused to do my first IV on a crying eight-year-old. I also refused to do it on an old man with absolutely no visible veins. Why? Because I had classmates who had been traumatized attempting to start an IV and failing or—even worse—blowing the vein and causing the patient to bruise.

I knew that if I were going to start my first IV, I wanted it to be special, like losing your virginity. Which is verbatim what I

NEW

told the nurse following that day in the emergency department. She laughed and said something along the lines of, "Ok, you little weirdo. Let's find you the perfect patient to lose your IV virginity to."

Long story short, this nurse did in fact find the perfect patient for me. They were young, probably only a few years older than me. Relaxed and had been in the hospital multiple times for diabetic ketoacidosis, so it wasn't her first rodeo. And she had lavender hair and sparkles on her face. As an avid face sparkle-wearer myself, I knew that we were the perfect match.

The nurse I was following told the patient that it would be my first IV start, and the patient calmly and encouragingly allowed me to go for it and— *I got it*. I felt so empowered. My waiting significantly paid off, because once I knew that I could successfully start one IV, I knew I could do it again.

Then, in the very next room we went into, the patient was an older gentleman who was very apprehensive about my starting an IV on him. He even asked, "Have you ever done one of these before?" to which my nurse responded, without missing a beat, "Yeah, she just did one in the next room over and it went great." Neither of us mentioned that it was the only IV I had ever done, but it was true all the same. At that point, I *had* started one before. Did he need to know that his IV was only the second one that I had ever done in my life? No. And do you know what? I successfully got his IV started, too.

We have to know when to fake it as well as when not to. Sometimes, faking it is exactly what we need to do, and sometimes, it is exactly what we should not be doing. Identifying that imperative distinction is part of being a continual learner. Fake it in front of the patient, client, customer, or whomever to help instill confidence, but do not fake it in front of your team. Just to reiterate, *never fake it in front of your team*, because that is when people get hurt. That right there is the distinction between healthy confidence and unhealthy pride. Healthy confidence is instilling confidence in your patient,

Chapter 4

even if it is with the help of the tried and true fake-it-till-you-make-it method. Unhealthy pride, however, is faking it in front of your coworkers because you don't want to look incompetent, because you want to save face, because you are scared to ask questions, or because of whatever the case may be.

Let's talk about what being shame looks like versus what healthy humility looks like. We are lumping these two together because the line between the two is just that thin and just that treacherous. Let me demonstrate how thin that line can be and also how powerful and freeing it is when we learn to discern it.

*****

Tomorrow, I officially finish my ninth month as a registered nurse. Let's discuss the last shift that I worked. I really wanted to try to help carry the team a little bit. When you are first a new nurse, you do not carry the team whatsoever. Instead, your teammates carry you. The charge nurse answers your questions, the more experienced nurses help you double check orders you don't understand, and the oncoming nurse ties up loose ends that you weren't able to. You just try and keep your patients alive and safe for the night. That is pretty much what being a new nurse is like for a long time.

This last shift I worked, I finally felt like I had a minute to help my teammates out. I called doctors. I tied up loose ends. It was the most productive night that I have ever had. At the end of it, I gave my report to a nurse who is known to be on top of things. Telling her about all the miscellaneous things that I completed so that she wouldn't have to made me feel good.

I worked exceptionally hard two nights in a row to get everything accomplished, but even after all of that, I still got two emails concerning things that I had missed. Frankly, the emails were merited, and needless to say, I went from feeling proud of myself to frustrated. I tried my absolute hardest, and it still wasn't enough. In reality, it's been nine whole months of trying my hardest and

NEW

falling short. It's hard. More specifically, it's humbling. That is one of the best ways to describe my first year as a nurse. Sometimes, we are humbled in good ways. Other times, we are humbled in ways that really hurt but that end up being conducive to growth.

I want to take a moment to highlight that I do mean humbling and not humiliating. A good environment is humbling in a healthy way. When we see challenges before us and recognize that we can't meet those challenges on our own, we ask for help, and we are met with gracious assistance. That is a perfect case scenario of how humility can be used to foster healthy growth.

Humiliation, however, is different. Humiliation stems from when we, or our mistakes, are met with chastisement rather than help. Honestly, I don't feel qualified to talk about the concept of humiliation, because my team is so wonderful, but if you feel like you are being put in situations that are humiliating, then you could very well be subjected to bullying which needs to be reported. You do not deserve that. But, I digress.

I probably have asked more questions than any new nurse ever has, but I would rather someone think that I am not that smart than inadvertently do harm. I would rather take up two minutes of my coworker's time than do harm. Not knowing can be humiliating if we let it be, but if we keep our mouths shut and pretend like we already know everything, then we'll never actually learn. Finding the courage to admit that we don't know everything, to humble ourselves, and to ask for help is what ultimately allows us to grow.

Maybe right now you are thinking to yourself, *Well, of course I'll ask questions. It is stupid not to,* or maybe, *Actually, I am already pretty humble, so I don't think I'll have a problem with that,* or even, *I know myself. I feel like I am a good blend of confident and humble.* But, I'll tell you what—I thought all those things about myself before I started as a nurse, yet I quickly found that I had a lot to learn about humility. In light of the emails I got coming off my last shift, I still have a lot to learn.

Chapter 4

If we don't learn how to be humble in a healthy way, we are going to sink, and fast. We are our own biggest enemies when it comes to the anxieties that we have regarding our own shortcomings. When we get in our own heads, we turn what could potentially be humbling in a healthy way into something that humiliates us. Let's extrapolate.

For example, you have a question and maybe you are thinking to yourself, *I have this question, but I'm afraid to ask*. You have two options, one that is true and one that is false. One leads to liberating humility, and one leads to stifling humiliation.

The true option is this: you only learn by asking. Everyone is a resource. Your coworkers know you're new and need extra help. Even the most experienced nurses ask questions when they don't know something. So, let the truth lead you to *humility*. It's ok to not know everything, so take that humble step and ask for help.

The false option is this: insert whatever self-deprecating thing that you think about yourself here. *This is a dumb question. I'm not competent. They'll think less of me if I ask.* This option feeds on fear. When we let our fear overtake our thoughts and we don't ask questions, it can lead to *humiliation*. Humiliation is what occurs when we let our own shame and fears speak louder than the truth of the situation in our minds. Even if no one else is inflicting humiliation on us, we often inflict it on ourselves.

The reality is, as we discussed in Chapter Two, none of us will ever be enough. None of us can carry the team on our own. None of us can provide perfect and complete care to any one patient.

******

Healthy humility is something that we all have to learn. In the middle of that lesson is learning how to let go of feelings of shame. One thing that helped open my eyes to this was the idea of nursing being twenty-four-seven care. I remember the first nurse who said this to me almost made me cry, in a good way, because she said it with so much kindness. I was still orienting on nights at the time, and I was supposed to have hung an IV antibiotic at 7:00 a.m. I didn't know it yet, but the night shift is supposed to take care of all the 7:00 a.m. antibiotics, and day shift takes over the 7:00 p.m. antibiotics so that nothing gets missed or is late.

While giving the oncoming day-shift nurse report, I realized that I had not hung the antibiotic. Upon realizing that I had not done what I was supposed to do, I immediately felt ashamed. But this bright soul of a nurse gave me a hug and said, "Don't worry about it. I'll take care of it. It's twenty-four-seven care. Never forget, it's twenty-four-seven care."

That simple idea re-framed my shame and brought me into a place of healthy humility, because she was right. As individual nurses, we cannot provide care to someone twenty-four-seven. We work twelve-hour shifts, we go home, and then it is up to the next nurse to continue the care from there. So, I found the grace in what she said, in the idea that I couldn't do it all. No one can. That lesson formatively impacted how I practice.

To conclude the definition portion of this chapter, I want to again quote the same portion of C.S. Lewis's *Mere Christianity,* but this time, with a focus on humility. Lewis concludes like this:

"If anyone would like to acquire humility, I can, I think, tell him the first step. The first step is to realize that one is proud. And a biggish step, too. At least, nothing whatever can be done before it. If you think you are not conceited, it means you are very conceited indeed."

But, what can we actually do to untangle the sticky web of pride and shame and instead foster healthy confidence and humility in both ourselves and others? Well, we need to look at it this way: while pride and shame feed off of one another in a cyclical downward spiral of eventual rot and decay, healthy confidence and healthy humility are woven together in an intricate dance. When

Chapter 4

we can find the balance of confidence and humility in life, then we are truly dancing. When we step into that kind of liberation, we go from cowering in the shadows of the nightfall of fear to dancing in the moonlight of freedom.

Like so many of the most important things in our lives, confidence and humility both need to be in balance. So, how do we do this? While the following list is tidy, actually doing these things and putting them into practice is not a tidy process because life is not a tidy process. In fact, life is the messiest of all processes. I even admitted to you that I did not learn this lesson the easy way. But you know what? I still learned it. Will I always be able to get the process down perfectly? No, but now I know what to do the next time I am staring down at the precipice of pride and shame and am thinking about jumping into its sticky cycle. Now, I know how *not* to jump.

The five ways we can all come one step closer to becoming moonlight-dancing human beings who balance healthy humility and healthy confidence in the midst of new situations are as follows:

1. Ask questions.
2. Ask for help.
3. Recognize that you are part of a team.
4. Give yourself grace.
5. Never stop learning.

Let's go over the choreography of this dance together.

1. Ask questions.

Asking questions helps dissolve unhealthy pride because the actual act of asking someone a question invites us to admit that we do not know everything. This then speaks into healthy humility because it not only allows us to admit that we don't know everything, but it also allows us to take the opportunity to learn something new. Thus, asking questions dispels unhealthy shame because instead of sticking us in an I-don't-know-anything or an I'll-never-be-able-to-learn-all-of-this spiral, it allows us to both calm down and break down our learning process into more manageable portions. You can learn one new thing, can't you? Consider it a small victory every time you learn one new thing, for those small things will soon build on each other, and we will come to find that we actually know quite a lot and have won a lot of victories.

This process cyclically brings us back into a realm of healthy confidence, because we now know something that we didn't know before, which is something we can feel good about and, in turn, share with others to help them learn, too.

In my research, nineteen nurses verbalized the importance of asking questions within the scope of their practice. One nurse said this on the subject in response to the question, "What is a common mistake that you see younger nurses make?"

"I would say not asking enough questions, feeling too intimidated to ask, or feeling like what they have to contribute to the conversation about the patient is not significant. You need to speak up. You are the nurse. You have valuable information and have observations and perceptions that need to be shared. There are no dumb questions and there are no dumb observations."

—*SF, professor of nursing, twenty-seven years of experience*

2. Ask for help.

This goes hand-in-hand with asking questions. Beyond that, it goes hand-in-hand with the idea of not going through life alone. Do you really think that you can make it up the mountain of life and death in the shadow of disaster and disease *alone?* I know I can't. So, how do we not go through life and up that mountain alone? We ask for help. Is asking for help easy? No. Is it fun? No. In fact,

Chapter 4

it is tremendously vulnerable and scary. But, is it necessary for our actual survival as humans? Yes. We are going to talk about this in depth in Chapter Five, but for now, let's just look at the idea of asking for help in the context of pride and humility.

When we ask for help, we are kicking unhealthy pride aside because again we have to admit that not only do we not know everything, but that we also cannot do and be everything. This, in turn, allows us to break away from the unhealthy inadequacy that misplaced humility brings because it allows us to stop being so anxious for a minute and say, "You know what? I can't possibly be everything because at the end of the day, I am human." This, too, lends itself to healthy humility, because it allows us to recognize that we are not always going to be enough and that that is ok. We won't always be able to measure up to the perfect standards and internal expectations that we have for ourselves, and that is ok. It all becomes ok when we are open to receiving help and to helping others. None of us are making it up that mountain alone.

This then leads us back to healthy confidence. When we see all of the ways that we once felt inadequate and all of the ways we were able to ask others to help us overcome that, we realize how to move forward and help others in that same way.

Asking for help was another central theme that came up in my exploration. Sixteen nurses stressed its importance. Two nurses said this on the subject:

"The other new nurse that was hired at the same time as me has kind of gone down a different path. We've talked about it, but I feel like it is because she kind of stayed in her own corner and felt like she had to put on a front of knowing everything and not asking for help. That has affected her greatly. It has been hard to watch. I have been able to walk through that with her. At first, I didn't know that she was struggling because she would say that she was doing great even when she wasn't. I think it has affected her relationship with the other nurses and some of her patients.

NEW

Watching that taught me that while it is hard to be vulnerable, it shows that you care, because it shows that you are humble enough to take whatever criticism comes your way in order to help your patients. Now, when I see new grads just starting out, I tell them, 'Come to us!' If you are willing to accept growth, then it really helps. Never be afraid to ask questions. It is on us, the more experienced nurses, to foster that."

—*MO, pediatric intensive care nurse, one year of experience*

"Nursing is about teamwork, so it makes you better to know who, when, and how to ask for help. I wish someone had told me that when I first started, because I was stuck on that for so long. One thing I noticed about new grads is that they obviously are struggling, and when I ask them if they need help, they say, 'No, I am ok.' They aren't ok, but they feel like they need to say that they are. But they need to know that it is ok not to be ok and to ask for help."

—*LC, medical-surgical respiratory nurse, seven years of experience*

3. Recognize that you are part of a team.

When you are a brand-new nurse, feeling like you are caught up in a mudslide of not knowing what is taking place around you, you find out just how much the team carries you. We can break this idea down in the following way:

> Pride is saying, *I carry the team.*
> Healthy confidence is saying, *I am a valued member of the team.*
> Shame is saying, *I don't belong on the team.*
> Healthy humility is saying, *I am so grateful to be part of the team.*

The dance of healthy confidence and healthy humility is woven together as follows:

Chapter 4

When I am weak, the team helps carry me.
When I am strong, I help carry the team.
When I felt like I didn't belong on the team, others welcomed me.
Now, when I gain new teammates, I will welcome them.

In nursing school, teamwork wasn't talked about that often. We were taught to delegate tasks, but that's about it. I personally have been beaten over the head with the idea of leadership my entire life. I have been fortunate to be part of some exceptional teams, but I have found that in society in general, if we are going to choose between the two, we often choose to sacrifice the principle of teamwork at the altar of leadership.

Look at the whole college admission process. Yes, schools care that you were on a team, but do you know what impresses them even more? If you were the leader of that team. This very idea contributes to the disillusionment that many of us feel when we first go into our professions: we have been made to believe that if we are not leaders, then we are wrong.

The profession of nursing is even more intensely invested in promoting leadership. If you have your Bachelor of Science in Nursing, suddenly you are supposed to be this spectacular nurse leader right out of the gates just because you graduated with that title, but truly, a title without life experience means absolutely nothing. Nobody cares about our leadership experience if we are a terrible teammate.

To even hope to one day become a leader, we have to become a team member first. There is tremendous beauty in that. What's more is that by being on a team, we have a better opportunity to learn the choreography of the balanced dance of healthy confidence and humility in the process because we get to rehearse the steps together. Therefore, strong teamwork is just as important as strong leadership.

In nursing school, we had to practice Code Blues and CPR frequently. You are made to practice like you are the only one running the code. In real life, there is an entire team of nurses, respiratory therapists, doctors, etc., dedicated to running codes. If it is your patient coding, your teammates, the other nurses who you work with, step up and help you. Someone else does compressions. Someone else puts the defibrillator on the patient, so on and so forth. They do this because they know that they have to carry you, so that you, in turn, can carry the patient. If it is your patient who is coding, your only job is to tell the doctors what happened. You hold the vital information that the other nurses don't. The team carries the tasks, so you can advocate for the patient.

Codes take teamwork, but those are the extreme cases. Let's talk about the more mundane aspects of everyday nursing. You are too busy to hang an antibiotic? Ask your teammate. You have an admission and need help getting them settled? Ask your teammate. One of your patients insists on going on a walk that very minute at 4:00 a.m. and you haven't had a chance to go to the bathroom all night? Ask your teammate.

When you are new, you are so stressed out and busy that you cannot carry the team, and that is ok. In life, we cannot be carrying the team all the time, so the team carries us. Then, when we are in a healthy enough place, we can help carry our teammates who aren't. Your teammate is too busy to hang an antibiotic? Offer them help. Your teammate has an admission and needs help getting them settled? Offer them help. Your teammate hasn't gone to the bathroom all night and one of their patients insists on going on a walk that very minute at 4:00 a.m.? Offer them help. Asking for help and offering help means having healthy humility and healthy confidence, which in turn means working together as a team.

In another one of the interviews that I conducted, a nurse said the following in response to the question, "How is nursing different from what you expected?"

"It is different in that, as a student, I thought I would have to have all my stuff together or I would be screwed, but really you are

Chapter 4

a team. You rely on your coworkers, especially in the emergency department. Everyone is indispensable—the doctors, the clerks, the aids, the techs. In school, you think you are on your own island, that you have to do everything. You can work at any hospital, but the people you work with make or break your experience as a nurse."

—CH, *emergency department nurse, ten months of experience*

In fact, this nurse was not the only one to bring up the theme of teamwork in the interview setting. Of the fifty interviews that I conducted, twenty of the nurses mentioned teamwork at least once. Much like the topic of *small love*, teamwork was a theme that kept popping up even though I didn't ask a specific question about it. That is exceptionally beautiful, because teamwork is showing up for one another, which is one of the most important tenets of *small love*, as we previously discussed.

Another nurse said this in response to the question, "What advice would you give students as they prepare to become RNs?"

"Know that you will never be alone. You will always have coworkers—your charge nurse and the code team—there to help you. In school, they make you feel like you are the only one, or the only one in charge, but in reality, you always have people on your side."

—CH, *transitional care nurse, five months of experience*

In response to the questions, "What kept you from not quitting?" and, "How did you deal with wanting to quit?" one nurse said this:

"A huge part of my not wanting to quit is my coworkers, because no matter what happens, no matter what situation I am stuck in, I one-hundred-percent know that they will be there. They'll be there for me. It's weird, because I hardly know these people. I've only been at my job for nine months, but there is this

deep connection that we have. We are deeply connected, because we are going through the same shit together. My coworkers are a huge reason I don't want to quit. They make it all a little bit easier."
—DY, *bone marrow transplant oncology nurse, nine months of experience*

We are going to talk about teamwork more in the next chapter, because it isn't enough to just talk about teamwork within the context of our jobs. There is a tremendous amount of teamwork that goes into simply existing as a human being. So, if you are sitting here thinking, *This is great and all, but I work from home as a graphic designer, so I am my own team,* well, guess what—you probably have a team, too. The players may just take a different form than that of coworkers. After all, none of us will make it up the mountain of death and inadequacy alone.

4. Give yourself grace.

Halfway through my eleventh month as a nurse, I wrote the following poem. I didn't understand how to give myself grace within the context of my job up until that point. That equates to eleven months of suffering, suffering over the work of my own hands and over the toiling of my own heart and mind. Now, I better understand the grace that we need to have with ourselves, which is illustrated below:

*****

Masterpiece.

Once I wrote a poem of the stars when I was very depressed
Once I painted a painting of the stars when I couldn't see past my own stress
Back then I knew what I know now, but only with my head
But now I have felt, breathed, and lived out that knowledge instead
Here it is, my less-than-eloquent conclusion

Chapter 4

What has helped my tumbling life feel like less of an illusion
We are all in different stages of becoming art, being drawn and hewn
We are not just trash jumbled on the ground on which we often feel aimlessly strewn
But unlike the stagnant medium of paint, we are ever moving, ever growing, and ever carved
And while we may not always feel beautiful or priceless, from eternal hope we are not starved
Masterpieces aren't made without error, patience, or time
But that is easy to forget when you feel like an unfinished poem that is missing all its rhymes
But if you give yourself grace to make mistakes and treat yourself with patient kindness
You will be able to see yourself for who you truly are, but first you have to strip yourself of your own blindness
Then, and only then, will you become a masterpiece, a walking piece of art
With a strong yet vulnerable mind and a soft yet fierce heart
Let the paint of your life dry, the clay harden, and the final notes of music play
Then, take a deep breath and remember that while you may not feel like it right now, you will be a masterpiece someday.

*****

Giving ourselves grace is the key to life. We are all in the midst of our own processes of refinement and growth. While we all will have tough people with exceedingly high standards come into our lives—whether that be in the context of work, family, friendship, or otherwise—more often than not, the only person who truly expects us to be perfect is ourselves.

It is most often our own internal expectations that pack the hardest punch and weigh the most heavily on our minds. I know, because I am guilty of this. I even have had other nurses at work rallying around me imploring me to have grace with myself. But I am not the only one who has had to work to recognize the importance of self-grace. In fact, much like teamwork and *small love*, showing one's self grace was another major theme that showed

NEW

up in my research. Fourteen nurses mentioned the importance of being gracious with one's self.

When answering the questions, "When was the moment that you knew that you were going to be ok? When was the moment that you knew you were going to make it?" one nurse responded with this:

"When I realized that everything is just one question away. Everything has grace with it. I can wait two minutes until my charge nurse can come help me. Not everything is on my shoulders, because I can ask for help. That has really helped me. Sometimes you just have to pass things off to the next nurse. [...] I know I will be ok, because I have help [...] Even though I feel like crap, I don't want to be the nurse that people complain about because I am new, and I don't want to be a burden, I was reminded that it is really ok to be in the spot that I am."

—*HW, medical-surgical stroke and diabetes nurse, six months of experience*

In response to the question, "What advice would you give students as they prepare to become RNs?" two nurses replied with the following:

"Any advice? Be gracious to yourself. Honestly, I am going to leave it at that. You are doing the best you can. You are not going to be perfect. We are humans trying to save other humans. People come to the hospital trusting nurses. For me, that is difficult. They expect you to have all the answers, and you try to give them the best answer that you can, but you don't always know. So, just find someone who does, ask them, and learn something."

—*SB, high risk labor and delivery nurse, five months of experience*

"Give yourself grace, that was something that took me a while to learn. I felt so alone thinking that I was the only one who sucked at my job. I felt so upset that I had spent all this money and time on a career that I wasn't good at, but seeing that you are going to make mistakes and feel inadequate is normal and ok. That wasn't talked about enough. It is going to be hard in ways that you couldn't have imagined, and you need to learn to tell yourself that it is hard and that you don't love your job most nights, or you are put in situations where other people have to pick up your slack—all those things are so normal. It is ok to struggle. You have to give yourself grace and keep going. Otherwise, if you believe those doubts, you will be hindered even more. Give yourself grace and move on."

—*JW, high risk labor and delivery nurse, ten months of experience*

Grace is an important component in mitigating pride, because pride heavily favors that which is perfect. Grace is also a pivotal point in promoting humility, because it allows us to rest from that which we are striving to be perfect for. Masterpieces are not created in the haste of a day. Grace comes in between brushstrokes, when the painter is just holding the paintbrush. Or, in a quote that is most often attributed to composer Claude Debussy, "Music is the space between the notes."

It is in those moments of life when we are not striving or creating, in the quiet moments when we show ourselves grace, in between the notes and brush strokes, that grace creates its own art within us. Life is everything all at once. It is the all-at-once nature of each that tends to overwhelm us if we let it, but it is grace amidst the whirlwind of the all-at-once, and not despite it, that instead takes the wild chaos of life, tames it, refines it, and ultimately makes it beautiful.

5. Never stop learning.

Continual learning is why many of us are drawn to nursing, and beyond that to medicine, and even beyond that to science itself. There are always new discoveries being made, new things to be improved upon, and new things to be learned.

NEW

One of my favorite memories from nursing school has to do with this very principle. I was precepting in an emergency department, and a woman came in with a dislocated jaw. She had been at the dentist earlier that day, and somehow when she got home, her jaw became unhinged. She was in a significant amount of pain, and all she needed was for her jaw to be put back into place. The hospital where I was doing this rotation was small, so there were only two doctors and a small team of nurses in the emergency department that night.

It was a simple problem that could be easily fixed—just shove the jaw back in its socket. The only issue was that neither of those two doctors had ever done that to someone before. Dislocated arms? Yes. Dislocated jaws? Apparently not. After discussing the case for a little while, the two doctors decided to watch a video on how to put someone's jaw back into place.

They literally looked up how to do it on the internet. What's more is that the internet delivered. They watched the video a couple of times and when it came time to do it, they did a quick bedside sedation for the patient and had me hold up the phone with the video loaded on it just in case. Then, one of the doctors climbed up on the bed, straddled the patient, and popped her jaw back into its socket.

People tend to think that nurses and doctors have everything figured out, but the truth is we do not. We just recognize that we have to be continually learning and, even more importantly, be willing to do so. We are willing to continually learn, and being willing to learn means being willing to grow.

We ended the last chapter by trying to get roses to grow, and I again ask, "How do we do that?" Well, a big part of that process is being willing to let them. That means embracing growth by going forward in both confidence as well as humility and being willing to learn.

Chapter 4

Of the fifty nurses I interviewed, sixteen mentioned the importance of being a continual learner. Three experienced nurses expressed the following:

"What I liked about nursing is that it really is a lifelong learning process. In other careers, you might learn occasionally, but in nursing, you are learning all the time. Every day you are building on the little things that you learned in nursing school. I knew I didn't know everything, but what I didn't fully fathom was that every day wouldn't just be a little bit of a learning curve but lifelong, serious learning. You are always finding something that is new—new medications, new research."
—*LS, university health nurse practitioner, thirty years of experience*

"I was afraid as a new grad in that I almost felt sorry for the patients who had me as a nurse, because I didn't know what I was doing. But it's ok to ask the patients to teach you. You can learn from your patients, too. That is therapeutic for them. Patients like to share what they know, and they like to share their experiences. I learn so much from patient stories as well. You can do it in a way that allows for you not to come across as scared but in a way that allows for you to be real and to ask them. You fake it till you make it, in a sense, but you still learn. In oncology, you aren't expected to know everything, because it is such a huge field and every person in that field is a part of learning how to see and fix the problem. So, we have to ask one another what we are each learning, glean from that shared experience to learn what is going on, and then do something about it once we have that information."
—*EE, oncology travel nurse, five years of experience*

"Get out there and expose yourself to as much as possible. Grasp every learning opportunity that you can. I was not that way. I was kind of like a shrinking violet in nursing school. I still have never had to put in an NG tube! I never really had an opportunity to, but also, I never volunteered for it. Now, I would want to be the one to do it. Get out there and expose yourself to as much as possible."

—*LC, operating room nurse, thirty-seven years of experience*

There you have it—the five steps of our dance of healthy confidence, humility, and dealing with our own internal expectations. If we are being honest, though, when these principles are put into practice, they don't always take the shape of some pristine moonlit scene because that isn't what life is. Life isn't a well-rehearsed eight count or a stardust-infused sway. Instead, it is much more often a down-in-the-dirt, back-alley brawl. At least, that's how I somehow always end up grappling with my own internal expectations. It starts as a dance, but when anxiety becomes mixed in with those internal expectations, all of a sudden, the dance turns into a fight scene, and the steps turn into wrestling moves.

Dancing and wrestling have something very distinct in common. They both require muscle. So, what are we going to do in the next chapter? We are going to learn how to weight lift.

Chapter Five:
Waiting Under Weight

When I started piecing this chapter together, I had the complete intention of jumping straight into the practical how-tos of healthfully dealing with the heavy weight that comes with responsibility. As I continued to write, however, I realized that before we can learn how to lift the weight, we first have to unpack the true nature of its heaviness. Before we learn how to be ok, we first need to admit that we are simply *not*. Then, we need to be ok with that fact. I don't know how many times my resident director, when I was a resident advisor in college, had to tell me before it sank in, "It's ok not to be ok. It's ok not to be ok."

It takes a long time to be able to accept that for ourselves. It takes a long time to be able to show ourselves that kind of grace. We are taught how to be strong but not how to be weak. In all actuality, we are often weaker than we think. I know I told you that we were going to be weightlifters at the end of the last chapter, but before we lift the weight, let's just hold it. You might be thinking to yourself, *You want me to hold the weight, face my fears, and make peace with my burdens?* Yes. None of us are strangers to feeling heavy, but if we run away from our painful feelings instead of learning from them, then we are missing out on the opportunity to allow the weight to make us stronger. So, in this chapter, we will be learning how to hold the weight, and that's it. Then, in the next chapter, we will learn how to actively lift.

Selfishly, this portion of the book came from a question that I myself was desperate to find the answer to during my first year as a nurse. It is one that I asked all fifty of the nurses that I interviewed. That question was, "How did you deal with the weight of responsibility that was put on you?"

Why was this on the forefront of my mind? Well, I personally didn't know how to answer this question in my practice as a nurse or in my personal life. I didn't know how to deal with the weight that I was presented with, and I was terrified that it was going to crush me. Life is heavy enough on its own, but having to deal with other people's lives on top of that? I had no idea how to wrap my head around that thought, but I was determined to figure it out. Of the fifty nurses I asked this question, twelve reported feeling extremely overwhelmed when they first started out.

One new nurse reported feeling the same way when she first began and said the following:

"I really thought I was the only person who felt that badly about my job. Is it ok that I don't want to go to work? When am I going to be able to go to work and feel happy and feel like I know what I am doing? When is it going to be easy? I was so stressed out all the time that it would never get easier. Other nurses would be sitting and laughing, and I would be so behind that I didn't have time to laugh. When would I be able to get to that point? Now I am able to do that, and there is another new guy, and he will ask, 'How are you guys done with all your stuff?' and I'll tell him, 'You'll get there!'"

—MO, *pediatric cardiac intensive care nurse, one year of experience*

As to what each nurse did specifically to combat those initial negative feelings? Results varied. We will be getting into that more in the next chapter. In this chapter, however, we will be focusing on three things and three things only. If you still haven't forgiven me for all the heavy content I threw at you in Chapter Two, I'm sorry, but this chapter is also pretty heavy. In this chapter we will be doing the following:

Chapter 5

1. Learning how to be ok with not being ok.
2. Asking for help (yes, we are talking about this again, because it is that important).
3. Recognizing the importance of pain in our development as human beings and how learning to cope with pain in a healthy way takes time.

Will we be doing this in order? No. These three lessons are, as with healthy confidence and healthy humility, intertwined. We cannot learn to come to terms with the weight that we carry if we do not come to understand the three items on this list first. If we cannot learn how to hold the weight, then we will never learn how to lift the weight. If we never learn how to lift the weight, then we will never grow stronger from the weight. The only alternative to lifting the weight is letting it crush us.

Let's look at some examples of what nurses had to say in response to the weight of responsibility predicament. We will be able to clearly notice how our tidy list messily fits into the reality of life and how all three components do in fact blend together.

"I was scared. It wasn't lost on me that I was in charge of keeping these people alive. I felt immense pressure and the expectation of having to be able to handle everything well immediately. I felt like I needed to do it perfectly, with no mistakes and all on my own. That is so false! Now that I am a year in, I have never asked for more help than I do now. But, that is how I survived when I first started, too. I realized that everyone around me knows more than I do. The people around me have the answers that I need."
—*EP, medical-surgical oncology nurse, one year of experience*

"I don't feel like I dealt with it well at first. It is a learned skill. It is something that needs to be taken very seriously, but you don't know until you face the hard situations where you need to step up. There are ways that can help you learn how to deal with the weight, but it doesn't really go away. You will always have to deal with it, because you are always going to be entering into new situations on the floor. I think that the best way I found to help deal with it was to let other people come alongside me and help me carry that burden. Asking questions is really important. I would not have been able to make it this far without asking for help. By being humble, you take the weight of responsibility seriously, and it shows that you want to respect the responsibility. When you ask questions, you are reaching out for help when you are not sure what carrying that responsibility looks like."

—*JW, high risk labor and delivery nurse, ten months of experience*

"The biggest thing was knowing that I wasn't carrying it alone, but that was because the support of the nurses that I had around me was so good. That's how I dealt with it—I didn't have to do it alone. I always had the peace and the confidence that there was always someone to ask and someone was always willing to help me. I had a great team. My manager was amazing. Honestly, I think that's it. It is a team thing. Being a nurse isn't a one-person job. It is always a team."

—*AB, women's oncology breast clinic nurse, four years of experience*

"The first six months, I cried a lot. I was fearful and scared. I am responsible for this person's care, but how exactly am I supposed to do that? I know I will, but I feel like I can't. I don't know if we ever fully understand the responsibility that we have. No one really talks about it, but I'd think to myself, 'Am I the one responsible for all of this stuff? What if it doesn't get done?' I was able to talk to my preceptor about it, and I am so blessed because the nurses on my unit really are a team. I felt alone at the beginning, but once I saw that I had people who would help me, I realized that I shared the responsibility, that I could ask them questions no matter what. It is expected that you ask for help, and once I knew that I could ask and share that responsibility, I could

Chapter 5

come to work and not kill someone, because I knew I had a team of people I could ask questions of."

—*MO, pediatric cardiac intensive care nurse, one year of experience*

"It is an amount of responsibility that no one outside of nursing will ever understand because you have lives in your hands and, beyond that, you have so many rules and policies placed on you. You have to take the responsibility seriously. Owning it is number one. Realizing that I am not going to know everything but that I still need to meet this responsibility and own it is important. If I don't know something, I have to seek out the necessary resources to find the answers. For me, 'owning it' means finding the resources to make it work and the rationale for how to proceed even if I don't know everything. It is my responsibility to go and find out for the sake of my patients and then follow up and do everything that I promised that I would do. Follow up and figure out how to pursue it in the future."

—*EE, oncology travel nurse, five years of experience*

"When I started working in oncology, I didn't know how to grapple with the weight of other people's stories. For the first year, when people would ask me, 'How is work?' or, 'How was your day?' I felt so inauthentic saying that my day was good or fine when I just took care of someone who was literally dying or someone who was getting chemo or someone who was suicidal. I think that there is an emotional wrestling that happens that you have to go through. It takes time and you really have to work through it."

—*BS, internal medicine hospitalist nurse practitioner, eight years of experience*

"I was freaked out about it for sure. I remember feeling terrified every day that I was going to work. I would always think, 'What are they going to throw at me today that I can't handle?' I

distinctly remember that feeling, and I distinctly remember when that feeling went away, but it was a while."
—*CM, pediatric advice line nurse, thirty-seven years of experience*

"Not well at first. I was constantly thinking and rethinking about my day, things I should have done, things I should have done differently. I would beat myself up about not knowing certain things. I would take responses from other nurses, doctors, and staff so personally. I couldn't turn my brain off. I would come home and keep replaying those thoughts. Now, I am able to clock out and shut my mind off, but that took a long time."
—*OR, medical oncology nurse, eleven months of experience*

To more specifically address the pain component of our list, I want to reference an interview that I had the chance to conduct with a nurse who spent eight years working at a maternity center in a low-middle income country. When asked what the biggest insight was that she took away from her time being a nurse in another culture, her answer was as follows:

"In terms of working cross-culturally, it better defines what health is. Health may not be freedom from pain or looking put-together on the outside. Where I worked, before the importance of health was the importance of having community, people to reach out to, people who reach out to you. It is mutual. People to walk the journey with you when sickness inevitably comes. In America, we are so afraid of pain that it has almost become an idol, and it has become isolating. It is regarded so highly, that it is known as the fifth vital sign. We would rather be home alone, narced up and numbed, not feeling pain, than be out with the community releasing natural endorphins that combat the pain.

"Having worked in a place that gets more natural disasters than any other location in the world, I have seen the importance that family and friendships and community have on the resilience

Chapter 5

of a person. In nursing, when you come to a place of hardship or wanting to quit, ask yourself, 'How is my community? How are my coping mechanisms? Who is going to hold my hand when pain, sickness, and hardship inevitably come?' That has been the greatest perspective that working internationally has given me: the aspect of quality of life versus quantity."

—*PE, labor and delivery nurse, ten years of experience*

In reality, humans are capable of lifting a lot of emotional weight, but our emotional and mental health muscles, like any other muscle group, have to be used regularly if it is our intention to get stronger.

Again, we will be building off of the previous chapter. While we talked about internal expectations in the last chapter, we predominantly discussed how to address them within the context of a *professional* setting. But, that leaves us with the question as to how we are supposed to address our internal expectations in the *personal* setting, in the I-am-crying-myself-to-sleep-every-night setting.

Fortunately, the steps of the internal-expectations dance are the same in both contexts. We need to ask questions, ask for help, recognize that we are part of a team, give ourselves grace, and never stop learning. Done, done, done, and done, right? Wrong. This dance is one that has to be performed daily. Some days, it is easier to do this. Some days, it is harder. Every day, it is important.

It is in the private, daily, and in-the-meantime spaces of life where the humility aspect of the last chapter truly comes in. Every day, we have to realize that we are finite. We have to recognize our own frailty in the shadow of the mountain of life. But, who said that finitude has to be a bad thing? Who says it has to be a prison? I like to think of my own finitude through the lens of a concert: when we can recognize our own smallness in front of the broad continuum of time, that is when life's music really becomes beautiful.

NEW

We practice, we do the dance over and over, we sometimes get the steps right, and we sometimes don't. But, do you want to know something about the musical image that I am painting for you? In the concert of life, we are not a member of the symphony. We are the audience, and life itself is the music. It is our choice as to whether we want to sit and listen, kneel on the floor and cry, or get up and dance. In life, there are abundant opportunities to take all three postures, none of which are wrong. There is a time for each of the three—the trick is figuring out when to take which stance. But, the humbling truth is that the music is going to continue to play no matter what we do. Time is a symphony that never stops. The notes started playing long before we were born, and they will continue to cascade long after we are gone. Depressing? Only if you let it be.

"Vapor (A Meditation)," by The Liturgists, profoundly says this; "Finitude, after all, is actually what makes life sweet." Does the eventual inevitability of death make life less beautiful? No. If we let our own finitude empower us instead of shrink us, then we will indeed be able to find the beauty in our own mortality. It is what makes us hold our loved ones tighter. It is what makes our small moments of joy and happiness brighter. It is what spurs us to claim our time on Earth well, and it is what turns us from cowards into fighters.

We are going to talk about what it means to have joy in the midst of the in-the-meantime in Chapters Eight and Nine. But, for now, we are going to talk about pain in the midst of the in-the-meantime. As I promised before, if we can do death together, then we can do life together, and if we can do pain together, then we can do joy together.

The interesting thing about music is that each note is a part of a greater whole. The notes turn into chords, chords turn into chord progressions, and chord progressions turn into songs. More fascinating still is that hidden within the comprehensive nature of music are distinctive minor and major chords. In Western music,

Chapter 5

minor chords often get stereotyped as being the sad chords, whilst major chords are often considered happy. But, actually, it is the way that the minor and the major chords are brought together into a chord progression that allows for a complete musical sound to occur and for the contextual feelings of a song to take shape. It is their progression *together* that adjusts the nature of the song.

While not all songs contain both sets of chords, due to the very fact that both minor and major chords are integral parts of musical structure in general, neither type of chord should be considered any more or less beautiful than the other. Additionally, while some musical works induce pain and others foster joy, each type of sound is equally important to the great catalogue of musical history. It is the unique ability of the musician to take the unseen and turn it into the seen, to take the seen and turn it into the heard, to take the heard and turn it into the felt, and to take the felt and turn it into the lived. Ernst Levy, musicologist and author of *A Theory of Harmony*, wrote this:

"Music is, before and above all, a matter of spirit and not of acoustics in the engineer's sense. Music—as we said at the onset—is not primarily 'something that happens in the air.' It is something that happens in the human soul on the basis of a response to universal norms expressed in the tone structure."

Music is the science of the soul, and the soul is what allows us to embrace life. Therefore, we need to view life as we view music, not in parts of equal or lesser value, split up by the happy and the sad, but as a whole. The song of life is an interlaced chord progression, not a segregation of the major and the minor. Musicians have to understand the individual components of music before they can learn how to compose. Only after that can the musician knit together a sound that truly encompasses all of the feelings that come with life itself. Similarly, we have to understand the roles that both pain and joy play in our lives before we can live our lives well.

NEW

But, in life, we often have to wait to see how the things that we go through will be made beautiful with time. This is where the idea we discussed in Chapter Three comes in, the idea of waiting under the weight of the in-the-meantime. It is in the space of the in-the-meantime where life is simultaneously the most painful and the most profound.

The weight of time is a burdensome thing, because we don't know how long certain times in our lives will last. Whether we are in a time of pain or a time of joy, the length of time's unknown variability can be an anxiety-producing factor. When we are in a time of sorrow, we are waiting painstakingly to be out of it. Then, when we are in a time of joy, we are afraid that it will end at any moment and we will be thrown back into pain again. Being a human being is an exhausting feat if all we do is let our mind wage war on time itself.

In the poem "The Old Astronomer" by Sarah Williams, Williams gives the reader insight into the conclusion that an old man arrives at as he comes to the end of his life and leaves his life work to a younger astronomer. His beautiful conclusion is this:

> "Though my soul may set in darkness, it will rise in perfect light;
> I have loved the stars too truly to be fearful of the night."

Often, we think of the hard parts of life as synonymous with the nighttime, with the cool darkness that inevitably replaces the warmth of the daylight. But, truly, if we didn't have the blackness of the night, we would never experience the brilliant beauty of the stars. As I said before, we will be discussing joy and beauty later on in Chapters Eight and Nine, but for now, let's talk about what comes before the starlight. Before the day gives way to the night, before we get to see the stars shine, we have to endure the dusk. While beautiful, the rosy hue of twilight—if we are equating the sky to life itself— represents the fading away of what was and the dawning of what is to come.

Chapter 5

If we take the time to look at the sky as it turns black, we will notice that it takes a while for the stars to come out. So, we sit there waiting, knowing that the darkness is impending but that with the darkness comes the stars. But, life isn't as rhythmic or as constant as the solar system. When we enter into painful moments or seasons of life, we stare into the deep abyss of depression, anxiety, and insecurity, wondering if the stars will ever start to shine. We wonder if what is hurting us will ever produce beauty. We have to wait to see the stars come out, and that waiting is the hardest part.

So, for now, let's wait in the waiting. Let's take a moment to lament and be ok with not being ok. Let's take a moment to feel the weight pressing down upon us. It hurts, doesn't it? Whatever we are wrestling with as individuals, it is heavy. Sometimes it feels like that heaviness is more solid than we are.

Like I said at the start of the chapter, the brutal thing about nursing is that it carries an additional weight with it: it carries the weight of being responsible for other people's lives as well as their burdens. Some nurses are empowered by this, and others are terrified of this. Either way, at one point or another, each nurse has to come to grips with this new type of pressing weight.

One nurse said the following on the topic of dealing with the weight of responsibility:

"There were times when I was overwhelmed and would cry on the way home from work. Having someone's life in your hands is a big thing. I was twenty-two when I started, and you have to learn and feel that weight at a young age. It gets heavy. So, I would cry every so often. My ways of relieving that were working out and finding things outside of work to balance those feelings. When you are twenty-two and watching someone die, it takes a lot out of you emotionally. I mean it does at any point, but it is especially difficult when you are first starting out."

—CR, *medical-surgical respiratory nurse, sixteen years of experience*

NEW

As for myself, I did not deal with this newfound weight well. In fact, I almost let it crush me completely, but only almost. Instead, I was able to learn how to use the weight to build up my muscles instead of letting it push me down into nothingness. So, for a moment, let's put away our telescopes, wrap ourselves in our blankets, and feel the full weight of the possibility of a night without stars. Let me tell you a story.

*****

During my sixth month, I got fired by a patient's family. Honestly, I could understand where they were coming from, but it was not a good feeling being taken off someone's care team. When I got home, I took off walking. The memorable thing about that particular excursion was that it was raining and quite possibly hailing that day. It was the clouds that made me think of it, the word "weight." According to *Scientific American,* the mass of a cloud can total around two million pounds.

As I was walking, noticing the weight in the clouds, I began to think about the weight that I felt as a new nurse. I thought about it all during that walk: the weight of responsibility, the weight of anxiety, the weight of inadequacy, the weight of how this whole thing could have been a huge mistake. With heaviness in my heart and tears on my face, I wondered how I was going to be able to carry that weight for the rest of my first year. My first six months were brutal. If my next sixth months were the same way, how on Earth would I be able to make it? What was I going to do with all that weight?

I repeated the question over and over again to myself, "What am I going to do with all this weight?" If I were going to make it through my first year as a nurse, I knew I would have to answer that question, and I realized that there were two ways in which I could respond. Option one, I could let the weight crush me. Option two, I could use the weight to become stronger.

Chapter 5

I resolved right then and there, soaking wet from the rain, that I was going to choose option two no matter what. As I write this, I am in my seventh month as a nurse, and I am still an anxious work-in-progress. But, deciding that I would not let the weight crush me gave me a boost of much-needed empowerment. Since then, I have felt that maybe, just maybe, I'll be able to make it through my first year after all.

Thus far, nursing has appeared like a looming mountain lying ahead of me, one that is seemingly impossible to climb. But, this realization was like discovering a trail on that mountain. While it may be a steep and rocky one, it is a trail nonetheless, and I decided that I was going to do whatever it took to climb it.

At the end of the day, however, even if I say I am going to use the weight to make myself stronger, I still have to carry it, and it is heavy. But, I realized that I didn't have to carry the weight on my own. Two million pounds is too much weight for any one person to carry. While we may not have to carry the weight of a rain cloud on our shoulders, sometimes the emotional and mental weight that we struggle with is just as burdensome.

Don't try to carry this weight on your own. The weight will get too heavy, and it will crush you. Maybe you're thinking to yourself, "But I can carry the weight on my own. You don't know me. I am strong enough." Let me tell you right now that you are not.

As a nurse, I have tried one too many times to carry the weight of responsibility on my own. I haven't thrown up in the bathroom from anxiety at work yet, but I've cried. I've cried in front of people, too. But, I am telling you that that's ok. It is ok to cry in front of your coworkers if that means that you are going to get the help you need. If we are going to make it in this world as human beings, we have to ask for help.

*****

After seeing what I've seen as a nurse, I understand why people drink. I understand why they do drugs. I understand why they numb themselves. The weight of life and time is heavy and none of us are able to carry that weight alone. Coming to terms with the fact that we will not survive the weight of the world on our own is truly healthy humility. It is humility that allows us to show ourselves grace.

But, this all begs the question, "How are we supposed to deal with that weight and endure its pain in a way that is ultimately strengthening rather than detrimental?" Well, it comes back to the healthy confidence and healthy humility dance that we talked about in Chapter Four—we need to ask for help and offer help. This, in turn, brings us back to the idea of using *small love*, which we discussed in Chapter Two—all we can do in this life is show up for one another.

I am not sure exactly when during my first year as a nurse that I wrote this following excerpt, but I was obviously feeling something particularly heavy when I wrote it. Are you ready to walk through the valley of the shadow of death with me? We won't be journeying into physical death per se, but we will be looking into something that can be just as sinister: the heavy weight of depression itself.

When we have finally broken free from the particular bondage of depression, the scariest thing in the world is the possibility of falling back into it. Maybe we are breathing. Maybe we are walking. But, we are afraid to even let ourselves live because of the fear that the weight of depression is looming on the horizon. When we live with depression, our bodies move, but our minds fester and wither away.

Let me just take a minute to encourage those of you who struggle with depression and anxiety. You are my brothers and sisters, and more importantly, you are my fellow fighters. For too long, the world has called us weak. For too long, religion has told us to just pray it away. For too long, we have been made to feel like something is wrong with us. But we have a unique strength that others do not, because we have had to fight for ourselves, for our

Chapter 5

minds, for our lives, and for our beings every single day. Keeping ourselves healthy is a valiant and imperative war that we wage daily against our own thoughts. But know this: we do not have to fight for ourselves on our own.

*****

Recently I have had a lot of people ask me if I'm safe. Also, recently, I have found myself asking my friends the same thing. You might be wondering, "Safe how?" Well, as I write this, I am depressed. And to answer the question I just posed, yes, I am safe.

If I were a patient at the hospital and you were the nurse doing a depression screening on me right now, I would have to tell you that yes, I have been feeling sad. Yes, I feel hopeless. Yes, in the last week, I have wished that I was dead. No, I don't think people would be better off without me. No, I don't want to actually harm or kill myself. No, I have never attempted suicide before. No, I do not have any lethal means to kill myself. I know my responses would still most likely merit a social work evaluation order, however.

More people have been asking me this lately, because I have been more honest about the depression that I feel than I have ever been before. I have been more open because I have learned the hard way that if I am not open about it—if I don't ask for help—then I am going to be responding yes to a lot more of those questions on that depression screening.

Author's Note: *My dearest reader, if you answered yes to any of those questions, I implore you to pursue help. Bravery is asking for assistance. You are too precious to be crushed. Your light is too bright to be dimmed. The world needs you in it. You do not journey or fight alone. If you are in need of assistance, please go to the National Suicide Prevention Hotline website; suicidepreventionlifeline.org for additional resources or call or text 988 for immediate help. If all else fails, go to the hospital. Walking with you in our time of pain is a nurses' greatest honor.*

NEW

Nurses, do you remember the psychiatric rotation you had in school? I do, *vividly*. It uniquely humbles you in a way that no other specialty does. Again and again, I found myself thinking, *I am just one bad day away, one bad circumstance away, from being the one in that hospital bed.* I remember posting on my nursing class' social media page, "Hey guys, if it ever comes down to it and you are in a bad spot, go to the hospital willingly, because if you have to be taken in on a 5150, your nursing license could be revoked." I saw the reality of the situation so clearly: we are only one moment away from that hospital bed. Even the strongest of us. We are *all* one moment, one breakdown, or one bad day away from becoming patients. I like to think I have a reputation for being the strong friend. If you are a nurse reading this, you are most likely the strong friend, too, because nurses are truly some of the strongest people around. But, regardless of how strong we think we are or how strong we think our friends are, we all need to check up on one another.

Fortunately, my family and friends are amazing and have been checking in on me. But, back to my original point. I have found myself asking more people, "Are you safe?" That is such a chilling question: "My radiant and beloved friend, are you safe?" So far, the answer has been yes for both my friends and myself, but it is imperative that we ask one another vulnerable questions. We need to watch out for one another, because many times, people do not ask for help when they need it.

This was demonstrated to me on a small level during nursing school when one of my classmates pulled me aside and said that she noticed that I never really ate lunch. "Is everything ok?" she asked me. "Do you want to talk about it?" We were not even the closest of friends, but she went out on a limb and out of her comfort zone to check on me. I gave her a hug and told her that I was absolutely fine. In reality, I would just eat after class when I got home.

Maybe I didn't need the help then, but she taught me a valuable lesson. It doesn't matter how well you know a person: if you see a

Chapter 5

red flag—if you see someone potentially hurting—ask them about it. Nurses spend all day and all night taking care of patients, but we also need to take the time to care for ourselves and for one another. It doesn't matter if we ask awkwardly, if we don't use all the right words, or if we don't get our therapeutic communication techniques exactly correct, we still need to ask each other.

It takes courage to ask someone—and I mean *really* ask someone—how they are doing, but it also takes courage to respond to that question truthfully. Being vulnerable is being strong. Of course, not everyone deserves to be trusted with your vulnerability, but if you can think of one or two people whom you can be vulnerable with—whom you can say, "Hey, I am actually not doing ok," to—then you are in better shape than you might have thought at first. We all need to ask ourselves, *Who is on my team right now?* and, *Can I talk to them?*

If there is no one on your team and you are in a bad place, there is still hope. During nursing school, I remember a girl about my age came into the emergency department, and I, along with the nurse I was following, had the opportunity to care for her. When we asked her why she came to the hospital that day, she said, "I am just really sad. I knew I couldn't be alone, and I didn't know where else to go, so I came here."

To which the nurse I was following replied, "You did the right thing."

To this day, that remains the moment in which I felt the proudest to be a nurse. When someone feels that alone—like there is no one in the world they can turn to—they can always come to the hospital, to us nurses, and we will take care of them. We will help them carry their weight.

We got her connected to social work. We created a safe space for her to feel, breathe, and process. She made some phone calls and told whomever she was talking to that she was at the hospital. When it was time for her to go home, she did not go home alone. It took having to go to the hospital for her to let people in and tell them where she was really at in her life. Even so, she showed extreme bravery that day by coming to the hospital and asking for help.

That is what I mean when I say that we are all one bad day away from being patients. Don't wait until you are in the hospital to let people help you. Be vulnerable. It's scary, I know, but people love you and will show up for you. You just have to let them.

*****

So, what does it mean to wait under the weight in a way that is healthy? What does it mean to find rest within the darkness before the stars start to come out? It means knowing that we do not have to face the darkness alone.

We will be thoroughly discussing practical tips on how we can best manage our emotional and mental health in the next chapter. But, for a moment, let's explore our spiritual health. In both my own personal life and in my research, I have discovered that finding solace in the development of our spiritual health is deeply important when it comes to how we respond to weight.

Four nurses revealed similar sentiments when asked, "How did you deal with the weight of responsibility that was put on you?"

Author's Note: *As we have discussed, holistic care is based on the mind, body, and soul. The NCLEX itself has questions pertaining to how nurses can best facilitate spiritual care for their patients. Whatever the patient requests, whatever faith they belong to or don't belong to, it is our job to try and help them achieve a sense of inner peace and wellbeing while they are with us. It is the same for nurses. Therefore, I wanted to include how I attended to my own spiritual care while in the process of becoming a nurse. The premise of this 'Lament, Remind, Praise' section is a framework of mindfulness that we can all partake in, in our own time and in our own way, no matter our faith affiliation or creed, because it is about making peace with how we relate to the world as humans and it is our humanity that we all have in common.*

Chapter 5

"I know that, no matter what, I don't have control over each situation. I have to keep surrendering. I know that my best will not be enough, and I have to rely on his hope. I had to learn to not take things too personally. If we did all that we could and the patient still didn't make it, I had to remember that I don't hold the fate of someone's life in my hands. You have to slow down and ask God, 'What am I supposed to do?' When you lose a patient, you can have peace and not carry that weight that someone has passed away, because it isn't on you. It helps me be kind to my patients, too, reminding me that God will take care of things, even if the patient doesn't want my help."

—MA, *emergency department nurse, ten months of experience*

"Now that I have a little more experience, I remind myself that the worst thing that can happen is a code, and that during a code, I can ask for help from my coworkers. I don't have to go through it alone. I remind myself that God is in charge of life and that there is nothing that I can do that will end a life sooner than he is planning. I know that ultimately it is not my responsibility to control when someone dies or doesn't die."

—CH, *transitional care nurse, five months of experience*

"I always prayed from nursing school onward, 'Jesus, please don't ever allow me to be in a position where I could seriously hurt someone.' I prayed that all the time. Even now, my hospice practice is very high acuity. [...] I pray, 'Don't let me hurt anyone. If something needs to be done, show me.' I just walk out in faith. I can't say that I am very fearful. I think my fears are in other areas now, but not in that. I feel like I am a child and am saying, 'Dad I'm going to jump! Catch me!' So, I pray that God will catch me."

—HG, *hospice nurse, ten years of experience*

"In general, what I did was speak truth over myself and affirm my identity in Jesus rather than my identity in work or in my

NEW

feelings of inadequacy. I would remind myself why God had called me into this profession to begin with and why I wanted to do this profession in the first place. Knowing that I care for my patients and that I want the best for them, then how much more does he care for them? And when we are weak, he is strong. Even in the feelings of my own weakness and inadequacy, I knew that I had a powerful God. We literally carry the Holy Spirit with us wherever we go, so remembering that is such a powerful thing we have as Christ-followers, because we get to bring that into work.

"Once, I had a patient who was septic with a systolic blood pressure of seventy and a fever. Later, the doctor came and told me that I had fixed the patient, but I said, 'No, Jesus fixed the patient!' Even when I was feeling inadequate, the Holy Spirit was still at work within me, pointing me to the resources that the patient needed, and healing people in front of my eyes. I dealt with it by realizing that the responsibility of it all was not something that I was meant to carry on my own, but that it was a partnership that I had with God. It was a year of learning, too, because early on, the Lord showed me that I could only do so much and the rest I had to learn to give to him. All those anxieties and fears? I had to give to them to the Lord because that is all that I knew how to do in those moments when I didn't have all the knowledge or know-how to do the specific skill that was required of me. I still had to learn. He has entrusted lives to you, but you don't take care of those lives alone. It is a partnership."

—*Al, bone marrow transplant oncology nurse, two years of experience*

The only way that I was able to get myself to go to work when I was just starting out was by praying in a very specific way. If it weren't for this, I would have quit. I would have had to for my own sanity. But, by praying in this manner, I was able to clear my mind enough to be able to leave my apartment and go to work. This didn't really help me lift the weight per se, but it did allow me—with the help of my mom, who let me call her every night

Chapter 5

on the way to work, and the unfailing support of the nurses who I worked with that first year—to hold the weight and not be completely crushed by it.

So, what would I do? I would lament, remind, and praise. To investigate these three principles further, let's turn to the ancient grief poetry in the book of Lamentations.

1. We lament.

> "He has broken my teeth with gravel;
> he has trampled me in the dust.
> I have been deprived of peace;
> I have forgotten what prosperity is.
> So I say, 'My splendor* is gone
> and all that I had hoped from the LORD.'
> I remember my affliction and my wandering,
> the bitterness and the gall.
> I well remember them,
> and my soul is downcast within me.
> —Lamentations 3:16–20

Does this sound like just praying the bad feelings away? No, not at all. This is recognizing and validating the weight of the pain that we feel and expressing it because we cannot contain it any longer. This is asking, "What do I do now that my endurance has run out?" and saying, "I'm not ok," and being real, raw, and truthful as we examine what it is that we are feeling. It is ok not to be ok. Sometimes life hurts. Sometimes we hurt, so we need to take the time to let ourselves reflect on and unpack that. Process your emotions, even the negative ones.

*Author's Note: *Some translations say 'endurance' instead of 'splendor.'*

2. We remind.

> "Yet this I call to mind
> and therefore I have hope:
> Because of the LORD's great love we are not consumed,
> for his compassions never fail.
> They are new every morning; [...].
> —Lamentations 3:21–23a

We let ourselves feel pain. We give ourselves the grace and space to feel those emotions. But the concept that it's-ok-not-to-be-ok has a Part Two. If we stayed in the not-ok space forever, then we would just be setting ourselves up for more pain. After giving ourselves some grace and time, we need to recognize, as one of my pastors once said, that, "It's ok not to be ok, but it is not ok to stay that way."

So, what do we do to transition out of lamenting? We remind. We cling to what is good. Remind yourself of the things that are beautifully and uniquely true about yourself. Remind yourself that people care about you, that you have resources, and that you are not alone.

3. We praise.

> "Great is your faithfulness.
> I say to myself, 'The LORD is my portion;
> therefore I will wait for him.'"
> —Lamentations 3:23b–24

I am actually going to stop us right here. We will be waiting to fully unpack the joyful portion of the lament-remind-praise trilogy until Chapter Eight. Why? Because human nature is such that we often want to skip over the pain to get to the joy. We either seek the stars at the expense of rushing through the dusk or we attempt to shut

Chapter 5

down the night in order to avoid the darkness altogether, beauty of the stars be damned. But in truth, hiding from the pain only makes the pain worse. When we let it make us anxious, pain steals from us and shields our eyes from any beauty that is to come. Therefore, we have to first finish our discussion on life's more lamentable moments.

Brené Brown—author, researcher, and licensed medical social worker—says in her book *The Gifts of Imperfection,* "We cannot selectively numb emotions, when we numb the painful emotions, we also numb the positive emotions."

Truly, that is the whole of it: the totality of life. Music isn't complete without both the major and the minor. It is only in the nighttime that we see the beauty of the stars. Without pain, we can never truly fathom joy. Times of pain play a profoundly important role in our lives, but we have to stop, hold them, and recognize them in order for those painful times to yield any growth.

Now, if we just left it at that—if we stopped at reflecting on our own pain—then we would never allow for any forward movement in our lives. Like my pastor said, "It is ok not to be ok, but it's not ok to stay that way."

Once we have held the weight, we then have to learn how to lift it. That is how we can actively address those confusing, messy feelings that come up in the space of the in-the-meantime. While we are waiting for the day when we can see how our pain has become beautiful with time, we can start by figuring out what we can actively do to become healthy, no matter the circumstances we find ourselves in.

So, my concert-attending, stargazing, weight-holding friends, I will wrap up all the metaphors that we have addressed in this chapter with one final metaphor that I know you'll be familiar with: at the end of the day, no matter how many lenses we look through, we need to keep the image of ourselves as gardeners at the forefront of our minds. Why? Because, as we have previously

NEW

discussed, it is how we allow the roses to grow out of our lives that makes our time on Earth beautiful.

To conclude, I will leave us with a quote from the song "I Have Made Mistakes" by *The Oh Hellos:*

> "Nothing is a waste if you learn from it
> And the sun, it does not cause us
> the sun, it does not cause us to grow
> It is the rain that will strengthen,
> the rain that will strengthen your soul
> and it will make you whole."

So, let's become whole people—people who healthfully embrace both joy and hurt—and let's learn how to do it *well*. If we can learn how to make roses grow even in the midst of the heaviness of sorrow, then we can make roses grow in the midst of anything. In this chapter we discussed how to hold the weight of pain; now let's discuss how to actually do some gardening and heavy-lifting so that the parched deserts of our weight-laden minds have the opportunity to grow magnificent super-blooms.

Chapter Six:
I Wish, If Only, My Fault

The sentiments expressed in the title of this chapter are weighty in and of themselves. How much weight do we add to the burdens that we already have in our minds when we start to say things to ourselves like, "I wish," "if only," and, "my fault." Not only do those thoughts wreck the steps of healthy confidence and healthy humility that we have so faithfully been trying to practice, but they go two steps further by fostering and perpetuating a cycle of unhealthy shame within us.

In the last chapter, we discussed multiple times how it is ok not to be ok. Now we are going to unpack the notion that while it is ok not to be ok, it is not ok to stay that way forever. As for the three sentiments highlighted in the title of this chapter? They are three things that we say to ourselves that make us stay not ok. So how do we fight them? How do we lift the additional weight that those ideas add to situations that are already heavy?

When asked, "How did you deal with the weight of responsibility that was put on you?" one nurse whom I had the chance to interview replied with the following:

> "Find out early on what the responsibility of nursing is, and try not to add personal interpretations to it. Then, when you go home, be able to separate from it. It is ok to put a cap on it when you go home and focus on your life and what makes you happy. Then, when you return to work, focus on that. Don't bring it home with you. It really is like you are changing gears."
>
> —JS, *medical-surgical renal telemetry nurse, three years of experience*

NEW

When asked, "What advice would you give students as they prepare to become RNs?" another nurse responded with the following:

"Be really honest with yourself about your own expectations for yourself, then be honest about if those expectations are realistic or not. I thought that I had it all together. I really thought too highly of myself and my ability, when in reality, I had such little experience. You see a lot in nursing school, but you don't know. I think I even had an expectation that I would get to work and look cute, and that I would get to the end of the day and not be exhausted, but there have been many times where I get home and go to bed with my makeup on. I didn't think it would bother me much, but it did, because I put that expectation on myself to look good and be on it all the time. [...] Being honest with yourself and with others about your expectations is important. Writing them down or saying them out loud really helps."

—OR, *medical-surgical oncology, eleven months of experience*

The ideas of *I wish, if only,* and *my fault* do exactly what these nurses are warning against. They allow us to add our own negative, personal interpretations and expectations to what are already hard situations. Wrangling these feelings is a learned skill. When I started as a nurse, I had the propensity to let those musings of *I wish, if only,* and *my fault* run completely amok in my mind long after I got home from work. The two nurses whom I mentioned above had to work to reach the conclusions that they came to. They didn't just magically have perfect boundaries for themselves. But, as we discussed for the entirety of the last chapter, pain is often what teaches us the most.

The first nurse I quoted above replied to the question, "How is nursing different from what you expected? How is it the same? Overall, did you feel prepared?" with the following:

"I didn't know what to expect, honestly. Nursing school gives you a good idea of what the job entails in regard to care-plans,

Chapter 6

discharges, etc. So, clinically, I felt prepared. But, emotionally and mentally, I got destroyed. The first three months were heavy. Then, by the eighth month, I felt better. I would tell myself that it is ok to trudge through the difficulties. You are in a new territory. You are taking off the training wheels, but you have your coworkers. Take the time to get to know them and lean on them, because they are going to be the ones that help you when things get hard."

—*JS, medical-surgical renal telemetry nurse, three years of experience*

In response to the question, "What do you wish someone had told you before you started? What do you wish was talked about more?" the second nurse I quoted above said the following:

"During Months Three to Five, I started having panic attacks. [...] I never had them at work, but I would have them before work or on my days off. Usually I sleep like a rock, but I started not being able to fall asleep. I was waking up every hour. I would have chest pain. I wouldn't be able to catch my breath. [...] I didn't realize it at first, but then, once it lasted a couple weeks, I began to think something was up. I had indigestion. I couldn't turn my mind off. I would think about all the things that I had done wrong, things that I had forgotten. What did I miss? Would the next nurse be upset?

"One night, I was crying, and I called out in prayer, and I said all my insecurities out loud to God. I sang a few worship songs to myself. Then, for a couple weeks after that, they were totally gone. Then I had one once a week for a little while. Now I haven't had them for months. [...]

"This was the first time that I really struggled. It didn't come naturally. I really had to work to become competent. Maybe that is a good thing, because if anyone could be a nurse, then would we really trust nurses with our lives? It really felt like a slap in the face. It was way harder than I thought it would be. I felt like I had a little bit of an identity crisis. For the first time, I felt like I sucked at something that I really couldn't afford to suck at. I felt really insecure. I definitely didn't walk as tall for a while. I was believing the lies of the enemy: that I wasn't good enough, that I was bad at this, that I wouldn't succeed. To combat it, I would pray the same prayer every day on the way to work. Now I have added stuff to it as I have gone along. One aspect is that there is not a moment of each day that I don't need God for."

—OR, *medical-surgical oncology, eleven months of experience*

A third nurse said this on the topic of mental health:

"In terms of mental health, it is really important to try and hold onto your own self in the taking on of any new job. Before you do that though, you need to do a thorough assessment of the state of your own mental health. How healthy is your mind? How are you doing as a human being? If I hadn't already been diagnosed with severe depression and anxiety before I started this job, I would have found out about it this year. But since I did know, I could fall back on my doctors, therapist, psychiatrist, and support system. If I didn't have that, this year would have been really hard on me, and that's ok. We need to be intentional through and through.

"Sometimes huge stressors open us up to being able to identify our own needs. Doing a thorough assessment of those needs is important in the midst of it all so that you don't get swallowed up by a sea of mental health issues while you are already drowning. Some things are just chemical imbalances, genetics, things you are born with, but they do come up in hard situations. At work, when I had a panic attack, I had to text my therapist and take my panic attack medications, but afterward I was able to feel ok. You have to have tools. You have to have tools to fight what is in front of you and know that you don't have to fight barehanded and alone. It is important to know that you can start these things short-term to help you through a short-term situation. It doesn't have to be long-term or signing a lifelong contract like, 'I have to take this medication until I die.' You can find assistance when you need

Chapter 6

help. You can walk on your own, too. You don't have to do any one thing for your whole life, but it is important to ask for help when you need it."

—EP, *medical-surgical oncology nurse, one year of experience*

Regardless of how we typically handle the difficult situations that we face—whether we are well versed in taking care of ourselves mentally or not—we need to keep in mind that new situations have the tendency to bring out those *I wish, if only,* and *my fault* feelings in all of us. There is nothing like the remarkable power of the unknown to make us feel incompetent.

As promised, we are going to talk about weightlifting. For the sake of this particular metaphor, I watched the 2019 Women's Weightlifting World Championship in order to better understand what weightlifting actually entails. These women are remarkable because they are lifting weights over their heads that weigh more than they do.

Watching it made me anxious. I was terrified that one of them was going to drop the bar on her neck, causing her a cervical spinal cord injury, leaving her paralyzed. But that isn't what happened. Competitor after competitor bravely walked up to face the weight that lay in front of them. Then each woman hoisted the weight that weighed more than she did, held it up high above her own head, and proceeded to triumphantly throw it to the ground to the sound of much applause.

Now, I didn't fully understand this beforehand, but there is a whole art and science to weightlifting. The weightlifter's stance, their squat, the way they lift, the way they straighten their elbows at the end of the lift—all of these factors are taken into account by the judges. It is by no means just picking something up and then setting it back down. It takes training. It takes work. For these women—these superstar Olympic-bound athletes—it has taken a lifetime of devotion.

NEW

Do you know what else takes a lifetime of devotion? Building the muscle to wrestle with our own inner thoughts. Those muscles, if conditioned and used in the right way, are the same muscles that we can use to grow stronger from the weight and the pain which afflicts us.

If correct stance is important in how one lifts physical weight, what are the key factors in lifting mental and emotional weight? Well, there are a number, and we are going to address quite a few in this chapter, but we are going to start with dispelling the idols of *I wish, if only,* and *my fault*.

How many of you out there have fed these ideas to yourself in futility as you lie awake at night, staring at the ceiling, unable to sleep? I used the word *futility* because the way we toil with these three notions is exactly that: futile. I also referred to them as idols, which may seem strange. For the context of this book we will be defining an idol as something one's mind has decided to place at the pinnacle of internal importance.

I wish, if only, and *my fault* are ways that we idolize the past, because we focus and dwell on them too much. Not only that, but they are not even accurate reflections of what has actually happened. They are simply our own fanciful notions of what we wish we could have done or said. Therefore, when we get caught up with *I wish, if only,* or *my fault,* we idolize a false past.

Rather than looking forward to how we can use the weight of a painful experience to strengthen ourselves in the future, we instead idolize what we could or should have done, trapping ourselves in spiraling, inaccurate narratives about our personal histories. That is the exact opposite of using the weight to lift and strengthen.

When we continually dwell on the *could-haves* of our past, never letting them go, we allow the weight to slowly crush us. When we operate solely based off of the *could-haves,* we attempt to lift the weight with an incorrect lifting-posture. *I wish, if only,* and *my fault* cause us to ignore the intentional stance that weight-lifting requires. Why? Because when we get so fully caught up in our own

Chapter 6

minds, we forget how to put into practice all that we have trained for.

This can in turn prove to be dangerous; when a weightlifter does not lift with proper technique, they run the risk of causing injury to their muscular structure. Similarly, when we don't lift our own emotional weight properly, we run the risk of sustaining injury to our mental structure. In truth, we are all going to have to do some heavy-lifting at some point, especially in the midst of new circumstances, so it is imperative that we learn what it means to lift correctly and then actually do it.

Like any new job, nursing is filled with many firsts. Some are awesome firsts and are anticipated with great excitement, but others are not awesome firsts and are anticipated with great anxiety and trepidation. Unlike with most jobs, the firsts that new nurses worry about carry a distinct layer of heaviness. I am talking about rapid responses, codes, and death (whether expected or sudden).

The first time that any of these three things happens to a new nurse, that nurse is changed forever. Not just as a clinician, but as a person. What we do is not a game. Our lives are not like medical TV shows in which the episode wraps up with a tear-jerking moment, a heart-wrenching song, and then cuts cleanly to the credits. This is the truth of our reality. This is the weight of which we carry.

Personally, I was terrified of these types of firsts. When other nurses would share their first encounters with the three aforementioned events, all I could think to myself was, *How do you ever make peace with that in your mind? How do you live with yourself after being part of something so horrific?*

I found myself adding the weight of the anticipated onto the weight of the active. Interestingly, the first time one of my own patients rapid responded, it was in the same week I met the artist who inspired this book. This experience with my first rapid response became one of the first things that I wrote about. Let's take a look back at my seventh month as a nurse.

NEW

A rapid response occurs when a patient is declining or showing concerning changes, but they still have a heart rate and are breathing. They might not be breathing well, and their heart might be doing something weird, but in short, a rapid response occurs in order to prevent a Code Blue from happening. The whole team of critical care nurses, respiratory therapists, and doctors come to the bedside, but hopefully no active CPR or defibrillation has to be performed. But, back to the story:

*****

As I write this, it is exactly two days after I had to call my first rapid response on one of my own patients. All the new nurses on my floor anticipate their first rapid response with dread. We are not the emergency department, nor are we the critical care unit, but on our floor, declining patients are very familiar to us, and rapid responses are frequent.

Usually when you hear the rapid response call go off on the hospital-wide overhead speaker system for another nurse's patient on your floor, you go help. But that night it was my patient who was declining. It seemingly came out of nowhere. When my charge nurse told me to make the rapid response call, I blinked once. Twice. Then I ran. I've said it before, and I'll say it again: I have an amazing team. As soon as that call went off, the other nurses immediately came in to help me.

The whole process ended up not being too bad. In a weird way, I am glad that it happened the way it did. I was able to give a thorough report to the rapid response team. The patient was safely transported to critical care. Her heart rate remained stable. She remained conscious. She even kept saying, "I'm fine, I'm fine," in between gasps. The patient's respiratory rate was through-the-roof high, but I checked her chart later and saw that she had improved once she had gotten settled in critical care. I heard no Code Blues called later that night, which is always a good sign. One of the

Chapter 6

experienced nurses did have to remind me to call the primary doctor as I was running around, and I had no idea how to chart the whole ordeal, so it was far from perfect, but it was over. I survived. More importantly, the patient survived.

Reflecting on the situation afterward, I thought to myself, *I wish* I had acted faster. *I wish* I could have caught onto the patient's deterioration sooner. *I wish* I had done a better job talking to the doctor. *I wish* that I had prayed for my patient's safety rather than praying, "Please, God, let the report that I give the rapid response team be good enough."

Then after the *I wish* was out of the way, the *my fault* came pouring into my mind. *Is it my fault* that the patient declined? *Is it my fault* that her disease progressed? *Is it my fault* because I missed something that I should've picked up on? *Is it my fault* because I didn't do a thorough enough assessment? *Is it my fault* because I didn't provide her with good enough care? *If only* there was something that I could have done to have prevented this.

I asked myself those questions over and over again. Do you know what, though? I don't really think there was anything else I could have done. But on the twisted path of anxiety, which my brain just loves to go down without my permission, the whole thing was *my fault*. Of course, I could have single handedly saved the patient *if only* I had acted sooner, *if only* I had thought more critically, *if only* my assessment skills had been sharper. *If only. If only.* Right? Wrong.

Here's the thing—sometimes patients get worse. Sometimes patients are visibly declining for days, circling the precipice of disaster, and you are the unfortunate nurse who has to rapid respond them. Other times, the disease brews dormantly and the patient seems fine—maybe they even seem like they are getting better—and then suddenly they become symptomatic. But at the end of the day, if a disease is going to manifest itself during your shift, it's going to manifest itself. All you can do is respond to it the best you can.

NEW

Two of the other new nurses on my floor had their first rapid responses recently, too. Both said the exact same thing: "I feel like it's my fault."

When I heard that, I immediately and vehemently told them, "No! It's not your fault. It's not your fault." We deal with very sick patients, and very sick patients often get sicker. I wish I could tell myself this the same way I told them, with such a definitive fervor. It wasn't their fault. It wasn't *my* fault. But even as I type this, I still feel that somehow it was.

The more experienced nurses don't seem to be like this as much. They pack their patients up and send them down to critical care, no problem. It isn't a jaded thing or a lacking-compassion thing. It is more of an experiential-wisdom thing. We are not the dictators of life; we are the stewards. The more we realize how fierce and unpredictable disease is, the more we realize how powerless we really are against it. So, we work our hardest, do our best to love others, and pray. That's all we really can do. And I pray, oh man, do I pray. I've prayed so hard at work that I have given myself headaches.

*****

I am not saying to just pray the anxiety away. I know that in the battle against *I wish, if only,* and *my fault,* praying helps, but it has to be done in conjunction with other strategies that are offered to us. We also need to have resources, a support system, and things that we can actively put into practice to protect our own minds from dwelling on the idol of a false past.

A rapid response with a fairly positive outcome is not the worst that can happen to you as a nurse, not by a long shot. I consider myself lucky that my experience ended as it did, with my patient safe and alive. Let's talk about the very worst that can happen. *What's the worst that can happen?* you might be wondering to yourself right now if you are not a nurse. But if you are a nurse,

Chapter 6

you already know the haunting answer to that question: the sudden and unexpected death of one of your patients.

The following is not my story. It is not my lived experience or my pain, and I have no claim to it as such. The new nurse that shared it with me is incredibly brave for doing so. I do not share this with you as a simple anecdote to bolster this chapter. I tell it to you with permission and with the respectful somberness that all nurses learn to carry with them when such stories are told. This nurse's experience is as follows:

"I had a Code Blue on one of my own patients a couple months ago. Since I had first started on my unit, no one had ever had to call a code. I never saw one in school, and real life is so different from any simulation. The patient crashed really fast. She had been talking, breathing, and everything had been normal. Then ten minutes later, we had to do compressions. She was on the younger side, too.

"Honestly, I felt like the code went as well as it could have in how the code team responded and how people helped me. But I felt like—as the primary RN, having never seen a code in real life—my communication to the necessary people was below adequate. Whether or not that was the case, I don't know. But it was really hard, especially because in the end the patient didn't make it.

"My coworkers were really supportive. They told me that sometimes patients just don't make it. I did everything that I could, and I did it in a fast time frame. We called a rapid response first, then a Code Blue. I was as fast as I possibly could be, but communicating professionally in such a high-intensity situation is just a whole other ballgame. The doctor would ask questions about the patient's history that I didn't know off the top of my head. When you have five patients and you don't know all the information off the top of your head, it's scary. One thing I learned is to bring your brain or notes into the room. Small, simple things like that I learned, but you only get confidence from experience.

NEW

"I really don't think the outcome would have been any different no matter what we did, but it is something that shook me up a lot. Afterward, dealing with those feelings, I really had to give credit to my coworkers. They were so supportive. Almost everyone sought me out individually. They either did something nice for me, texted me, or shared with me how their first code went, how they dealt with the guilt of it all, and what people did for them.

"At the end of the day, they reminded me that we do everything that we can, and sometimes people still die. I was adequate. That's just what happens. People waited for me after the shift even though I had to stay late to chart. They asked me if I wanted to get breakfast. The next night there was a potluck. People brought food. Then the next day, other people who hadn't seen me since it happened brought me food, too. The charge nurses even sought me out to talk me through it. Having someone die is really heavy.

"The thing that helped me the most was hearing other people's stories and how exactly they felt in their first code. The honesty of it all. I felt so responsible for what happened. I knew I wasn't the one who was responsible for making her code, but that is still how it felt. It took me the next six shifts that I worked—almost back to back that next week—to start to feel better, because the people who were around me at work all got it. They understood. It wasn't like I was back in regular life at the grocery store with strangers. They understood, and it was a safe place to talk about it. That was good because I could acknowledge the reality of what happened, but I also knew that I couldn't live in that space of guilt forever.

"Having an experience like that, it all makes you become a better nurse. Zipping the body-bag felt so surreal. Then having to come back with the same friendly, 'Hi, I am your nurse,' for the next patient was really hard. Somehow, I get that room assigned to me a lot now, and it's hard, because I remember being in there with the patient who was talking to me, then coding her, and then at the end, I had to clean up her blood. It's difficult. It sucked. But, with support, I was ok. Even the day-shift nurses checked in on

Chapter 6

me. In the break room, they wrote on the board, 'Good job, MK!' and I thought, You guys! I don't deserve you! It was the worst-case scenario, but it couldn't have been avoided. Patients just crash sometimes."

—*MK, medical-surgical telemetry sepsis nurse, eight months of experience*

"Then at the end, I had to clean up her blood." That is the weight of which we carry. The day we lose someone out of the blue is the day our hearts break in a way they have never broken before. But while we have lost that patient, that family member, that friend, or that coworker, saying *I wish, if only*, or *my fault* to ourselves will never help. No matter how hard you try to re-rehearse the past, the underlying truth is that *we* will most likely get a tomorrow, so the important question we need to ask ourselves is, *How will we choose to move into it?*

We *choose* how we deal with the pain. As always, we can let it crush us or we can use it to make us stronger. First, we grieve, we give ourselves space, we give ourselves time, and we hold the weight. It's ok not to be ok. That is imperative. But eventually we have to choose to lift the weight, because it's not ok to stay that way.

After experiencing great loss and great devastation, we will never be the same. Things will never go back to the way they were. Things will always be different. Things will always be weird. All of that is ok. It's ok. We will dissect these ideas in full in Chapter Eight, but for now, know this: as another one of my pastors once said, we have to choose to "make our pain our power."

If we choose to allow that pain to empower us, to let it strengthen us rather than crush us, then we will come out the other side of that hurt with muscles we never even knew we had.

In order to do that—in order to transition from not being ok to being ok and to lift the weight rather than drop it—we have to fight to protect our own mental health. That fight needs to be an everyday fight. While death doesn't usually happen to us on a personal level every day, life does. We are actively living, fighting, and developing as human beings every day that we are on this Earth. If we want to grow stronger through our pain instead of being crushed by it, then we have to actively reframe our minds and anxieties and remember our proper weightlifting techniques and stances.

Admittedly, I have not always been the best at doing this because I have the propensity to do something that I call "crazy spiraling." Crazy spiral: (definition by me) the act of latching onto a negative thought, not being able to detach from it, replaying said thought over and over in your head until you feel like that negative thought has become the truth and is definitive of who you are as a person.

I used to crazy spiral like it was my job. Any time an even remotely negative feeling—no matter how trivial or fleeting—ran across my mind, I would start to spin out of control with anxiety. Every once in a while, I still do it, but now I know what to look out for in order to keep the spiral from taking over.

Let me break it down for us. Feeling, exploring, and unpacking all of our feelings is healthy. Crazy spiraling, on the other hand, is not. But can we avoid it? How do we allow ourselves to process our feelings without being sucked into a crazy spiral of overwhelming, negative thoughts?

Feelings can be exceptionally difficult to navigate. But truth be told, we have more power over them than we may initially believe. As someone who has struggled with anxiety for years, the idea of having complete control of my thoughts sounds fictitious. What I am saying, however, is that we have more power over our feelings than we tend to think, because we have the power to choose to either crazy spiral or not. I am not saying that we need to mute our feelings, push them deep down, and never speak of such negativities again. Not at all. Instead, we can respond to our feelings in positive ways rather than in negative ways. Insert a thousand and one quotes about changing one's attitude here.

Chapter 6

Here is one quote that I have actually found to be helpful. Authors Kyle Strobel and John Coe wrote the following in their book, *Where Prayer Becomes Real:* "Your feelings do not tell you true things about the world. Your feelings tell you true things about your heart, which is why they are so important. Our feelings and emotions are not adequate signals about the way things are outside of us."

When I asked one nurse whom I had the chance to interview, "How did you deal with the weight of responsibility that was put on you?" she responded with the following:

"I definitely am an anxious type of person, so I tend to feel anxious and really feel that weight of responsibility. It is about having to learn that positive mental attitude and learn one moment at a time and one task at a time, and then surrounding myself with positive thoughts rather than dwelling on things when they don't go right. One thing I struggle with is self-confidence, and I doubt myself a lot, so I have to be confident in the things that I do know and then ask questions when I don't know. It is so important to ask questions. In the ICU environment, you are never alone. There are always people around. Especially since my hospital is a research hospital, we always have residents, doctors, and more experienced nurses on the unit.

"So, at this point, I know that I don't know it all and that I will be asking questions fifteen years down the line, too, which is ok! [...] I have to have grace with myself, however, because I know that, while I cannot do it right now, one day when I am not so focused on just keeping the patient alive, I will be able to care for the patients more holistically. I had to come to that conclusion though, because at first, I felt really guilty about it. I think it comes down to thinking positively by holding your negative thoughts captive, and then reframing them into positive ones. That is really important."

—*SK, pediatric critical care nurse, two months of experience*

NEW

We have to work hard to identify the truth amidst the lies we are telling ourselves. If we don't, the lies of our own internal expectations will swallow us whole. This is something that we are all still learning to do in every aspect of our lives for our entire lives.

Whenever I am on the verge of a crazy spiral, I give myself two choices. Option one, I am going to let the lies of my unhealthy feelings take over and allow them to crush me. Option two, I am going to approach my feelings in a healthy way by identifying the truth in the situation.

In the moment, Option One is easier to choose because it does not take work to be pulled down into a crazy spiral. When we feel anxious or depressed, it is easy to go along with the negative feelings. They are not easy feelings to have, by any means, and I am not trivializing their weight. What I mean is that they are easy feelings to get swept into. It is extremely hard to get out of those feelings once we are swallowed by them. It is hard to say no to the crazy spiral. Once it's got us, it's got us. But at the end of the day, Option One is only going to hurt us more, especially in the long run.

Option Two is the harder initial choice by far, both in the moment we are presented with an opportunity to crazy spiral, as well as in our day-to-day lives. It may be the harder choice, but it is ultimately the healthier one. But choosing Option Two and staying out of the crazy spiral doesn't just happen easily. It takes work. In my research and in my own personal life, I have found that the best ways to stay out of a crazy spiral, and to allow the weight of difficulty to strengthen rather than crush, is to do the following five things:

1. Recognize that it is ok to not be ok and let yourself feel your feelings.

We already spent a significant amount of time on this topic, so I will keep the extrapolation of this particular step short, although it

Chapter 6

still remains imperative to practice. One new nurse expressed the following sentiment on the topic of anxiety;

"I was very anxious going into my first day. I couldn't sleep the night before. I took a sleeping aid, but even then, I still woke up. It was more than uncomfortable, but I wouldn't say it was painful. Feeling anxious is the feeling of being unsteady and that is one of the worst feelings to have. It is different from physical pain, but it is more like a head or heart or psychological pain. I think, just on a side note, that it is easier when someone says, 'I fell, and I hurt my hip, and I have eight-out-of-ten physical pain,' and the x-ray shows a fracture, and the doctor tells you how long it will take to heal. But when it comes to psychological issues, it is so subjective that people don't know how to respond when you feel those things. There is that added anxiety and depression because you feel like you are alone."

—RL, *medical-surgical sepsis nurse, three months of experience*

To summarize, emotional and mental pain need to be taken just as seriously as physical pain. If it is ok for someone to have pain from a broken hip, it is ok for someone to have pain because of an emotional or mental injury as well. Both are real, both are valid, both need to be addressed, and both need to be met with compassion.

2. Approach your feelings in a healthy way by identifying and processing them, and then by finding the truth in the situation.

The key component to this is being able to show yourself grace. We also talked about this one in depth, so again I will keep it short. When I asked one nurse whom I interviewed, "What is a piece of wisdom that you have for someone in their first year? What advice would you give your younger self?" she said the following:

"I would say that you definitely need to be kind to yourself. It is so challenging. I have trained over twenty new grads and the hardest thing is finding this balance of needing to be perfect but knowing that that isn't possible and having to have grace for yourself in that. You are inevitably not going to be perfect, but you still have to continue to press into trying to improve."

—*BS, internal medicine nurse practitioner, eight years of experience*

In Chapter One we discussed that while there is a person in that hospital bed, there also is a person inside of those scrubs, and if you are a nurse, then that person is you. Whoever you are, wherever you are, and in the midst of whatever new situation you find yourself to be in, you have to be kind to yourself by remembering your own humanity.

My sister and I have a rule that whenever one of us engages in negative self-talk, the other one promptly yells, "Hey! Don't you talk about my sister that way!" In reality, we would never say the hurtful things that we say to ourselves to another human being, so it is important to remind each other not to talk about ourselves that way either.

Once we are done showing ourselves grace, we have to actively pursue the truth in the situation. This step is of vital importance when moving from the space of the not-ok to the space of the ok. As the nurse quoted above said, "You are inevitably not going to be perfect, but you still have to continue to press into trying to improve." One way to improve is to healthily engage and grow by identifying the truth in the situation.

3. Talk things out with someone.

This is really just asking for help, in disguise. Talking things out with someone, being vulnerable, and letting a safe person share the weight of our pain are different ways of asking for help. In all the interviews that I conducted, nurse after nurse talked about the

Chapter 6

important role that talking with someone played in their lives. This very simple yet profound act transcends the realm of the workplace.

Of the fifty nurses that I interviewed—regardless of whether or not the nurse in question had an easy transition into nursing or an easy time separating their home life from their work life—twenty-three reported that they found solace and mental well-being in talking with someone. This was reported again and again as the nurses answered the following questions:

- How did you deal with the weight of responsibility that was put on you?
- What kept you from quitting? How did you deal with wanting to quit?
- What is a piece of wisdom that you have for someone in their first year? What advice would you give your younger self?
- What did you wish someone had told you before you started? What do you wish was talked about more?
- What was a mistake that you made? How did you cope with it after the fact?
- How have you prevented yourself from becoming burnt out? What did you do to recover when you were burnt out?

One could ask these same interview questions of any person in any job, but when one asks them of a nurse, there is a certain critical weight to the answers one receives. It is imperative to pursue open and honest communication in order to deal with heavy situations. This is something that transcends the limitations of the professional sphere and can be applied to anyone, anywhere, because it is a universal component of developing as a healthy human being. For as we discussed in Chapter Five, no one person can carry the full burden of life's weight on their own.

One new nurse stressed the importance of talking to someone in the following way:

NEW

"Share how you are feeling with others when you are overwhelmed. Don't feel like you have to keep it all inside. Find people to talk about it with, whether it be people on your staff or outside of it. You need to talk to someone."

—*AH, medical-surgical respiratory, ten months of experience*

Likewise, an experienced nurse said this on the same subject:

"We all need to talk to people. If we feel like we are not doing a good job, we need to get someone else's perspective. We need to share our feelings and get their feedback, even if it is just one person in our work situation. Sometimes we are too hard on ourselves."

—*WB, hospice nurse, thirty years of experience*

You are not being a burden by sharing your heavy feelings with someone. Being a human is simply a weighty thing. To quote Hayao Miyazaki's film adaptation of Howl's Moving Castle, "A heart is a heavy burden." Having a heart means having the feelings that come with it, and sometimes things just get heavy. There is no shame in that. Do you know those professional weightlifters who we previously discussed? They have people nearby to spot them as they lift. Why? Because they are lifting heavy weights, and lifting heavy weights can be dangerous. That being said, we all need people to spot us to make sure that we aren't going to get crushed.

One of the most experienced nurses that I had the privilege of interviewing remarkably said this:

"A mistake that new nurses make is they try to do things on their own and don't ask for help. The newer ones need help, and the older ones need to be needed. There is something about being needed that is really beautiful."

—*CM, pediatric advice line nurse, thirty-seven years of experience*

Chapter 6

Life is symbiotic. There is a whole lot of teamwork involved. We said it before in Chapter Four: ask for help and offer help.

4. Do something that you enjoy doing.

This is an area that we are going to talk about in depth in Chapter Ten, but for now, just as a sample for what is to come, let's look at what one nurse said this in response to the question, "How have you fought burnout? What did you do when you were burnt out?"

"Do what you love with who you love, that is my motto. There's life outside of nursing. You can't forget that."
—*TH, professor of nursing and burn ICU nurse, twenty-five years of experience*

I'm just going to leave it at that.

5. Identify strategies that will help you become ok again.

Here we are—the practical how-tos of weightlifting. One analogy that we can use to help ourselves identify healthy coping strategies is the analogy of the tool belt. In fact, one of the nurses who I quoted at the start of the chapter brought up this very analogy. Here is a refresher:

"You have to have tools. You have to have tools to fight what is in front of you and know that you don't have to fight barehanded and alone."
—*EP, medical-surgical oncology nurse, one year of experience*

So, what can the tools in our tool belt of mental health look like? They can take many different forms. Let's look at a few as we conclude.

NEW

The Tool of Community

"The main thing is to identify a mentor that you feel comfortable being transparent with. I wish that I had sought out or identified a mentor, ideally in nursing, but someone who was older and seasoned in the working world. I didn't have that, and I feel like I would have perhaps avoided some significant mistakes that I made in coping with the stress of being a new grad. As a Christian, I would say to make sure to continue in an accountability group or a small group. Stay connected to your community. I think the encouragement to focus on what God is doing in your life instead of focusing on self-doubt, personal needs, or feelings of insufficiency is important. Those are two things that I lacked."
—*SF, professor of nursing, twenty-four years of experience*

The Tool of Professional Counsel

"The first year is really taxing mental-health-wise. In nursing in general, no matter what stage you are at professionally, in my opinion, we all can use therapy, and it is absolutely ok to go get help in that way. I think it should be more encouraged to really take care of yourself. Your life isn't just your career. There is always other stuff going on outside of that. Having a stressful career can make things more difficult at home. I waited a long time to go into therapy, but I wish that I had done it sooner. A lot of hospitals offer it for free, too—mine does—so it is good to know your resources."
—*KE, acute care rehab nurse, five years of experience*

The Tool of Medical Assistance

"I remembered that to cope with just the thought of going to work in the beginning, when I was stressed out of my mind and having some serious anxiety issues, I would have to take a Xanax

Chapter 6

just to even get myself there. I want people to know that that is ok. There shouldn't be a negative stigma over needing medication for mental health problems especially for anxiety. There are those people that will say, 'Toughen up,' and, 'Don't be so weak,' but it's not a matter of weakness—it's a matter of a real illness, and that is ok."

—*HH, surgical-telemetry step-down nurse, nine months of experience*

The Tool of Self Accountability

"I am still dealing with it right now, but initially I worried and was anxious a lot. But over time, and as I continue to grow in my role, I have learned that I just have to really be on top of my work, whether that be planning my day well or being in contact with the people that I need to be in touch with. Remembering that there is a lot of responsibility but at the same time as long as I am doing my best that is the most that I can do. I can be at peace with that. There is only so much that I can do, too. Actually taking the time to sit down and list what those things are and visualizing them so I can hold myself accountable helps. Then, when I have completed and done all those things, I know that anything beyond that is really out of my hands."

—*DH, registered nurse consultant, seven months of experience*

The Tool of Prayer

"A wise person told me, 'Make a written list of all of your daily frustrations, things that you want to change about where you work or what you do. Pray over it every night, or morning, just every day, I guess. Then, mentally move on. Wait to see what God will do. Wait for his timing.'"

—*PE, labor and delivery nurse, ten years of experience*

NEW

The Tool of Choosing to Let Things Go

When I was watching the 2019 Women's Weightlifting World Championship, one of the athletes scratched her lift when she dropped the weight that she was trying to lift. She did it very gracefully and kind of tossed the weight and rolled under it in order to stay out of harm's way. One of the commentators said, in response to the athlete's actions, "You have to know when to let it go."

In the circumstance of actual weightlifting, that is what one physically has to do in order to not become crushed and paralyzed. But do you know what you have to do in real life? Sometimes you have to let that weight go in order to not get crushed and paralyze yourself.

"Let it out, let it go. That's my motto. Otherwise, it will eat you up."
—*AN, medical-surgical respiratory nurse, nine months of experience*

"I feel like I am a very calm person, so even when things would get hectic at work, I would go to the bathroom and give myself two minutes to breathe. Then, I would think to myself, Ok, let's prioritize and regroup. When I would be on my drive home, I would think about what had happened, but once I got home, I would stop thinking about it. I would give myself that barrier. "
—*KR, medical-surgical respiratory nurse, nine months of experience*

"One thing I learned from my new grad program was when one of the educators taught us this: at the end of your shift, on your drive home, pick a spot, kind of like halfway home, and forget about your shift and everything that happened during it. I really took that to heart, and that's really helped with not bringing my work home. That is one way that I dealt with the mental pressures."
—*DY, bone marrow transplant oncology nurse, nine months of experience*

Chapter 6

The Tool of Resting in Tension (For When You Can't Let Things Go)

"I had to find the balance of leaving things at work, but also talking about it outside of work. In school we learned mixed things. Some people would say to leave it all in the breakroom at work and don't think about it at home. But then, I felt like I was never resolving any of my thoughts that way. But then, when I took it all home, I felt like it was making me crazy at home. It was a process and a balance of being able to talk with my nursing school friends, getting to hang out with them and vent and discuss the frustrations of having doctors scream at you or the terror of having G-tube contents spilled on you. Being able to talk with them was a Godsend, but also having friends that have nothing to do with nursing that you can dance and have fun with and forget about nursing with is important, too. Once I found that line between those two tensions, I could carry the weight better, because I was able to process it better with the support systems that I had built."

—EP, *medical-surgical oncology nurse, one year of experience*

The Tool of Guided Imagery

This last tool is one that I have personally relied on a lot. There is one image in particular that has, in all actuality, held me back from the brink of disaster. A number of years prior to writing this book, I was on the precipice of a complete mental breakdown. I remember sitting in my car, giving myself two options: I knew that I could either go to the hospital or I could call people who I knew cared about me and ask them for help. Either way, I knew that I couldn't do nothing. If I had chosen to do nothing in that moment, I would have chosen to let the weight crush me in a way that I wouldn't have been able to come back from.

We are all one moment, one bad day, away from that hospital bed. I had spent an entire year prior to that near-breakdown building up

NEW

community for myself. I had practiced asking for help in small ways. I had practiced vulnerability with safe people. I had re-enrolled myself in therapy. I had found and participated actively in a healthy spiritual community. It was a good thing that I did those things, because in that very bleak moment of breaking, I knew that I wasn't alone. It was the tool of community, used within the context of the tool of guided imagery, that gave me the strength and the courage to be vulnerable and ask for help that day so that I didn't have to take myself to the hospital.

You are probably wondering, *What could you have possibly envisioned to get yourself out of that spot?* It is a mental image that I like to call *Team Tenley*. It takes the form of a very large, pitaya pink poster, covered in sparkling star stickers. There is a picture of me in the middle of it, surrounded by the photos of people who I know will pick up the phone if I call them and will come help me carry my weight if I tell them that I am struggling.

When I picture this over-the-top poster in my head, it reminds me that I am not alone. It reminds me of the resources that I do have. It allows me to identify the truth hidden in the sweeping darkness of my feelings. In that moment, I felt alone—*alone, alone, alone*—until I remembered that I wasn't. I made some calls, and my community showed up for me. One friend skipped class and took me out for boba. My mentor invited me over for dinner. My mom drove the three-hour drive between us to visit me. My boss let me call out from work. People showed me an unfathomable amount of kindness, but I had to let them.

Depression and pain, while often isolative, can ultimately be used to point us to community. They can be used to point us to one another, so that we have people to spot us, to train with us, and to help us lift the weight of our own lives even when our elbows shake. While these themes are exceedingly important in all areas of life and in dispelling the lies of *I wish, if only,* and *my fault,* do you know where they become even more imperative still?

Chapter 6

They are at their utmost importance when things are actually our fault. We all make mistakes, and there is nothing that will crush us faster than lifting the weight of the mistakes that we have made poorly, without help. Trying to navigate our mistakes alone is a sure way to paralyze ourselves and stunt our growth. So, let's move forward from the lies of the false *my faults* to the stark reality of the times when we find ourselves saying, *Oh shit, it actually is my fault.*

After all, roses don't stop growing just because they get pruned. We don't stop growing just because we make a mistake. Therefore, we need to learn how to let our mistakes refine and reshape us, rather than stunt us. That is, after all, what pruning does to a rose bush. Pruning allows the plant to grow more purposefully. It will hurt, but when we are done, our lives won't just look like haphazard briar patches: they will look like well-sculpted topiaries. So, however reluctant you might be to face the realities of your own mistakes, get your hedge trimmers ready, because we are going to be doing some clipping.

Chapter Seven:
When It Is Actually Your Fault

Mistakes undoubtedly contribute to some of the most unpleasant parts of our lives. Whether they stem from times when our actions were brash and brazen, or from times when we were too cautious and timid, mistakes unmistakably *hurt*. Not unsurprisingly, mistakes tie directly into the aspect of unhealthy pride that we discussed in Chapter Four, because who wants to be wrong? Who wants to take ownership of their own shortcomings? Where mistakes occur, shame can abound, but only if we let it. This latter concept, the fine line between humility and shame, is one that we discussed in Chapter Four and then again in Chapter Six, where we discussed how to stay out of the *crazy spiral*.

Now we are going to talk about mistakes specifically. While mistakes happen in all areas of life, in the field of medicine, we *have* to admit our mistakes to our team. While mistakes can be detrimental, many can also be resolved. Damage and harm come, however, when the mistakes that we make get swept under the rug. The only thing that is worse than making a mistake is making a mistake that hurts another person. Is having this discussion painfully vulnerable? Yes, but it is imperative to do so because, in nursing, our mistakes never affect just us.

To reiterate a sentiment that was expressed in Chapter Four, one nurse wisely stated the following:

"We are humans trying to save other humans."
—*SB, high risk labor and delivery nurse, five months of experience*

Chapter 7

It is a heavy thing to think to one's self, *Today is the day that I might save somebody,* or, *Today is the day that I might kill somebody.* Both sentiments are terrifyingly true. But if we were to think about life only in the framework of those two lenses, then life itself would be extremely anxiety-inducing. Not just for health care professionals, either. Many of us get behind the wheels of dangerous machinery every day to get to work. But does the fear of a car accident keep us from driving? No.

This brings us to a false idol that we didn't talk about in the last chapter. This idol is not one of a false past but is instead one of a false future. It is the future idol of *what if?*

There are many *what ifs* that we ask ourselves, both within the context of our jobs as well as in our daily lives. But we can't let the *what ifs* of life stupefy us and keep us from living or from loving. If we are honest with ourselves, we probably can pinpoint areas in our lives in which we have sacrificed our own hopes, dreams, optimism, and childlike faith at the altar of this particular idol.

Instead of learning all that we can in the here and now, we fall prey to the futuristic *what ifs* that trap us in that same sort of false past *crazy spiral,* except this time, it is in the spiral of the inaccurate narratives of our own personal futures. With the *what ifs* come a weight that we are not even meant to be carrying, because it is a weight that might not ever even come. Nothing steals our joy faster than the heaviness of the *what ifs.* If we dwell on the fanciful ideologies of the *what ifs,* the weight of responsibility will crush us instead of build and strengthen us each day.

Of course, the big question in this chapter is, *What if I make a mistake?*

I picked up this following notion at work during my first year as a nurse. Whoever said this to me opened my eyes, not just to the possibility of mistakes but to their imminent reality. They said, "It is not a matter of if you make a mistake, it is a matter of when."

One would think that this would have added more weight to the heaviness that I was already feeling as a new nurse, but surprisingly, it did not. In fact, it actually lessened the self-imposed burden of having to be a perfect clinician and, beyond that, a perfect person.

Now, if you have ever met me, you would know that I am not a perfectionist. In my day-to-day life, I am a very carefree person. I usually answer the question, "What if?" with, "So what?"

But you cannot be that way in nursing. You cannot be that way *at all*. So, my whole personality had to be reshaped in order to make me a safer nurse. That was extremely hard for me to do, but consciously rewiring my brain was not the hardest part. The hardest part was living with the consequences of becoming *overly* rewired. I went from being a sunshine soul—a borderline hippy of a human—to being a no-nonsense, no-room-for-mistakes, ice-cold clinician.

For me, there was no middle ground. I went from zero to one-hundred and I went there fast. Somebody should've handed me a red lightsaber, because, to quote Obi-Wan Kenobi: "Only a Sith deals in absolutes."

How did I become the bad guy? By turning everything into an absolute in my mind and by giving myself zero room to make mistakes. I had jumped on the perfectionism-train, and it was only this idea of *it is not a matter of if, it is a matter of when*, that allowed me jump off of it. I am eternally grateful for whoever said this to me, because the perfectionism-train has no other destination than a place of burnout, isolation, and ruin (which is literally what happens in *Star Wars*).

Having someone say this to me reminded me that mistakes happen. They happen to all of us; to the strongest, to the smartest, and to the most experienced of us. Just as none of us are making it out of this life alive, none of us are making it out of this life without making mistakes. There is a distinct component of healthy humility to this idea as well as a distinct sense of community.

So, by changing my mindset from *what if* to *when*, I allowed myself to breathe a little bit more easily. It allowed me to face the

Chapter 7

weight head-on and use it to strengthen me instead of crush me. I saw that no matter what happened in the mistake-making process, I wouldn't have to go through the consequences alone, because everyone has been in the same position.

Though we all make mistakes as humans, as nurses, we have to actively put the fear of the false idol of *what if* aside and learn to wholeheartedly embrace the truth of the *when*. Why? Because if we do not, we would never have the courage to show up to our jobs. While we have to intentionally endeavor to put the *what ifs* aside, we do not have to go into our work environments blindly. We know intimately that each day that we show up to care for others, we risk that day being the day that we either save someone or lose someone. But we do it anyway. We willingly traverse the landscape of life and death, because no matter what happens, as we know from Chapter Two, it is a beautiful day to love people.

The great painter Vincent Van Gogh once said, "It's by making mistakes that one sometimes finds the way." It is only when we fall that we have to rise. That is how we learn how strong we truly are. And even though we put safety measures in place to make sure we set ourselves up for success—we still make mistakes. We can't let the fear of our fallibility and the weight of the *what if's* stop us from doing our jobs, head into new situations, and, most importantly, fully live our lives. We have to let out love be stronger than our fears

This all sounds nice in theory doesn't it? But words are just that—theories until we put them into practice. So, here we go. Let's practice making mistakes and getting through them together. Just as I was desperate to find out how nurses dealt with the weight of responsibility, I also wanted to know the answer to the question, "What was a mistake that you made and how did you cope with it?"

This particular question was met with a variety of different reactions. Some laughed nervously. Others said, "There are too many to count!" Some simply blurted out, "Oh God," and buried their faces in their hands.

But most commonly, no matter how much experience the nurse had, or how far away in time they were from the mistake, they would be visibly transported to the painful memory of that incident.

I am no mental health professional, nor am I a proficient body language reader, but more often than not, when this topic was discussed, there was a little bit of a shift in the interview. There would be a pause, and the nurse across from me would take a deep breath and look off, staring into an inward space where time stood still; a time in which they had done something they wished with every fiber of their being that they could undo. I know, for I have felt that same feeling.

Realizing and acknowledging that one has made a mistake is truly a shattering experience. We all want to do our best to provide the best possible care for our patients. There is no malice involved. But, the simple truth is, as the nurse we cited at the start of the chapter commented, we are humans trying to save other humans. As humans, we are fallible. We are messy. We err.

What is interesting is that, in general, people don't like to talk about their mistakes. But the unique thing about nurses is that we do. Participating in these conversations isn't happy or enjoyable. But there is a communal realization that we have to have these discussions out of necessity, for both our own sanity and for the betterment of the profession itself.

Three nurses expressed this idea as such:

"My advice would be to talk it out and don't keep it in. Even if it is something small. Everyone makes mistakes, and when we talk about them, it helps encourage others to share as well, and then we all can learn from them and not to do the same."

—*CS, professor of nursing and nurse house supervisor, twenty five years of experience*

Chapter 7

"Mistakes will happen. Don't be discouraged, but learn from them. As a group, we learn the most in medicine from our mistakes."

—*SP, associate dean of collegiate nursing, twenty nine years of experience*

"Being a good nurse and a good teacher is to admit that you are not perfect. We learn more from other people's mistakes than from their successes."

—*TH, professor of nursing and burn ICU nurse, twenty five years of experience*

In Chapter One, we discussed nurses as being a family. There is a solidarity among nurses that makes us a very unique community. We show up for each other. We have each other's backs, and one of the tangible ways which we do that is by helping each other navigate the mistakes etched into our minds.

I can't tell you how many times other nurses have hugged me as I've cried in the medication room over the errors that I made. I can't tell you how many times I've hugged other nurses as they have cried in the medication room over errors that *they* made. We show up for one another in the wake of our mistakes.

Admitting our own failures takes a tremendous amount of humility, vulnerability, and bravery. I am honored and privileged to have been allowed into that space by fifty of the most courageous individuals whom I know. I hold their vulnerability with love, respect, and gratitude.

In all honesty, I didn't know what this chapter was going to look like at first. Fifty nurses answered this question with open hearts, but if vulnerability is a sacred space, then we have to help one another protect it. So, while these stories were shared with me, it is important to remember that I had a direct relationship with each of these individual people. We sat down and talked nurse to nurse, human to human. Therefore, it felt imperative as I wrote this chapter, to uphold and honor their personal narratives and boundaries.

NEW

Now, if you are not in the medical profession or are new to it, you might be wondering to yourself, *What really happens when a nurse makes a serious mistake? What happens if you kill someone? What if, what if, what if?* As we ask those questions, we are all actively worshiping at the altar of a false future. Let's take a minute to explore it before we go on, for those are fair questions to ask. For a moment, let's jump to the worst that can happen. We all have the tendency to do that anyway, so let's do it together. Let's process it together, so that we can come to terms with the weight of it, hold it, lift it, grow from it, and move on.

In reality, the medical profession is quite precarious. Every single action we take while working with a patient runs the risk of being detrimental to them. Some actions have positive results, and some have negative results, even if there was no mistake at all. Likewise, some mistakes bear little or no consequence, while others have extreme consequences. This is the immense pressure that is placed on nurses. With every single helping action that we facilitate, there is the possibility of harm. And that is tremendously difficult to get one's mind around.

Therefore, it is not necessarily the action or mistake itself that is important, it is the outcome. It is uniquely difficult to differentiate a minor mistake from a major one in nursing, because all of our actions—correct or incorrect—have the capacity to become disastrous. The outcomes of some mistakes are critical, and nurses ultimately have to care about the patient's reality. And we do. We do, we do, we do.

As I mentioned, every nurse's biggest fear is doing something that will cause harm to a patient. We recognize in earnest that some mistakes are not recoverable. Death is always a possibility, but it is still just a *what if*, a false idol, and therefore we can neither worship it nor let it hinder us from doing our jobs. *Let your love be stronger than your fear.*

Truly, if one were to kill someone, it doesn't really matter to the patient or their family what you are going to do about it

Chapter 7

after the fact. Some mistakes are definitive in that way. But after it all, when the storm settles, what matters is how we are going to address the weight of the mistake within ourselves.

That is why it is so important for nurses to be able to learn how to deal with mistakes well, because if our actions do end up bringing harm to someone else, we have to figure out a way to live with ourselves and keep from shattering in the wake of the mistake. With that in mind, we are going focus less on the errors and more on what was done about them. Ultimately, in order to not be crushed by the weight of our mistakes, it is of the utmost importance that we learn and grow from them.

I will tell you that while there was a lot of crying in the medication room, there was also a lot of laughter, because sometimes, when you make a mistake, or have had a close call, you have to laugh about it. There is nothing more comforting than when you say, "Oh my gosh you will not believe what I just did," and another nurse responds, "Oh yeah, I've done that too." There has to be solidarity in the wake of mistakes, because otherwise we would all be smashed flat beneath their weight.

So, in the spirit of solidarity, I will present to you *our* mistakes. But I will do it in the context of data—not to protect my fellow nurses from shame, but to uphold and respect their vulnerability and sacred space.

Shame? We don't live that way. We can't afford to.

Before we get started, it is imperative that we talk about shame for a moment. Of all the nurses that I spoke with—in fifty out of the fifty interviews I conducted—no one answered this question from a place of shame. They all answered the dreaded-mistake question bravely. They owned it. I'm not saying it was easy for them. I told you I cried with other nurses in the medication room. Well guess what? I cried over coffee with some of the nurses that I interviewed too.

But it wasn't in shame that they shared their stories. It wasn't in shame that the tears rolled. They shared their mistakes from a place of courage and strength, the kind of strength that comes from learning how to use the weight of mistakes to make us stronger. The tears flowed from a place of courage. So, just to reiterate and make myself abundantly clear, it is not in shame that I am keeping this section more anonymous than the other portions of this book. It is out of respect for the power of personal story.

Let's dive into some numerical data. In the interviews that I conducted, the most common mistake regarded medications. The words "medication error" spark flames of anxiety in any nurse's heart. Medication errors? Even with all the systems we have in place to check ourselves, somehow they still happen. Why? Because we are humans trying to save other humans.

If you are a non-nurse and are unfamiliar with what a medication error is, or if you are a nurse who has made a medication error yourself and are looking to find some companionship, I will explain.

Twenty-five nurses reported a mistake that had something to do with the administration of a medication. These mistakes included giving a medication at the wrong time, giving a medication in the wrong route, giving a medication outside of its required parameters, giving a medication to the wrong patient, giving the wrong dosage of a medication, pulling the wrong medication out of the medication machine, losing a medication that was pulled, giving the wrong dosage of tube-feeding, miscounting the narcotics in the medication machine, and—the bane of every new nurse's existence—forgetting to unclamp the patient's IV antibiotics.

In nursing school, we practice something called The Five Rights, which, in short, means that if we are going to medicate a patient, we have to make sure of five things:

1. We have the right patient.
2. We have the right medication.
3. We have the right dose of the right medication.

Chapter 7

4. We are giving the medication through the correct route. (Is it an oral medication? A shot? Etc.)
5. We are giving the medication at the correct time.

This is drilled into nursing students in school. In fact, if you make one of these mistakes during clinicals, you run the risk of getting kicked out of the program. Why? Because medication errors are serious. We have to make sure that we keep our patients safe. In school we were taught to be perfect at our trade, but once one enters the real world, you quickly realize that you are not perfect at anything, even the things that you thought you would be perfect at. I mean, you think you would never do that, and then suddenly you find yourself saying, "Yikes. I did *that.*"

Even the best nurses are not exempt, and the nurses that I interviewed are truly the very best. But nurses have to work smart and we have to work fast. It isn't just a simple task of giving a medication either. It is giving a medication while someone is crashing, while someone is yelling, while someone is being admitted, while someone is trying to hit you. Sometimes it is a simple, "Here is your medication," the patient swallows it, and you can move onto the next thing. But, a lot of the time, it is not that.

Another theme that came up was communication errors. Six nurses reported issues with this. Whether it was a miscommunication with a doctor or a miscommunication with a patient, these nurses felt that a breakdown in communication was their biggest mistake.

Other mistakes that were brought up included but were not limited to patients falling, charting things incorrectly, misplacing equipment, prioritizing incorrectly, not listening to or incorrectly assessing the patient, stepping out of the patient's room during a critical situation, missing an important order put in by the doctor, not implementing important orders quickly enough, not responding to a patient quickly enough, and making minor procedural mistakes in terms of caring for Foley catheters, IVs, and PICC lines.

NEW

Interestingly, four nurses reported mistakes that had more of a psychosocial impact. These mistakes included blurring personal and professional boundaries, not asking coworkers for enough help, and not seeking out community in their own personal lives.

There you have it. You name it, one of these fifty nurses has probably done it. No, scratch that. One of these fifty-*one* nurses has probably done it, because I, too, have made mistakes. But do you know what? Of these mistakes that were reported, not one nurse made a mistake that was responsible for killing anyone. While we tend to think every single one of our mistakes is somehow going to greatly contribute to the demise of our patients, in all actuality, they very rarely do. In truth, while sometimes minor harm does come to the patient, most things can be fixed if you quickly own up to your mistake and ask for help.

Of the mistakes listed above, some were easily fixable. Give the patient fluids to boost their blood pressure, and they will be fine. Reschedule the antibiotic and it will be fine. But in other circumstances, rapid responses had to be called, safety meetings had to be held, policies had to be put into place, and so on.

As we have discussed, errors in nursing carry an additional weight. That weight can only become one that strengthens instead of burdens when we ask ourselves the question, "What am I going to do about the mistake that I made?" That moves us from a matter of *if* to a matter of *when* to a matter of *what*. This isn't a matter of *what if,* either, because at this point, the mistake has already happened. It has moved from the realm of the possible into the realm of reality, and the only question that matters now is, "What are we going to do about it?"

I remember this was something that one of my charge nurses would always say to me. I would run up to him in a panic, scared out of my mind, declaring, "I made a mistake!"

To which he would calmly reply, "Ok. What are you going to do about it?" This response would simultaneously allow me to do five things:

Chapter 7

1. Calm down and stay out of the *crazy spiral*.
2. Make a plan.
3. Get help executing that plan.
4. Keep my patient as safe as possible in the meantime.
5. Learn, so that I wouldn't make the same mistake again.

The last thing on that list is incredibly important, because it is what gives us the strength to grow. When everything was all said and done, this particular charge nurse would say, "Well, you'll never make that mistake again will you?"

To which I would respond, "No, I will not."

There was a time when I didn't believe that only making a mistake once was possible. How are we supposed to remember to never make that same mistake again in the chaos of a hospital? But, in truth, a lot of the times we simply *do* remember to never make that mistake again. Other times, we remember for a while, and then down the road, we do unfortunately make that mistake again.

My mom always talks about how when you have your first child, you don't even understand how you could ever love someone so much, and then when you have your second child, somehow that love is magnified exponentially yet again. Somehow the human heart becomes capable of equally loving that second kid, that third kid, or that seventh kid without diminishing effect.

Likewise, it is through error that the human mind becomes capable of remembering not to make the same mistake twice.

"What happens when you make a big mistake is that you remember to never do it again."
—DH, *registered nurse consultant, seven months of experience*

"You learn more from the things that you do wrong than you do from the things you do right. [...] Now I know never to make that mistake again."
—KR, *medical-surgical respiratory nurse, nine months of experience*

NEW

We've talked about the act of making the mistake. We've talked about how they are normal and how they happen to all of us, but now let's talk about what this actually looks like. We are going to do this a little bit uniquely. I am going to share the biggest professional mistake that I made during my first year as a nurse. In the midst of that commentary, we are going to address the four ways that I was able to address the mistake that I made in a healthy way. Then, to substantiate the validity of each of those four points, I am going to include insights from the other nurses who I interviewed on how they used similar methods to cope with their own mistakes. It might get a little messy, but mistakes themselves are always messy.

*****

Well, well, well. Here we are. Making mistakes is probably the biggest fear that new nurses have. Have you ever thought to yourself before you start a shift, *Please, don't let me hurt anyone tonight?* I have. I pray that prayer before every shift—in the car, in the elevator, and as I pick up my patient assignment for the night. Making mistakes is a very real fear in day-to-day life. It isn't an irrational fear, either. It is a reality.

It reminds me of the people who are deathly afraid of needles. I feel badly for them because at some point or another, they are going to have to get a shot, have their blood drawn, an IV inserted, and so on. For me, my biggest fear is getting stuck in a tsunami. Is that going to happen? Probably not. One guy I went to school with was insanely afraid of hot air balloons. Is that something he is ever going to have to deal with? Again, probably not.

But for all the new nurses out there who are afraid of making mistakes—which is all of us—I'm sorry, but it's going to happen. You are going to make a mistake. In fact, you are going to make lots of mistakes, some big, some small. Whether you are religious or not, at one point or another, you are probably going to pray that your mistakes aren't going to hurt anyone.

Chapter 7

As I write this, I am in my eighth month as a nurse, and these eight months have not been without mistakes. At the end of my seventh month, I made a pretty bad one, one where my manager called me at home and arranged to meet with me. I am writing this now because I just had to meet with both of my managers yesterday.

Remember when I talked about my first rapid response? Well, following that, I had to admit another patient at 5:30 a.m., which is possibly the worst time to admit someone because it is far enough away from the start of the next shift that you theoretically could get all the admit tasks done in a perfect scenario, but it is also right before the 6:00 a.m. medication pass, which is a busy time in and of itself. It was also my third night in a row at work, so I was extremely tired, and I had just used all of my functioning brain cells to handle the rapid response earlier in my shift.

None of these are good excuses, however, because I should not have done what I did. *What did you do?* you might be wondering. Well, I put the wrong identification armband on the wrong patient.

As I said, this should not have happened. This is the simplest, most easily avoidable mistake that someone could make. The cherry on top of it all is that my hospital was having a big crack down on patient identifiers at the time. I should have checked the armband before I put it on the patient, but in my tired, rushed admit of the patient, I didn't. That is my fault. *Mine.* Luckily it was caught less than an hour later before any harm could actually be done, and the patient was not affected in any way, but still, putting the wrong armband on the wrong patient is not good.

I told one of my closest and dearest friends on the unit about it, and she just stared at me. It was not one of those *you-did-that-guess-what-I-did,* story-swapping kind of times. It was a *what-you-did-is-actually-pretty-bad* kind of times.

Needless to say, I got in trouble. And I deserved it. I got reported to our chief nursing officer, and I got a final written warning, as in, "If you make this mistake again you could likely be

NEW

fired." Having the words "final written warning" spoken over you is not a fun experience.

Now, I could beat myself up over it. I could make myself feel terrible about it. But I am not going to. Let's be honest. I do not feel great about this situation. Like I said, it should not have happened. But it did. I can't go back and change that. So now what? Is it enough to simply say, "I won't let it happen again," and walk away?

Actually, yes. That's exactly what I did, and yes, it was enough. Usually this kind of stuff would sucker punch me in the face into a downward spiral of aggressively negative feelings. But this time it didn't, which was nothing short of a miracle. Aside from it being miraculous, the practical side of my not going into a *crazy spiral* over my own shortcomings was due to the following reasons:

1. I chose to own my mistake.

There is something freeing about saying, "Yes, I did that. I made a mistake." It doesn't feel good, but I am a firm believer that shame does more damage if we internalize it. As both a nurse and as a person, the second I think I've done something wrong that needs to be corrected, I tell people about it because I know that I am most likely going to need help to fix it. On a more selfish note, I also know that if I don't get some outside input, I will be left to my own anxious devices, and I will legitimately make myself go crazy and inevitably do more harm.

If we press that mistake down, shut it up, and put it away, it is going to linger in our minds like a monster in the closet. It is eventually going to show its ugly face right when we are trying to go to sleep each night. It is going to stomp around in our brains to remind us that we can't escape it. It will stir up shame and guilt, making a mess of all our clothes and whatever else we have stored in that closet of ours. We had our shirts nicely folded? We had our lives all sorted out? That monster doesn't care. It is there to cause

Chapter 7

chaos, and it will not go away until we tell it to get out. So, what are we going to do about it? Are you going to let your mistakes mess up everything you have worked so hard for? I'm not.

In the case of the armband, I made a mistake without knowing it. The I-did-it-without-knowing mistakes are a scary kind of mistake to make, because, if you are like me, then you might think to yourself, *If I made that mistake without knowing, what other mistakes have I made that I don't know about?*

If you are thinking that right now, stop, because that is one big monster trying to get into your mind closet, and you do not want to let that guy in. Like I said, the best way to combat the negative feelings that mistakes bring with them is to own up to them. Own up to them and quickly ask for help.

If we are going to take this metaphor to the next level, owning up to our mistakes is like putting on our armor and drawing our swords. Our asking for help in the midst of our mistakes is like building an army up so we don't have to fight that monster alone.

This takes me back to when I was in therapy during college. I remember my therapist at the time had me draw a monster of all the things I was feeling. The monster I drew was a scaly yellow, with big pink warts, a cyclops eye, and huge horns. But my therapist wasn't just having me draw for fun. She had me write a speech bubble filled with what the monster was telling me. She then had me draw where I felt like I was in relation to the monster I had drawn. That was the hardest part of all, because I drew myself all curled up on the floor, backed up into a corner, cowering in a little ball. Well, at least I drew that to the best of my abilities.

Now I ask you, who would you rather be? Would you rather be the person crying on the floor, letting shame and guilt kick the life out of you? Or would you rather be the person standing up to your fears, all decked out in some awesome armor with a cool sword and a posse of your closest friends, ready to fuck some shit up?

NEW

I want to be the second individual. In fact, I fight to be the second one. Believe me; it is a battle, because those kinds of monsters are big and strong. But, let me tell you right now, you are bigger, and you are stronger than your mistakes. So, don't cower in fear from the mistakes that you might make in the future. Don't let the shame from past mistakes overtake you. Own up to them. Grow from them. Mistakes are heavy things, but as we talked about before, we have to choose to take their weights and use them to make us stronger.

Another reason to own up to our mistakes is that it allows us to better prepare ourselves for their consequences and ramifications. Sometimes we hide them because we are afraid of getting in trouble. To be honest, that's fair. Having the words "final written warning" spoken over me was not a good feeling. But do you know what? With those words and that letter, the issue was over. I owned it. I got written up. Now it's done. I don't have to worry about whether or not someone is going to find out about my mistake, because I dealt with it. The mistake monster cannot cause havoc if the door is open and my personal army is staring at it with their swords at the ready.

When I met with my managers, things were pretty straight forward because everything was out in the open. Yes, I put the wrong armband on the wrong patient. Now what? I am hopefully not going to put the wrong armband on the wrong patient ever again. How? By checking it. By checking it with another person, if need be. With my mistake out there, we were able to discuss how we could improve the system so that this would not happen again, not just to me and my patients, but to any of the other nurses and their patients as well. Together, we were able to open that door, slay the monster, and discuss how we were going to prevent any other monster from moving in and taking its spot.

I originally was going to end my wristband story there because I thought it was over, except we went over patient identifiers at the next staff meeting, which, as I write this, happened this morning.

Chapter 7

I wasn't looking forward to it, mostly because the staff meetings are at 8:00 a.m., and that is a hard time for a night-shifter to be up, but also because I knew that we would be talking about patient identifier issues specifically, and I wasn't exactly excited to be going over that again.

Sure enough, we had a whole chunk of time in the agenda devoted to patient identifiers. Not only that, but there was a time for people to voluntarily talk about mistakes that they had made in that area if they wanted. I didn't know if I was going to share or not, because I didn't want people to think that I am an incompetent nurse that everyone has to look out for to keep me from killing people. It would have been easy to just slump in my chair, not say anything, and hope no one would notice me turning pink. But then I thought to myself, *this is my team here. This is my family.* One thing families do is share their lives with one another, and mistakes and the lessons learned from them are a huge and important part of life.

I don't think my managers were expecting me to share. In fact, I partly wonder if they were having people share to help me not feel so terrible about myself. But I thought to myself, *time to practice what you preach. Own your mistake.* So, when they asked if anyone else wanted to share, I raised my hand and laughed a little when I got up, and I said, "I'll share. Because mine is bad."

My mistake was now out there in the open. There was no hiding it. Maybe people thought that was the dumbest thing to have ever happened. Maybe some people felt better about their own mistakes because they saw that they weren't alone. I don't know, and I really don't care, because do you know what the bottom line is? I owned my mistake before it owned me.

I chose to tell everyone that I made a mistake rather than internalize it to the point of thinking that I am the mistake. Because I am not a mistake. I'm just human. We are all just human. After the meeting, my manager came up to me and gave me a hug. It was a better ending than I could've hoped for. My mistake held no power over me. The monster was slain.

The importance of owning our own mistakes was clearly stated by the following nurses:

"As time goes on, I am quicker to own my mistakes instead of defending myself, which doesn't serve anyone well. If the patient is upset, it is better to acknowledge their frustration because, at that point, they usually just want to be heard. Of course, this doesn't apply in every situation, but it can help in many of them. Same with mistakes of attitude or team tension with coworkers. Listening and empathy go a long way."
—CM, *pediatric advice line nurse, thirty-seven years of experience*

"I went to the doctor, fessed up and apologized, said I would never do it again, thanked her for noticing, and asked her what I could do to fix the situation. It was hard to own up to it, but now we have a good relationship, and I think she respects me for that, but it was hard to do, and I felt really badly... I try to learn from things and make the mistakes not happen again. I really try to fess up to it, too, at least to my staff."
—MA, *emergency department nurse, ten months of experience*

"There were so many times I would come home as a new grad and I would come home, go to sleep, and wake up two hours later because I realized, 'Oh my gosh, I did that wrong!' Or, 'I forgot something!' So, for me, it was a lot of verbal processing and getting validation from more experienced nurses that making mistakes didn't make me a bad nurse. You obviously try to avoid mistakes at all costs, but it is ok that they get made occasionally as long as you learn from them."
—BS, *internal medicine nurse practitioner, eight years of experience*

Chapter 7

2. I chose to let good come out of the situation by learning and growing from it.

We are going to expand upon this idea of growth later in the next chapter, but it is worth mentioning this principle here as well. So, we just defeated the mistake monster in our closet. Now what? What are we going to do with its dead body? Are we going to leave it in there and let the closet get smelly from its decomposition? No. We have to get that thing out of the closet. Do you know what makes great plant fertilizer? Dead things. So, take that dead monster's body, put it in your mental garden, and let something beautiful grow from it.

The nurses I interviewed also highlighted growth and learning as things that can come from dealing with mistakes healthily. Three nurses had the following to say on this topic:

"They saw, after that incident, that I could handle that kind of stuff really well. Being ok with not being ok has strengthened me so much and has allowed me to handle my freak-outs and all those terrifying moments much better."
—*EP, medical oncology nurse, one year of experience*

"I was really hard on myself, so I talked to one of the other nurses who had been a nurse for three years, and she told me, 'Thank God that the patient was ok. He was watching over both of you. I guarantee you that there is not a single nurse that hasn't made a mistake. You learn from them, and you grow from them, and then you don't make the same mistake again, and that is what matters.'"
—*LC, medical-surgical respiratory nurse, seven years of experience*

"I remember asking one of the charge nurses what I could do that would be better for the next time because, in that situation, I was basically just frozen and didn't know what to do. How I dealt with it was that I asked a trusted older nurse what I could do the next time to improve. I think that what has been such an important part of my process and growth is being able to ask people, because you are not always going to know, and that is ok. We all have different experiences. Someone who has a lot of experience with one thing might not know much about something that I do know, and vice versa. But you need to ask to improve, to be a better nurse, and to improve patient outcomes."

—*AI, bone marrow transplant oncology nurse, two years of experience*

3. I chose to move on.

The thing about mistakes is that we can dwell on them, or we can move on from them. Who wants to be stuck in a closet with that disgusting mistake monster? I'd personally rather be out in the garden, tending the flowers that I grew from its remains.

Right now, you might be wondering, *didn't you just have to meet with your boss yesterday? Is that really enough time to move on?* Well, apparently, it is because, in all honesty, I have moved on from the situation. Mistake made. Hard conversation had. Twice. Lesson learned. There is nowhere to go but forward.

An experienced nurse had this to say on the topic of getting help in the midst of making mistakes:

"In relation to any kind of mistake, it is so important to have community around you. This is important in all of life, but especially as a nurse, and especially starting out. You have to have people around you. It is a hard job, whether you make a mistake or have a bad day, you need to be able to talk about it, and you need to have people who understand. Being able to process that with another nurse, or with community, is so important. There is something unique about being able to talk to other nurses. I have personally done a lot of counseling over the years as well. When I am worried about something that happened, or something that

Chapter 7

could have happened, having that professional to help me process has been really helpful."

—KS, *community health nurse, eight years of experience*

Whether we run the race of life with wobbly toddler steps or with perfect Olympic form, we still need to move forward. We also need to help one another out in each of the races that we run. Sometimes we have to have a friend or teammate drag us across that finish line. Don't let one mistake—or one fall—get you down for too long. Choose to move forward, and when it is impossible for you to do so on your own, ask for help.

This act of choosing to move on was brought up by multiple nurses who said the following:

"You can't dwell on things forever. You have to learn from it and move on. But, then again, I'm not sure what I would've done or how I would have felt if the patient wasn't ok. But these things happen to every nurse, so talking through it with other nurses really helps."

—AB, *women's oncology breast clinic nurse, four years of experience*

"I was just on high alert after that, and then, after some time, I just moved on. That's kind of the reality of nursing."

—JF, *PICC line insertion nurse, six years of experience*

"When we face challenging circumstances, we can let it haunt us, or we can let it make us grow and improve."

—PE, *labor and delivery nurse, ten years of experience*

"Knowing that because God got me this job—He wants me here, He'll protect my license and position—I don't need to cover anything up. I can do my job and enjoy it because God is ultimately going to fight for me and protect me. It just sucks being a worry wart for your full twelve hours. I straight up block the mistakes

out. I will pray that God will help take them from me, and that helps, but some things do stay with you."
—CH, *emergency department, ten months of experience*

But I didn't just move on blindly. I also chose to try to make sure that I never did it again. Moving on doesn't mean that we flee from the negative feelings that come from our mistakes with reckless abandon in the hopes of throwing ourselves into the arms of a chaotic, forgetful future in which we never learned anything from our pasts.

We do have to let things go, and we have to do it in a way where we are able to accept ourselves for who we are, but we also have to be responsible for what we have done. Coming to terms with what we have done largely stems from learning and growing from our mistakes. We learn, we grow, and then we act. We have to conscientiously decide to try to not make that same mistake again, and also to set up parameters in our own lives to try to make sure that mistake doesn't happen again.

Multiple nurses stressed the importance of this very concept:

"I don't always get it right, but I do pay more attention to it. It is hard because you learn the most from the mistakes that you make. But now I know to never do that again and to triple check things."
—HW, *medical-surgical stroke diabetes nurse, six months of experience*

"My system that I have made for myself (because I am definitely an over thinker) is this: I think about what I can do differently on my drive home, and I ask myself, 'What is one thing that I could've done better?' Whatever the situation is, what is one thing I can do differently the next time. I try to pinpoint it to one thing that I can do better, one thing I can incorporate into my workflow. Then I forgive myself and let it go. That is easier said than done, but that is what I do in my head. If I can find

Chapter 7

something that I can specifically fix, then that helps. There are always things that we can fix and do better, and that is just part of our career, learning and improving ourselves, not getting caught up in the negative stuff, moving forward, and doing better."

—KE, *acute care rehab nurse, five years of experience*

"It was one of those things where you have to learn from your mistakes and make sure that you have a plan in place to prevent it from happening again. You always have to have a Plan B in place."

—LC, *medical-surgical respiratory nurse, seven years of experience*

*****

You will notice that each of the three aforementioned steps started with the phrase, "I chose." That is not without purpose. In reality, I had to choose to fight, much like I had to choose to stay out of the *crazy spiral* we mentioned in Chapter Six.

I decide what I do with my mistakes. My mistakes do not decide what they do with me. Is making that choice exhausting? Yes. But, again and again, it just points us back to the principles of asking for help, teamwork, showing ourselves grace and patient kindness, and utilizing all of the tools in our tool belt that we talked about in the last chapter because we cannot carry the weight of our mistakes alone.

Despite all the healthy ways we talked about dealing with mistakes in this chapter, it really boils down to this: Do not let your mistakes define you. Instead, let them refine you.

We are not defined by the mistakes that we make, but we must choose to let them refine us. Only then will we find that those mistakes have reshaped us into something more beautiful than we thought possible. But in order for this to happen, we have to do two things: we have to reclaim our own identities as not being based on or beholden to our mistakes, and we have to remind ourselves of what our identities are *actually* rooted in. These two things are only made possible when we show ourselves grace as we learn, grow, and become refined.

Four nurses summarized this process well in the following quotes:

"I have to remember that, yes, I could've made a better choice, but no one was hurt. I am still learning. You have to give yourself grace. You don't know what you don't know, and you have to have grace with yourself while you learn."
—*PM, medical-surgical float pool nurse, two months of experience*

"I had to go through a time where I was concerned that I would be terminated from my job. That got me thinking about how that would affect my identity, because I had put so much time into being a nurse. I came to the realization that my identity was in God, and that I was doing the best that I could with what I had, rather than just placing my identity in nursing itself."
—*EE, traveling oncology nurse, five years of experience*

"You have to make sure there is a balance in your life outside of work. You need to have healthy interests and connections out in the regular world. For me, coping looked like plugging into community and finding someone I could process with. That was really course-correcting."
—*SF, professor of nursing, twenty-four years of experience*

"No one knows what's going on all the time. No matter how experienced you are, you need to ask questions and ask for help. Everybody needs help sometimes. You are not expected to be perfect."
—*HH, surgical step-down nurse, nine months of experience*

To bring us back to the pruning metaphor that we ended the last chapter with, a healthy rosebush is one that has been pruned. Does

Chapter 7

the plant itself like having pieces of it hacked away? Probably not. But, as we discussed, pruning is what makes the plant grow more purposefully. Similarly, refinement is what makes us as humans grow more purposefully. It is what allows us to be reshaped, to regrow, and eventually to be renewed.

I laid out for you my biggest professional mistake I made during my first year as a nurse, but now let me tell you about the biggest personal mistake I made during that time. My biggest personal mistake during my first year as a nurse was having an incorrect understanding of what it means to truly be resilient.

Actually, no. This has been the biggest personal mistake of my entire *life*. I thought that I knew what that word meant. I thought that resilient was something I knew how to be. But it turns out I was very wrong. Now I know, but I only came to this conclusion after being painfully pruned and refined by this particular mistake.

Resilience isn't just a buzz-word or a romanticized ideology. It is a raw and active choice, and beyond that, it is a daily lifestyle. We may have been punched in the face and knocked down by our mistakes, but we have also chosen to get up and to move on from them. So, now what? In this chapter, we talked about what it looks like to be pruned. Pruning isn't always just taking off a few branches; sometimes it is cutting the rosebush down to a measly clump of stumps. Sometimes roses are pruned to the point where you are unsure if those remaining twigs were ever once roses at all.

That is where true resilience comes in. It is when we think that we have nothing left that we are given the opportunity to rise more fully than we ever have before. It is in the ascent that we grow the most. So, in the next chapter, we will talk about what it means to regrow.

An Addendum to This Chapter:

I would like to take a moment to address something before we move on. To be very honest with you, I did end up making the same mistake twice. It was almost a year later, at a different job, at a different hospital, in a different specialty. Again, it happened at some dreadfully early hour in the morning. I was handed a patient's chart. Thinking it was for my own patient, I, again, put the wrong identification armband on the wrong patient. I escorted the patient upstairs as per usual, gave the chart to the staff on the receiving unit, and then I went back downstairs to my department. Upon returning, I saw a chart lying next to the computer at which I had been charting prior to transporting the patient. When I realized that it was the chart for the patient I had already put an armband on and taken upstairs, all I could think was, *no. Not again. I cannot believe I made the same mistake twice.*

I quickly blurted out what had happened to my preceptor and then took off running to the complete opposite side of the hospital and five floors up. Now I knew that the patient would be ok as far as their safety went. It had been less than ten minutes since I had dropped them off, and if the receiving nurse had tried to give any medications or anything, they would have quickly realized that the patient had the wrong armband on.

Selfishly, as I ran, all I could think was, *what am I supposed to do about Chapter Seven?* After all, the majority of this chapter talked about how one of the best ways to cope with making a mistake is by making sure that the same mistake never happens again, yet there I was, running across the hospital because I had made the same mistake again.

When I got to the unit that I had transported the patient to, the charge nurse laughed and said, "We know. We fixed it. Don't worry about it."

I probably apologized six times and was so thankful to be met with such grace, but, to be honest, I was frustrated with myself, not just because I had made the same mistake twice, but because I failed to do what I promised myself I would never do again. I promised myself that I would always check a patient's armband before I put it on them, and, once again, I didn't.

Chapter 7

I came back to this chapter not feeling defeated but feeling like I would be lying if I didn't add some sort of addendum. Part of me was a little bit nervous about addressing this, but as I reread this chapter, I was re-reminded of the grace that all of this takes. It isn't telling ourselves that we will never make the same mistake again that is the most important part of healthily dealing with our mistakes. The most important part of dealing with a mistake well is giving ourselves the grace to make mistakes at all. Then, when the mistake does occur, we can give ourselves the grace to rebuild instead of crumble. Then and only then, after we have given ourselves grace, can we put strategies into place to try not to make the same mistake again.

One nurse profoundly said this:

"A few mistakes here and there do not define you as a nurse. The whole process is trial and error. Without our errors, we would remain unchanged, and that doesn't help us grow. Have grace with yourself when you fail because it will happen a lot. Whatever happens, you will be ok. One bad thing or shift does not define you, but it is so easy to get in that mindset. You need to roll with the punches and laugh things off."

—JW, *high risk labor and delivery nurse, ten months of experience*

I made the same mistake twice, and that is really not great, to say the least. The patient was safe, and I was reminded of my own shortcomings. I relearned what I needed to do to be a safer nurse. But, above all, I was healthily humbled, humbled because, even though I wrote a whole chapter on how to make mistakes well, I still fall short. I still can't practice all of this perfectly; try as I might. So, I am reminded and re-reminded again and again of how life is a journey and a process in which we are constantly learning and relearning, growing and regrowing. All of that is perfectly normal, so we need to give ourselves grace in the midst of it all, and then, after that, rebuild, regrow, and improve.

Chapter Eight:
The Lock and Key: Resilience and Joy

You have patiently waited and actively sifted through pages of emotionally difficult content, but at long last, here we are. We are at the turning point of the book. Finally, we are going to turn our mourning into dancing. This might seem a bit odd to you, considering I ended the last chapter by telling you that we were going to be talking about the biggest personal mistake that I have made in my entire my life, but as we also discussed in the previous chapter, we learn and grow the most from our mistakes.

This chapter serves as a foil to the pain that we discussed in both Chapters Five and Six. We have greatly explored how to live life well in the midst of pain, and now we are going to analyze what it means to live life well in the midst of joy. You will notice that some of the content of this chapter is familiar. We will be revisiting past topics, but we will not be doing so redundantly.

We have discussed pain in depth and alluded only slightly to joy in the previous chapters, but since pain and joy work the most profoundly when they are magnified together, allowing their contrasts to be illuminated, we will conversely be discussing joy in depth and only slightly alluding to pain from here on out. It is a subtle reversal but an important one all the same.

So, let's take a breath and celebrate the importance that experiencing joy plays in each of our lives. We aren't just going to stop there, either. We are going to investigate three extremely important components of what it means to be holistically healthy human beings. I am going to supply us with another metaphor

Chapter 8

here, a metaphor of three parts; a chain, a lock, and a key: pain is the chain that is wrapped around living life well; resilience is the lock holding that chain together; and joy is the key to unlocking the lock and undoing the chain.

Three parts; one whole. If we are going to live life *well*, we need to learn how to define, reconcile, and utilize all three components of this metaphor. We have spent a copious amount of time discussing pain, so now we are going to talk about resilience and joy. We are going to explore the unified dance between these parts of human nature and how that dance ultimately produces remarkable beauty in our lives. This is why I am able to say that my biggest life mistake thus far has yielded the most joy in my life.

My biggest mistake was my own misinterpretation of what it actually means to be resilient. However, this may not be a mistake I made entirely of my own accord: looking back, this misconception may have stemmed from the false narrative regarding what it means to be resilient sold to us by society. If the idea of resilience is interpreted incorrectly, then it does more harm than it does good. Now, maybe this was my fault. Maybe it was presented to me in truth, and I made the mistake of interpreting it in an incorrect way. If that is the case, I will take ownership of that, but whatever the case may be, I have been hurt by the idea of resilience because I have understood its true nature incorrectly.

According to *Merriam-Webster.com (2019),* being resilient is defined in the following two ways:

"Definition of Resilient (adjective): characterized or marked by resilience such as:
a. Capable of withstanding shock without permanent deformation or rupture
b. Tending to recover from or adjust easily to misfortune or change"

Do you want to know something? I hate that this word is used so often, because it is usually wielded with an unintentionally false premise. More upsetting still is that this word, this hijacked concept of true resilience, is not only spoken—it is celebrated. We already talked about the false idols of the past—*I wish, if only*, and *my fault*—and we talked about the false idol of the future—*what if*. I am going to make a controversial claim here: the commonly accepted definition of resilience is the false idol of a perfect present.

Why? Because all the dictionary does is provide us with stagnant words. As for the words included in this particular definition? They don't accurately reflect the indescribability of the human condition. The word *resilience*, used in this particular way, points us to an idyllic present, one in which we have to react to things perfectly without any scarring or ramifications. If we operate off of this definition of resilience, we forget the role that pain plays in our lives. Why, then, are we letting this unrealistic definition define and shape us as people?

The simple dictionary definition of this complicated word and practicing being resilient in a healthy way in real life look very different. But truly I tell you, that "withstanding shock without permanent deformation or rupture," and "tending to recover from or adjust easily to misfortune or change," are not what it means to live life well. In life, when hardship befalls us, three things will be true:

1. We will always be different.
2. Recovery takes time.
3. Adjusting will never be easy.

Answer me this: when you've personally experienced great loss or pain, were you the same after it? Was it a quick recovery for you? Was it easy for you to adjust? No. I tell you on all accounts, no. So why are we trying to force ourselves to submit to the standards of something that is written within a perfect context? When life befalls us, if we expect ourselves to react quickly and painlessly, then we are running directly into the arms of that false idol of a perfect form of the present.

Chapter 8

The idolatry of *resiliency* simply tells us to get it together and move on. But the reality of the present is much rawer and less simple than that. If we chase the false idol of resilience as solely moving on as quickly and painlessly as possible, then we will never process, learn, or grow from what has happened to us. It doesn't matter if the idol is one of the past, present, or future—when we set our hopes in idols, they will rob us blind.

During my first year as a nurse, every time I heard the word resilience, my soul would flip over itself in discontent. I would constantly think to myself, *I already am resilient, so why does this hurt so badly? What is wrong with me?* It turns out that it didn't hurt because I wasn't resilient or because I wasn't resilient *enough*. It hurt badly— and this is where my biggest personal mistake comes into play— because I was buying into the dictionary's false idol definition of what it means to be resilient and not the reality of what a lived resilience actually looks like.

If we get trapped by this false idol of the present, we don't give ourselves the chance to regrow *well*. When we depend upon this particular idol, our own growth is often muted by the fear of the pain that comes with doing the work of unpacking our pasts. But if a rose bush is pruned badly or incorrectly, it will not regrow well. Similarly, if we allow our past mistakes, tragedies, and traumas to go unaddressed and allow them to define us instead of refine us, then we won't regrow well, either. We will keep living, but we will never flourish. Our pasts are what have happened to us in life, but they are not what have to ultimately define us as human beings. This is where true, lived resiliency comes into play.

Thus far we have talked about the dictionary definition and the theory of resilience, but now let's talk about resiliency in its fullness. Let's talk about resiliency in a way that will actually allow us to regrow and, beyond that, thrive. In other words, what does resilience look like in real life?

The following is not my own lived experience, but it is the lived experience of a community very near and dear to my heart. I do not have any claim to this pain, but when something happens to a place and people that you love, it unmistakably hurts.

It is a true story of great tragedy and pain, but it is not a story that stays in a time of mourning. This community will always be different, its recovery took time, and adjusting in the wake of the aftermath was not easy. This tragedy was, and always will be, painful. But the presence of pain does not rob one of their true resiliency. If anything, it magnifies it.

Now, through the passage of time and regrowth, this same community has used all of those things to turn mourning into dancing. When it comes to real-life resilience, it is not just about the present—it is about reconciling the past with the present to secure a better future. This is what healthy, lived resilience looks like. This is what it means to live life and reclaim our time well.

*****

I am from an area in Southern California where there are a lot of wildfires. In fact, we often categorize summers and years by the fires that happened within them. During December 2017, there was an exceptionally large one. At the time, it was the largest wildfire to ever hit the state of California. To make matters worse, it was so devastating to the terrain that shortly afterwards, when a storm rolled in, the rains disrupted the Earth, rocks, and foliage on the mountains, causing an enormous debris flow that claimed many homes, businesses, and lives. The slide shut down the 101, which is a major highway and the only one that allows passage through the entire area. Things were awful. Subsequently, people in all sectors of the community have worked tremendously hard to rehabilitate the area and make sure something like that never happens again. But it is still a process, and the area is still healing.

About two years after the fire and debris flow, my mom and I went hiking in that very same location. We went in March, in the middle of my first year as a nurse, following a winter that had plenty

Chapter 8

of rain, so the hills were a lush and brilliant green. Remarkably, there were wildflowers everywhere. But do you know what was even more striking than the flowers themselves? It was seeing those flowers growing out of a fire-scarred, mudslide-devastated hillside.

Flowers sprung up from ash darkened Earth and wrapped themselves around charred trees. Water flowed peacefully in the crevice that the mud, giant boulders, and toppled trees had torn through when the hill came crashing down. Trees, which bore the marks of the debris some twenty feet up, still stood tall. Birds sang. Bees buzzed. Construction was going on as someone rebuilt a home nearby. People hiked with their families, pets, and friends. There were even signs posted for a community trail restoration day that was coming up.

My point in all this? Beauty will come out of disaster if we let it. One of the pastors at my church, who led the sermon the Sunday right before I went on this hike, poetically said, "We are not a people of the winter. We are a people of the springtime." We are not meant to wither away and die like plants in the winter. We are meant to grow and regrow. We are meant to produce beauty. If there ever is a fire in our lives, we are meant to grow back from it.

About a month after we went on that hike, I returned to the area for a family celebration, and we went to dinner at a resort on the seaside that had been directly impacted by the debris flow. When the hill came down in the flooding that took place after the initial havoc of the fire, it brought mud and devastation all the way to the sea line, covering much of the town and resort with it. Because of this, in the wake of the disaster, the resort closed for three months in order to repair the damages.

While three months might not be that long of a time in the entire spectrum of reality, in the face of tragedy and loss, it is an eternity. But after three months, the mud was cleared, the resort was cleaned up, and people were able to go back to work. While it would never again be business as usual given all the loss, the resort—and beyond that the community—was alive again.

NEW

Sitting at the restaurant with my family, I saw something exceptionally striking on their menu: they were serving a handmade cocktail featuring honey from bees that got their pollen from the wildflowers that grew in the wake of the fire.

If that is not resilience, I don't know what is. If that isn't making beauty out of pain and rising from the actual ash and the actual dirt, I don't know what is. No one would deny that both the fire and the debris flow were both horrifically devastating and painful, but I believe what they are saying with this cocktail is that they have chosen to rise and dance once again. Time moves on, and while we don't forget the pain, or the loss we can find beauty again. After a hardship, three things will be true:

1. You will always be different.
Dancing will always look differently from what it looked like before, but even so, it is still dancing.

2. Recovery takes time.
You might not be able to dance right away. Maybe you will be lying face down on the floor for a while.

3. Adjusting will never be easy.
Once you do decide to dance again, it will take work to relearn how.

And all of that is ok, because even so,
you are choosing to dance.

You are choosing to rise, and you are choosing to regrow. As for this community that I am talking about? It is one that is actively choosing to keep dancing. That is what true and tangible resilience is.

*****

Chapter 8

Now I can say that I understand what it means to be resilient in the full sense of the term, but it was only through the example of this community's great tragedy and process of regrowth that I was able to learn this lesson. It wasn't through a vacant word in a perfect dictionary—it was through loss, life, and time.

Maybe it sounds a little bit crazy to you that the simple presence of a cocktail on a restaurant's menu caused me to have such an epiphany. But I think that it struck me so profoundly because about nine months prior I had the privilege of attending the annual Trauma & Critical Care Symposium put on by this community's local hospital. There, first responders presented to us in detail what had actually happened during the disaster and what it took to rebuild a community in the wake of it all.

Seeing this menu item was strangely a concurrent moment of both fully mourning and fully dancing for me. That simultaneous experience of such different feelings is the final component of real-life resilience that the dictionary leaves out. We are still hurting, but we are also still dancing. In an effort to better understand this new facet of resilience within my own person, I ended up writing the following poem.

*****

This Is Where the Fire Was.

This is where the fire was
Where the flowers once grew and the bees used to buzz
This is where it all came down
With a crushing weight and a rushing sound
Setting the garden of our hearts into a fierce blaze
Turning what was once beautiful into an ashen haze
Some pains don't just etch, they cut and they carve
Making us feel like our wounds won't ever heal into scars
But being resilient doesn't mean that we've never gotten hurt

NEW

It is growing from the pain and rising from the dirt
For one day when the shock of the past has worn
We will rise from the cinder with our strength reborn
Stronger this time, with our hearts freshly healed
Though the scars on its surface will never fully yield
Because some kinds of pain we can never forget
But we can make that pain our power and use it to live in a way that we won't regret
And through the passage of time, though it may seem daunting
The shadows and grips of our hurt will slowly become less haunting
While we can never go back or reclaim the past
Devastating sorrow is not meant to last
We move on and let go
And allow the burnt matter of our hearts to regrow
We let life start anew
And with life and time, the garden of our hearts will be healed, too
Though the process is never easy, and it will most likely chide
We can move forward if we want to, we just have to decide
Instead of shrinking and fading, let us be bold
Let us march towards the future, whatever it holds
And someday when we look back into our once-charred hearts
The truth will ring out loudly in harmonious parts
We will be able to proclaim and unashamedly sing,
Do you see where the flowers now thrive and the bees now buzz?
This is where the fire was.

*****

Being resilient doesn't mean that we've never gotten hurt
It is growing from the pain and rising from the dirt.

The truth of the matter is that resilience doesn't mean that we are immune to pain—it means that we have experienced pain, held it, learned from it, and used it to create something beautiful. That is

Chapter 8

what people tend to forget. I know we spent quite a bit of time previously discussing this notion, but allow me to quickly tell you about what that means in this context, the context of resilience, and how it can be used to produce joy.

It doesn't matter that we have been knocked down—what matters is how we rise after we've been knocked down. It doesn't matter how fast we recover—what matters is what we learn while we recover. It doesn't matter how similar we look to our old selves—what matters is how we let our new selves regrow.

All the things that we have mentioned in the last four chapters—vulnerability, admitting that we are hurting, asking for help, talking with others—are part of what helps us become resilient in life. Those tools, in conjunction with time, are what allow us to take the excruciatingly painful moments in our lives and turn them into beauty. These things will allow us to one day say, *Look how far I have come. Yes, that experience was hard, and this is what I learned from it. Now I can see the growth that has been produced from the pain.* That is what rising from the dirt looks like and that is what making our pain our power looks like.

Towards the conclusion of my first year as a nurse, I wrote the following which speaks into this very idea of this dirty, messy kind of growth.

*****

Do you know what my whole story is right now? At this very moment? In this one-month-and-one-week-until-the-end-of-my-first-year-as-a-nurse moment? My whole story right now is this: I don't know how far I have come. I don't know why this has been so hard for me. I don't really know what I've learned. So, in all truth, I haven't risen from the dirt. But do you know what? Just because I am currently in the dirt doesn't mean that I always will be. I just haven't risen *yet*.

NEW

So, can I encourage you for just a second? You are going to rise, too. Maybe not today. Maybe not tomorrow. That rising may be a very slow and very painful process, but you will rise. Maybe that ascent will not look the way that you expect it to look, but it will happen. We might not ever fully know why we have had to go through all the things that we have gone through in life, but if we choose to grow from our pain instead of letting it shrink us, then we at least put ourselves on the trajectory of finding some of the answers.

*****

Choose to let beauty arise from the ash, even if you don't know what that beauty is going to look like, even if you don't fully know how your ascent is going to appear. Take the heavy weight of your pain and use it to produce something beautiful. In time, the flowers produced from your own growth will overshadow and outweigh the weight that the pain once held over you. I am not saying that we should erase and forget our pasts, not at all. That would cause us to fall victim to the very definition of resilience that we discussed as being ultimately incorrect. But I am saying that we can choose not to let our pasts hold power over us. Instead we can use them to empower our regrowth and rising.

But truly, we can't have true resilience without the key component of joy. Resilience, while a unique portion of the human soul, isn't the only part of our beings that is multifocal in its nature. As I said at the start of this chapter, we are at the turning point of this book. We have gone through death together. We have learned how to hold pain together. We have learned how to mourn together. Now, let's go through life together. Let's dance. Let's sing. Let's talk about one of the most robust things in life that makes our time on Earth more worthwhile. Let's talk about joy.

You might be wondering, *Why are we introducing joy in conjunction with resilience?* Well, as we said, joy is the key to unlocking resilience.

Chapter 8

It is joy that provides the hope that allows for resilience to grow within us and is ultimately what enables us to rise. If we want roses to grow out of our lives and if we want to claim our time on Earth well, we need to work to understand joy in its fullness.

Joy, like resilience, is multi-focal. It is multidimensional. Somehow, it is both happy and sad. It is aching and healing at the same time. It is duplicitous, but in a positive sense of the term, if there were such a thing. What both joy and resilience have in common is that they both rely heavily on the reality of the "even so" of the chain of pain. We hurt; *even so,* we have joy. We mourn; *even so,* we dance.

Again, this is not despite pain. Joy—true unadulterated joy—can be found most robustly because of pain. Do you know who has to grapple with this idea tangibly? Nurses. Nurses not only utilize the trinity of pain, joy, and resilience, but we quite uniquely live it out daily.

It is a natural human tendency to question why painful things happen. This is a valid and weighty question that needs to be addressed, and I am not diminishing the asking of it in any shape or form. But I will tell you that in life we do not always get an answer to that question. Regardless of if we are able to find the answers which we seek or not, we cannot let that stop us from living holistically healthy lives.

In Chapter Three, we talked about the *why* phase and the *what* phase with regard to our own disillusioned expectations and concluded our exploration with this statement: the question of *why*, while important, needs to eventually take a back seat to the question of *what*. There is pain—*what* are we going to do about it? If you are a nurse, you cannot get stuck on the question of *why* there is pain and suffering. If you do, nursing will chew you up and spit you out. While mulling over the *why* is important, at some point we have to move onto the *what*. As in, what are we going to actively do to address the pain and suffering that we see? This takes the ability to recognize the pain for what it is, the determination to

NEW

find joy in the midst of all of it, and the willingness to do it again and again in order to build up true resilience within ourselves. This skill is not just a nursing skill, either. This is what it means to turn mourning into dancing. This is what it means to live life well. *This is for all of us.*

Nurses just have to do this every single time that we go into work. The profession of nursing is all about finding joy, beauty, and brightness in the midst of the darkness of death and disease. In my interviews, I was able to find clear examples of the swirling dance of pain, joy, and resilience. The examples that most brilliantly illuminated this very concept were produced when nurses answered the question, "What is a good memory that you have from your first year (or beyond) in your nursing journey?"

"We had one of the first HIV patients in the 1980s, and everyone—his family and friends—had abandoned him except for his sister, and he was dying a horrible death. There was no one left for him, so being able to care for him was special. When he was assigned to you, you felt like you really were the hands and feet of Jesus, because everyone else in his life had shunned him for his lifestyle choices and said that this was the consequence of his life, and he had no one but his sister. Back then, people didn't understand the HIV disease, so when you went into the room, you had to wear a gown, mask, gloves, and goggles. They didn't know if it was respiratory or how exactly it was spread. It was a scary time because people were afraid and didn't understand the disease. Or I would have patients with cardiomyopathy who just wanted to live till their fortieth birthday, people who had a goal and then would die right after. That might sound depressing, but being able to help them reach that goal and be a part of that process is really special."

—LS, *university health nurse practitioner, thirty years of experience*

Chapter 8

"It is hard. I have good memories mixed in with the difficult memories, because we have a lot of death on our floor. I remember it was the Fourth of July, and I had a confused patient who was obtunded and not really there. I told her, 'Look out the window! The fireworks are going off!' So she looked over at the window, but I wasn't sure if she was really understanding what I was saying. She was on our floor for a long time, and she had a lot of complications following her treatments, so a couple months later, I had her again. She was one of my primary patients, too, so I ended up having her almost every time I worked. Then, one shift, she was telling me that before she was really sick she used to journal every day but stopped doing it for about a month because she was so sick and didn't know what was going on. But she said that in the middle of the month that she was really out of it, she remembered that a nurse told her to look out the window at the fireworks. That was so powerful to me because she didn't remember much, but she did remember being with me for a moment and watching the fireworks together. I feel like God was able to use that and that the small moments in life are so important when you take the time to help someone focus on something other than how badly they are feeling. It was such a sweet moment of feeling like what I do matters."

—*AI, bone marrow transplant oncology nurse, two years of experience*

"I don't know if I would call this a good memory in a warm-fuzzy sense, but while I was working in a low-middle-income country, we had a pregnant patient present who was from one of our outreach clinics. It was her third baby, and the mom appeared to be fine. She was sent to labor on the ward and suddenly, less than an hour later, we heard screams, and we went running. The baby was born in the amniotic sack. When we tore open the sack, there was hardly any fluid in it, and the baby was covered in thick meconium. The baby made no efforts to breathe on her own, so we started resuscitation efforts. Our pediatrician was called, and we were able to revive the baby girl. After several hours of Bubble CPAP, it was clear that the little girl had enormous challenges ahead of her, so we transferred her by ambulance to the leading children's hospital in the area. Halfway there, the oxygen tank ran dry right in front of another hospital. We rushed inside, and they gladly swapped our empty tank for a full one without charging us, and they sent us on our way. The miracle made it seem like, again, she would be ok.

"The next morning, we woke up to a text that had been sent from the mom in the wee hours of the morning asking for help. The hospital had run out of oxygen and was asking for her to pay $200 for the deposit on another big oxygen tank. This family didn't even have $2, but the nurse on the ward said that she could appeal to the Social Service Office. So, the mom, leaving her struggling baby girl with another patient's family, sharing their crowded hospital bed, frantically scrambled to get to the Social Services' Office, and she spent hours getting all the paperwork, and it came down to getting the last required signature of the doctor on duty before the funds would be released to get the tank.

"The overworked doctor took one glance at the paper that the mom timidly placed in front of him and he said, 'What is this? Get this paper out of here. I don't have time for this.' Within an hour, the baby girl died. We were devastated. But it is redeeming in that in nursing, or in the medical field in general, we sneak on the spandex and the cape without thinking. There are often times when our work feels heroic and there are times when outcomes don't happen as we hope, and when we face those hard situations it can feel demoralizing and make you question your calling.

"Later, when we gathered to debrief with our pediatrician, the doctor shared a passage from Mark, when Jesus was preparing to be crucified. This passage is quoted a lot in scripture about caring for the poor, but when this passage was read to us, one phrase stood out: Mark 14:3-9, which reads, 'While he was in Bethany, reclining at the table in the home of Simon the Leper, a woman

Chapter 8

came with an alabaster jar of very expensive perfume, made of pure nard. She broke the jar and poured the perfume on his head. Some of those present were saying indignantly to one another, "Why this waste of perfume? It could have been sold for more than a year's wages and the money given to the poor." And they rebuked her harshly. "Leave her alone," said Jesus. "Why are you bothering her? She has done a beautiful thing to me. The poor you will always have with you, and you can help them any time you want. But you will not always have me. She did what she could. She poured perfume on my body beforehand to prepare for my burial. Truly I tell you, wherever the gospel is preached throughout the world, what she has done will also be told, in memory of her.'"

"The phrase that stood out was that *she has done what she could*. When we look at the vast need of humanity, especially as nurses, it is easy to take on the needs of the world, but it is good to remember that we can only do our part. We went to the hospital, picked up the mom and her lifeless baby girl, and helped dress the little girl and got her to the funeral home. We visited the mom daily in her shanty shack, and the mom freely donated her breast milk for other babies until her milk ran dry. That was pivotal for me. There is so much hurting in the world. One of our family medicine doctors grew up in the Midwest and talked about how he would often drive past huge fields of corn, and we often think that we need to be the ones to water all of that corn, but really we are just one raindrop, and it is God's job to make sure that all the fields are watered. We just need to focus on the one job that he has given us."

—PE, *labor and delivery nurse, ten years of experience*

"We had one patient with ALS that really stuck with me. We took care of him probably for about ten years off and on. His wife was his main caregiver, and we really bonded. We even went to his funeral. I was on maternity leave at the time when he passed, but I still went to his funeral. To me it is all about bonding with patients. It isn't as much about the job—it is about being able to care for someone, and it makes me feel like I really am making an impact getting to care for them and care about them. I'm not just passing medications. It is so special to get to be with the patients, to hold hands with them as they are dying. There are lots of opportunities like that in our career."

—*CR, medical-surgical respiratory nurse, sixteen years of experience*

"One that will stand out forever to me was this five-year-old that I got to take care of with a brain tumor. He was basically on palliative care, but not on hospice yet. They were a Christian family, and they would always ask how I was doing, and I would tell them, 'You have so much going on! You don't need to ask me that!' They were an incredible family that I got to journey with during a really hard time. They ended up losing their sweet five-year-old boy. I got to go to the funeral, and it was devastating, but amidst it all, I had the privilege of working with this wonderful family. It is amazing that nursing provides that moment in time for you to be able to enter that space with people. After it all, you have a different appreciation for life, so that no matter what happens inside or outside of work, you can be thankful for what you do have and reflect on the joys and blessings in life."

—*RV, director of university nursing, twenty-one years of experience*

"Once, when I was on the floor, we had a patient who was in the same room for at least a month. He was such a sweet man, and he had a ukulele which he would play and sing, and we would be sitting there charting, listening to him play. It changed the atmosphere because it brought so much light and joy. One day, the patient next-door to him passed away, and the family was there, and this man heard what was going on outside, and he could tell that something hard had happened, so he started playing a song for them. I don't remember what song it was, but that's what he could do to bring peace and comfort to that family. Patients loving patients really is a beautiful part of humanity."

—*AB, women's oncology breast clinic nurse, four years of experience*

Chapter 8

"I remember there was a patient that I had as a new grad that had just had a knee amputation, and he was having severe phantom limb pain, which is a sensation that isn't really able to be relieved by medication. I had given him everything, all the medications that I could. I was trying to call and work with the doctors, but he was just writhing and crying in pain. I noticed that he had a Bible with him and I asked him if he wanted me to read him anything. So, I stayed there for probably twenty minutes and I just read him Psalm 23 over and over again until he managed to fall asleep. That memory sticks with me because a lot of times we think of nursing and medicine as just trying to make the pain go away, or we are just trying to solve the problem in front of us, but really what it is about is presence and making suffering more bearable. I saw that especially in oncology. That lesson has really stuck with me throughout my career."

—BS, *internal medicine hospitalist nurse practitioner, eight years of experience*

"When I first met one of my patients, she had a black eye and missing teeth after fleeing her abuser. Over the course of about a year, I have witnessed her life completely change as she continues to grow and learn and take courageous steps forward. Her smile is full of confidence, and it's incredible to see how she has grown and to be even a small part of her story. Nursing is such a rich career. Sometimes it is really hard, but I have to remind myself that it is still good. I get paid to connect with people and bring good into the world."

—KS, *community health nurse, eight years of experience*

"I have a lot of good memories of things that have happened. One of the more recent ones is that I had a patient who was a professor at a Catholic university, and he had just recently been promoted. He was under a lot of stress because of his new job, and he was having trouble sleeping, so he started taking sleeping pills. One morning, his wife found him lying face down on the

NEW

kitchen floor, and it turned out that he had overdosed on the pills. They took him to the hospital, and he had a psychiatric evaluation done. They ended up clearing him because he said that he had been sleepwalking and that he took the extra pills in his sleep. So, they discharged him. A week or two later, he got up to make breakfast for his kids while his wife had gone to church. He told his kids that he was going to get a prescription filled, but instead he went to a parking lot, poured gasoline on himself, and lit himself on fire. Thank goodness the fire department was a block away. Through a series of events and my sharing with him about forgiveness and love and spiritual warfare, we ended up having a lot of intimate conversations. From the burn, he lost both arms, his nose, and one of his ears.

"The Lord kept putting it on my heart to pray for him, and at one point, the Lord spoke to me and said, 'I want you to share Me with him.' In my home Bible study, I had been studying the book of Acts, and Acts 10:1-2 says, 'At Caesarea there was a man named Cornelius, a centurion in what was known as the Italian Regiment. He and all his family were devout and God-fearing; he gave generously to those in need and prayed to God regularly.'

"Essentially, it talks about the story of Cornelius and the Apostle Peter. It starts off talking about Cornelius, who is a centurion and for all intents and purposes, he appears to be described as a Christian, but it turns out that he wasn't yet at that time. Peter goes to Cornelius' home and speaks with him, and that is when Cornelius and his whole family get saved.

"God told me that I needed to share this story with the patient and that this patient was my Cornelius. I said to God 'Who am I to doubt this man's faith? He is a prominent man at a Catholic university. Won't he be offended?' But God told me to trust him. That day, I was a break nurse, and the nurse I was covering asked me to feed this particular patient his breakfast. Over breakfast, I shared the story of Cornelius and then I asked him, 'Would you like to have a God moment with me? Would you like me to pray

Chapter 8

for Jesus to become your Lord and savior?' And he said that he did. Six years later, at our last Burn Conference, he was leading his own support group. He asked me to be a part of it. It is a support group for people with self-inflicted burn injuries. He shared that he was so filled with anxiety and depression before his injury, but now, with no nose, no ears, and no arms, he is more content than he ever has been. He even would take off his glasses with his prosthetic nose attached to show everyone. The moral of the story is that we are more than the sum of our parts. God literally makes beauty from ashes."

—*TH, professor of nursing and burn ICU nurse, twenty-five years of experience*

These stories signify joy done well, for they demonstrate the allowing of pain to magnify beauty instead of allowing pain to steal beauty away.

I was hesitant about becoming a nurse for a long time because I didn't know if I would be able to witness suffering at such a magnitude and be able to handle it in a way that was healthy. I was expecting the weight of the sorrow of it all to crush me. Then, the summer before I officially became an RN, I read J.R.R. Tolkien's *The Lord of the Rings* all the way through for the first time, and I came across the following quote in the second book of the trilogy, *The Two Towers:*

"All that day they walked about the woods with him, singing, and laughing; for Quickbeam often laughed. He laughed if the sun came out from behind a cloud, he laughed if they came upon a stream or spring; then he stooped and splashed his feet and head with water; he laughed sometimes at some sound or whisper in the trees. Whenever he saw a rowan-tree he halted a while with his arms stretched out, and sang, and swayed as he sang."

Though seemingly obscure, this quote has played a key role in the way that I have come to define what joy is in my own life. Allow me to explain briefly. Quickbeam is an Ent, an ancient species that Tolkien created that very closely resembles trees. You come to find out that this particular species has nearly been wiped out. Not only that, but they haven't even seen their female counterparts, the Ent Wives, in a very long time. The Ents are starkly aware of the evil and destruction that is about to befall them as inevitable war looms on the horizon. Yet, even so—and not despite—Quickbeam the Ent still chooses to bask in small moments of joy, and his joy is what is radiating in this passage.

Now, if you are not a *Lord of the Rings* fan and could care less about some random tree beings, that is ok, because there is also a real life example that stems from this story. Tolkien himself was a World War I veteran and one of his initial purposes for writing *The Lord of the Rings* was to cope with the Post Traumatic Stress Disorder that he sustained from the fighting. According to writer and lecturer Hank Green in his educational YouTube series *Crash Course*, specifically in the episode entitled *Trauma and Addiction: Crash Course Psychology #31*, written by Kathleen Yale, the following is true:

"It took Tolkien years to process his experiences. To help him do it, he turned to writing fiction and in time he constructed a world that helped him and all of us better understand war, human nature, loss, and growth. His novels were the bi-products of trauma, and they're among the more beautiful reminders of how it can affect us. Most of us will experience some kind of traumatic event in our lives, and most of us will exhibit some kind of stress related behavior because of it. These symptoms usually fade, but for some, those reactions can linger and start to disrupt their lives or the lives of those around them. These reactions can develop into full blown psychological disorders including post-traumatic stress disorder and, in an effort to cope, sometimes addiction. But it doesn't always have to be that way.

Chapter 8

"Ultimately, Tolkien was able to harness the effect of his trauma and shape them into something important and to reclaim his own life, because there is such a thing as post-traumatic growth, too. As it does with many other things, psychology approaches trauma-related disorders with different perspectives, but they all tend to ask the same questions. How do you identify and diagnose these disorders? And how do you treat them so that the patients can recover with the understanding that they might never be the same as they were before the trauma, but they still can be healthy and happy? In a way, psychology helps patients ask themselves what Tolkien asks his readers, and what Frodo asks when he is finally safe back in The Shire: 'How do you pick up the threads of an old life? How do you go on, when in your heart, you begin to understand that there is no going back?'

"If there is any silver lining to all of this, it's that some people may actually experience positive change after a trauma. Treatment and social support help some sufferers achieve post-traumatic growth, the 'positive psychological changes resulting from the struggle with challenging circumstances and life crises.' That's in part what Tolkien did. Though he suffered great trauma and loss on the battlefield, he was eventually able to use those experiences to drive those powerful, allegorical stories, stories that helped not just himself, but many readers of all ages around the world. It seems that while whatever doesn't kill you might not necessarily make you stronger, sometimes it really does. We're amazingly resilient creatures. When nurtured with the proper support and practice, we can overcome a lot."

Tolkien's greatest trauma is what led to one of the literary world's greatest beauties. I am not in any way, shape, or form saying that we should call the evil, harm, trauma, and hurt that befalls us in life good. In fact, the pain and suffering that occurs both in ourselves and in others should be something that actively breaks our hearts. What I am calling good, however, is the strength and resilience that we can find within ourselves to seek joy and perpetuate beauty in a hurting world even after such things happen to us. As for Tolkien having to fight in World War I, having to witness extreme violence, and sustaining PTSD from it? That is a horrible thing that should deeply upset us. But his writing *The Lord of the Rings* as he healed and rose from the trauma? That is a beautiful, joyous image of resilience and should be celebrated as such. That is turning mourning into dancing, living life, and claiming time well.

While I have no claim to the level of pain that Tolkien experienced, by witnessing his lived resilience through both his personal narrative and his created art, I realized that no matter what kinds of death and suffering I would come to see as a nurse, I would still ultimately have the hope of joy on my side to sustain me. From then on, I decided that instead of cowering in fear of the possibility of tragedy, I was going to challenge myself to actively seek out joy in the midst of all things and allow beauty to permeate all of my circumstances. What's more is that I have found that it is this type of joy that has given me the resilience to get back up when pain has beaten me down.

This moves us back into the practice that we talked about in Chapter Five: lament, remind, and praise. Remember how I previously and purposely omitted the praise component of this practice? Well, we have lamented, we have reminded, and now let's talk about what it means to praise. In Chapter Five, we discussed Lamentations 3:16-24. Again, just to reiterate, it reads as follows:

"He has broken my teeth with gravel; he has trampled me in the dust. I have been deprived of peace; I have forgotten what prosperity is. So I say, 'My splendor* is gone and all that I had hoped from the LORD.' I remember my affliction and my wandering, the bitterness and the gall. I well remember them, and my soul is downcast within me. Yet this I call to mind and

*Author's Note: Some translations say 'endurance' instead of 'splendor.'

Chapter 8

therefore I have hope: Because of the LORD's great love we are not consumed, for his compassions never fail. They are new every morning; great is your faithfulness. I say to myself, 'The Lord is my portion; therefore I will wait for him.'"

It is the last two sentences that point us to praise. Praise, after all, is demonstrating gratitude. Gratitude is thankfulness actively practiced. It is the power of gratitude that takes us from the unknown of pain, to the known of what we have to be thankful for, to the lived experience of joy. Whatever our personal belief system is, it is imperative for us to practice gratitude. It is the capstone to how we can respond to and receive joy, whether it be joy that stems from happiness—in which our joy is too great to contain—or joy that stems from pain—in which learned resilience is fostered and becomes ultimately triumphant.

It was only by being thankful for what I did have that I was able to go to work each night during my first year as a nurse. When I was thankful for the good things that had *already* happened, it made me less afraid of the bad things that *might* happen. Tangentially, it also allowed me to slowly let the pain go and not be permanently hardened by it. It permitted me to focus on the joyful promise of hope, rather than focus on the heavy weight of fear.

It was also the act of using praise to foster gratitude that enabled me to strip myself of the hold of all the idols that we have previously talked about: the past idols of *I wish, if only, my fault;* the present idol of *perfect resiliency;* and the future idol of *what if.*

When we praise, when we rejoice, when we are thankful, we are able to find joy no matter the circumstance. With joy comes peace. I waited to share this, delayed the praise, not only so we could learn how to hold and grow from the pain, but so we could also recognize that this is not an easy, seamless, or quick process. If we jump straight into praising without taking the time to both lament and remind, then we set ourselves up to chase after a false sense of joy, a joy that won't fulfill or last. Easy joy is just a feeling.

NEW

It is working through the hurt that gives joy more meaning. It is resilience that gives us the capacity to find the sparks of joy in the midst of what is otherwise dark and tumultuous.

In Chapter Five, we talked about the possibility of a night without stars. Joy is about finding the stars in the middle of the dark expanse. By seeking the stars, we can look forward to the night sky's beauty rather than cower in fear when the sun goes down. Through joy and gratitude, we are able to seek out the stars more readily, and through resilience we are able to learn how to sing of their beauty more easily, but that takes practice and time.

I say this all in full recognition of the weight that life carries with it. The stories that I shared in this chapter can attest to that. Pursuing joy, becoming resilient, and actively practicing gratitude are no easy feats; we all have known significant pain. It is what we choose to eventually do with that pain that matters. But that process takes time and self-discipline. This again brings us to the precipice of the question, *What do we do in the meantime?* Isn't that somehow always the question? Before we asked how we can manage pain in the midst of the *in the meantime* in Chapter Five, but now, let's discuss what it means to seek joy in the midst of the *in the meantime*.

Beauty in life comes and goes. Rose bushes don't flower year-round, but we can still be gardeners, tending diligently to our own souls and our own hearts, by seeking beauty daily, *in the meantime*, one day at a time, no matter the season.

Chapter Nine:
One Day at a Time

Looking back on my first year as a nurse, there were an inordinate amount of times that I wanted to quit. In fact, if you talked to me in person at all that year, you probably would have thought to yourself, *Yikes. She seems really tense right now.* You would have been correct, because I was tense all day, every day, for the entirety of that year.

I remember the week before I was about to get off of preceptorship and begin my autonomous practice as an independent nurse, I went out to lunch with two of my dearest friends and coworkers who had made that same jump right before me. If it hadn't been for those two women, I would have quit. I was terrified. This was before I knew anything about what we have discussed in the last eight chapters.

As we mentioned at the start of Chapter One, the biggest lesson that I learned from my first year as a nurse had nothing to do with the profession of nursing itself. Instead, it had everything to do with what it means to be a human being. I can now say that I know what it means to be a holistically healthy human being, but it was only *because* my first year as a nurse was so hard, and not in spite of that fact.

Furthermore, I can only say that in retrospect. In the midst of the *in the meantime*, I was a mess. I would become almost paralyzed with anxiety when it came to even thinking about my job. I had no idea where to go or what to do, but I knew that I didn't want to *stay* paralyzed. I knew that, somehow, I was going to have to move forward. As for how I did it? As for how I was able to go from being an actual mess on the floor to an autonomous nurse to a holistically healthy human being who lives life and claims their time well? I did it one day at a time.

You might resent me for saying that. Living life one day at a time is equal parts brutal and beautiful. As for what allowed me to make it through the brutal? It was clinging onto the beautiful one day at a time. Full-time nurses in the traditional hospital setting work twelve twelve-hour shifts a month, split up into three shifts a week. I would count down how many shifts I had left in the year and there were numerous times when I thought, *That's it! I'm not going to make it. I'm going to my manager on Monday and I'm quitting!*

But I began to realize that those negative thoughts were the most pervasive when I thought in terms of the entire year. When I broke the year down, however, and thought of my job in terms of shift by shift, day by day, week by week, things became a little bit easier for me to manage. In my ninth month as a nurse, one of my non-nursing friends kindly encouraged me by saying, "It will never be as bad as your first day."

It was this advice that helped me get through Months Ten, Eleven, and Twelve. This sentiment didn't strike me in a way that played into any sugar-coated sort of optimism. It struck me in a way that allowed for me to find joy in the middle of the difficult without minimizing life's rough edges.

Was my first day practicing on my own as a nurse the worst day that I had that year? Actually, no. I was graciously given an easier patient assignment. My coworkers all pitched in to help me. My charge nurse checked in on me all night. I was surrounded by nothing but support and love. But the thing that was exceedingly difficult about my first day was that I simply didn't know if I could make it through the shift as an independent nurse because I had never done it before. In the lead-up to that first shift on my own, I would tell myself that I would be able to make it, but I didn't

Chapter 9

believe it. I didn't believe it, because I hadn't done it *yet*. I didn't know if I could rise to the occasion, because I had *yet* to do so.

The weight of both the unknown and my anxiety hung over my head ominously, which is why I almost quit before I even started out. But once I did one shift on my own, I realized that I could do another. Then another. I still had terrible anxiety going into work every shift for the entire year, but when I realized that *it would never be as bad as my first day*, I found a small amount of glimmering freedom. At least now I knew what to expect. At least now I knew that I could make it through a shift and keep everyone alive, even if that shift ended badly and with me driving home in tears.

I don't usually like to operate in the realm of at least because it tends to minimize the validity of the weight of the things we feel. But in this case, it actually did that in a helpful way, because it allowed me to reframe my fears, anxieties, and expectations. It reminded me that I had done it before so I could do it again. The anticipation of starting the journey is often worse than actually starting it. Therefore, it will never be as bad as our first day, because we've already done the hardest part. We've already started the journey. We're already doing the damn thing, even if we are terrified. We don't have to be perfectly unafraid or anxiety-free to keep going, to keep fighting, or to keep living life well.

It's ok not to be ok, and it's ok to be afraid, but it's not ok to stay that way. It's not ok to let our fears stop us. In my first year as a nurse, I was very afraid most of the time. But do you know what? I was still doing the things that I was afraid of. I still showed up for that first shift on my own. Then, I did it again and again for an entire year, but I had to take it one day at a time.

I wasn't the only nurse to feel this way. One new nurse similarly said this on the topic of fear:

"One thing my charge nurse told me was that if you are afraid of coming back the next day for whatever reason, if you don't come back, you are going to stay afraid of it, whatever it is. If you come back and show up, you are conquering the situation and not letting that fear grow, even if you come back afraid. It is rarely as bad as the first day or rarely as bad as you think it is going to be. Even if it is bad, you prove to yourself that you can do it by making it through that shift, and that builds your confidence."

—KH, *medical oncology nurse, eleven months of experience*

A second new nurse shared the following on taking things one day at a time:

"At the end of the day, it is only twelve hours. The sun is going to rise, and the day shift will take over. [...] Life isn't meant to be comfortable. We grow as nurses when we have hard patients. I become a better nurse on the days that are difficult. I am always going to be a better nurse on my next shift, and I am way more appreciative when I have a good shift when I've had difficult ones. I have to rely on God more during the hard ones, which is what he wants."

—CH, *emergency department nurse, ten months of experience*

I knew that it wasn't a matter of solely attempting to white-knuckle through the day-to-day because the thing about just white-knuckling through things is that eventually we will burn ourselves out. This is a topic we will be discussing in the next chapter, because burnout is a significant part of both nursing and life. What instead allowed me to hang onto both my job and my mental health was finding joy *one day at a time*.

Living life one day at a time and finding joy in the midst of the everyday is an active and often grueling process. Even joy doesn't come easily. Everything in this life takes work. And the good things? Sometimes they take even more effort, because staying healthy and bright in a dark and hurting world is a difficult endeavor.

Chapter 9

Let me share with you a story from my tenth month as a nurse that highlights the very idea of what it means to take things one day at a time and, beyond that, one step at a time.

*****

A week prior to writing this excerpt, I went to the Grand Canyon with one of my friends. We were hiking, having a great time going down into the canyon, but when we decided to turn around, we just about lost our minds. We knew that the hike back up was going to be rough, but seeing the shadow of the canyon looming over us made us both physically weak in the knees. I am an experienced hiker, but I have to admit that for the first time out on a trail, I was scared.

It was hot. It was late. The only way to get out was to hike straight back up. Staring up at the miles-away rim of the canyon's cliffs, we were daunted by the reality of our ascent. Had we gone too far? Were we overzealous? Yes and yes. But did we still have to get out of there? Also yes.

It dawned on me that things could get serious quickly. The chance of one of us passing out was high, and if that happened, then what? My nursing skills weren't going to help either one of us. So, we began climbing. Being crazy, I didn't want to stop too much. But my friend, being sensible, said that we should stop at every switchback. After both of us began to feel like we were going to faint, we began to stick to the stop-at-every-switchback plan.

Now, that is not the way I usually like to do things. I like to power through. I like to fight as hard as I can and go as fast as I can, but in that situation, that was not possible. I had to be patient and listen to my friend's wisdom. And do you know what? We made it out of there, and we were extremely proud of ourselves for having endured.

I have to tell you though, it was scary beginning that ascent. You know how people say that if you hit rock bottom, you have

NEW

nowhere to go but up? What no one seems to talk about is just how difficult that climb is going to be. When we begin an ascent, we can't even look backwards and see how far we've come because we really haven't gone anywhere. We have the whole climb ahead of us and no reference point to say to ourselves, *Look how far I've come,* because we are at the bottom. We are at the start.

Our hike back up was nothing less than brutal. But I soon realized that every time we stopped at a switchback and I looked back and saw how steep that last little part of the climb was, even if it was just a short distance, I felt re-energized to keep going. If we could make it up that last switchback, then we could tackle the next one as well. So, we took it step by step, switchback by switchback, until we made it back to the top of the canyon.

I spent the three hours that it took us to ascend not only praying in earnest that we would make it out of there alive, but also thinking about how this particular hike was a very poignant metaphor for what it is like being a new nurse. When you embark on your first year, it is like you are at the bottom of a canyon. You have nothing to prove or show from your downhill descent, and now you have a whole year ahead of you, a whole summit to climb up.

Just like getting out of the Grand Canyon, thinking about climbing the entirety of my first year was too overwhelming for my mind to comprehend. So, I had to take it shift by shift, switchback by switchback. Each shift that I have had has moved me an inch, a day, a month closer to the summit of my one year. Our daily journeys will not be easy, but if we seek out joy, if we know where to look, finding our switchback moments, then we will be able to find those sparks of beauty amidst all the hurt and make it to the top of our own personal canyons.

*****

Beginning that ascent at the start of my first year as a nurse was the most anxiety-ridden trek that I have ever had to embark upon.

Chapter 9

Prior to that, in the times in my life when I had been the most depressed or the most anxious, I would think to myself, *I used to feel like sunshine, and now I don't. So, what happened?* But during that year I came to realize something. The thing about the sun is this: even on the days that are cold, when we don't feel warmed by its rays, the sun is still shining. The sun is still the sun even when the weather is cold. It still shines brightly, even when clouds loom overhead and mute its brilliancy. When the sky appears ominous, it just means that we have to fight a little harder to discover the sun that day.

Living holistically healthy lives is the hardest thing that we will ever have to do because as we all know, this is a dark and hurting world. But sometimes, when things get heavy, we tend to forget that it is also a bright and beautiful one. Somehow, we must learn how to navigate it in such a way that allows us to stay bright like sunshine in the midst of it all. Now, that doesn't mean that we have to feel, act, or be sunny and cheerful all the time. Requiring that of ourselves would just be adding more unnecessary and unrealistic weight to our already heavy loads.

Sometimes we need someone else's rays of sunshine to warm us up when we are cast down. Sometimes we need people to remind us that the sun still shines when all we can see is a never-ending sea of storm clouds. But that goes both ways, and as we discussed, living life well means perpetuating beauty not only in our own lives, but also in the lives of others. But that begs the question, how do we stay like sunshine no matter what circumstances befall us? No matter how pervasive our own anxieties and personal pain?

S.E. Hinton's novel *The Outsiders* speaks profoundly into this very topic. In what is probably the most famous line of the book, one of the supporting characters urges the main character, in a moment of farewell, to, "Stay gold." Without giving too much away, it has been speculated that this character is urging his friend to hang onto his sense of hope in the middle of a circumstance that is filled with excruciating loss. This particular line is also often held in comparison with Robert Frosts' poem *Nothing Gold Can Stay*, which reads as follows:

> "Nature's first green is gold,
> Her hardest hue to hold.
> Her early leaf's a flower;
> But only so an hour.
> Then leaf subsides to leaf.
> So Eden sank to grief,
> So dawn goes down to day.
> Nothing gold can stay."

Paired together, it seems as if the two sentiments conflict with one another. How can someone "stay gold," if "nothing gold can stay?" Nothing in this life will stay—not the beautiful, radiant, golden times nor the painful, dark, gray times. But do you know the one person who is going to stay with you from the moment you are born until the moment that you die? The one person whom you have to live with for the entire time that you are on Earth? *You.*

Neither times of gold nor times of gray can stay because our own small lives and personal times of mourning and dancing are nothing but smoke through the lens of the great span of time. But as long as you have breath in your lungs, you are going to stay with you for the rest of your life. So, who do you want that person to be? Beyond that, how are you going to keep that person golden? How are you going to keep the cold calamity and pain that comes with being a human in this world from stealing your hope, your joy, and your own sunshine? The world is going to try and rob us of all of those things, but to live life well, we can't let it. Life itself is full of *in the meantimes*, so how do we make *all* of that time count?

This is not a call to full-blown hedonism. If it were, we would not have stressed the importance of pain so much. Living *one day at a time* and seeking to find joy in the midst of it is not chasing pleasure, neither to spite the pain nor to numb it. Living *one day at a*

Chapter 9

time is a pursuit of joy in the midst of the pain, anxiety, or moments of trepidation that we find ourselves to be in at the present.

What then can we practically do *in the meantime* until things start to get better? How do we go from surviving one day at a time to *living* one day at a time? That small, yet vitally important distinction must be unlocked by the key that we talked about in the last chapter: the key of joy. It is this key, the key of finding joy in the daily, that allows us to "stay gold." It is what allows us to unlock true resiliency, and it is that resiliency that allows sunshine to permeate our lives. Beyond that, it is also what allows for us to make our time on Earth beautiful no matter what circumstances befall us. Do we go through times in life where we just get by and survive? Sure we do, and that is ok. But living life well means to actually live fully, and we can best do that by finding joy daily.

Here is one question that I have had to ask myself time and time again: *have you let the thickness of your skin calcify the softness of your heart?* I initially asked myself this question in my ninth month as a nurse, and back then, the answer unfortunately was yes. And now? After all that I have learned, after all the nurses whom I have spoken with, the patients whom I have cared for, and the writing that I have done? My answer to that question is still sometimes yes. Why? Because our hearts are quick to protect themselves from the unknown, and tomorrow is always unknown. I wrote the following back when I was first grappling with this idea.

*****

Being in a helping profession where you are constantly caring for the downtrodden is extremely tiresome. At this point I am depressed, burnt out, and frankly just done. There have been two large factors contributing to these heart hardening feelings. The first is that I quite literally don't have time to care for my patients in a way that meets all their needs, and that makes me sad. We are taught in school that nursing care is comprehensive—mind, body, and soul—but somehow I am barely scraping by just to give adequate physical care.

The second is that I am so stressed out that I don't have the time to love my staff the way I want to. I love them with my whole heart, but more often than not, I am so busy running around that I don't really get to talk to them. Or if I do, it's while I am charting, so only part of my attention is given to them. While those are normal and valid things for new nurses to feel, I recognize that there is something wrong with my heart if I am letting the anxiety that I feel for my job become so great and so all-consuming that I am missing the people in front of me.

What is wrong with my heart is this: I have built a very big and solid wall around it. This wall is rooted in fear and my own sense of twisted control, because in my head if I am afraid of something, then I am prepared for the worst. If the worst happens, I won't be surprised. But do you know what? Maybe I won't be surprised, but I also won't be more equipped. At the end of the day, I'll just be anxious.

As nurses know, you have to be tough and you have to be strong. Your skin has to be thick, or you won't survive in our line of work. But I ask you, as I have been asking myself, have you let the thickness of your skin calcify the softness of your heart? In all honesty my own personal answer is yes. I have always had thick skin and I used to have a soft heart, but out of the fear of my job, I let that thick skin turn into a hard heart, and I have missed seeing and loving a lot of people because of it.

*****

Keeping our hearts soft while simultaneously keeping our skin thick is not an easy task. We often build fortresses around our own hearts again and again in attempts to keep the anxiety at bay. But when we barricade our hearts in fear, it just erodes our minds. Beyond that, it blocks out any potential joy that might come our way.

Chapter 9

We have to take risks and actively choose to unfurl our hearts to the potentialities of life, both the good and the bad, terrifying though it may be. What's more is that this is something that we have to do multiple times a day. To live well *one day at a time* we have to open our hearts to life, to whatever comes our way, whether that be pain or joy. If we lock ourselves in the caverns of our own fortified hearts, we will atrophy and mummify, never growing, never living, and never loving, just slowly turning into dust that is held together by the linen of our own desperation to control everything around us in the hopes that we won't get hurt.

Well, I certainly didn't think that we would be talking about mummification in this chapter, but here we are. It is a little bit ironic, because mummies are often surrounded by that which is physically golden, and here I am urging us all to keep *ourselves* golden. In order to not become mummies in this life, held captive in the tombs of pride, greed, and the fear of it all being stripped away, we have to let it all go. In fact, we have to surrender the anxiety-built walls of our hardened hearts, strip our eyes of the fog of worry and discontent, and look for what is truly golden, which is in fact joy.

Our hearts go before us exposed, soft, and vulnerable. It is resilience that keeps our skin thick, but it is joy that keeps our hearts soft. Beyond that, it is joy that keeps us golden, and not the type of gold that fades or the type of gold that is buried with kings as their mummified remains shrivel. It is the type of gold that allows our souls to sparkle and shimmer and remember the beauty of the sun even on the grayest of days.

But what can we actively do to keep our hearts soft? What can we do to keep the scales of our skin from calcifying and petrifying our hearts as well? Well, I propose four strategies that will allow for us to surround our hearts with the golden glow of joy rather than the cold stone of worry. I do not offer these things to you proudly as a master. Instead, I offer them to you humbly as someone who is learning alongside you. To find joy *one day at a time* we need to:

practice gratitude, facilitate kindness, seek beauty, and focus on *what's now*, instead of on *what's next*.

1. Practice gratitude.

We talked about gratitude in the last chapter, but I wanted to touch on it again in how it specifically relates to keeping a soft and golden heart. There is something special about gratitude that allows the heart to open up, because it remarkably dissipates fear, but that isn't all that it does. My mom was the first to look over this book in its entirety. When she initially read Chapter Four, she wanted to add a sixth point to our five-step dance of healthy confidence and healthy humility. The sixth point that she suggested to add (after we ask questions, ask for help, recognize that we are part of a team, give ourselves grace, and never stop learning) was this: *we say thank you.*

Of course, she was right, because gratitude is healthy humility at its best. The golden warmth of joy can be seen clearly in such moments. It is healthily humble for us to give thanks, because it frees us from unhealthy pride. It is also humble in a healthy way to receive thanks graciously, which fosters healthy confidence. It is an ebb and flow, a give and take, but what is more is that practicing gratitude allows us to bond with one another and perpetuate the joy that comes with community.

The theme of being thankful for good community in the form of coworkers became largely apparent in the interviews that I held. In fact, seventeen nurses mentioned how great an impact their team had on their daily work lives. Multiple nurses attributed some of their best experiences to their coworkers. Whether the connection happened in the middle of chaos, in times of laughter, or over the sharing of food, nurses found joy by being thankful for their community no matter what stressful circumstance they found themselves in.

Chapter 9

"I have so many good memories. In the first year, my favorite memories were getting to work with my nurse best friend. I can't pinpoint a specific time but getting to work shifts with your work best friend where you pull through what would have been a stressful and horrible shift otherwise, but because they are there, you turn it into fun. It becomes less stressful. We would laugh and help each other. That's my favorite part of nursing: suffering through a shift with your best friends and having fun."

—*LC, medical-surgical respiratory nurse, seven years of experience*

"Look for the little joys, the little things in your shift. One of the best responses to having a bad shift—and I mean in general any nurse can do this—is saying 'Lets get UberEats!' We will all be having a bad day, and then someone will say, 'That's it! We need to get tacos!' and we'll order food to the floor. Then, we are able to come together and laugh over how insane it all is. We bond over food. It changes the whole tone of what would've been a horrible day otherwise or what could've put you in a horrible mood for the next shift. You have to look for those little things."

—*EP, medical-surgical oncology nurse, one year of experience*

"I have made really good friends through work. I just got to hang out with two friends last night who used to work with me in the NICU. We worked together for several years. Having friends at work, especially in nursing, is important. You spend so much time together in a twelve-hour shift and you go through really hard stuff together, so there is a bond there that is awesome."

—*AK, NICU nurse and pediatric nurse practitioner, eleven years of experience*

"One of the most influential people in my earlier career was a nurse named Renee. She would disappear into the room where we did procedures right after report for about ten minutes every morning. I asked her what she would do in there, and she invited me to join her. She took time to pray for each of her assigned patients, asking that she be just what they needed today, that she would say the right words, ease their pain and fear, help in their healing, and she would add anything specific that she knew about them. She invited me to do the same. She was amazing. She lived her career and her life in a very intentional way every day. She wasn't there just for the paycheck, and she inspired me to live in that same way."

—CM, *pediatric advice line nurse, thirty-seven years of experience*

In addition to being thankful for one another, we can be thankful for what we have. This allows for the stripping-down of the walls of anxiety within our own hearts. When we are thankful, we are able to see the specks of golden joy in our lives, and therefore are able to step out of the shadows of the fortifications of our own fears. This inner gratitude helps foster a joy within us that allows us to keep our hearts soft even when the haze and hail of the storms of life close in around us, for it reminds us of the sun that still rises within our own hearts. Praise—or in other words— be thankful and practice gratitude.

In response to the question, "How do you feel your first year as a nurse shaped you into who you are today?" three nurses said the following:

"My whole first year helped me get out of myself and my own head. It helped me to be others-focused and to be thankful for the health that I have. When you are with people that aren't healthy, it helps you appreciate what both you and your family have. It also helped me in that I don't take people for granted or take my kids' health for granted. It made my problems seem smaller to me, too."

—CM, *pediatric advice line nurse, thirty-seven years of experience*

"Nursing has made me not necessarily cynical but more aware that we are in the midst of suffering as nurses. It is a reality check of life and what people go through. It has made me more realistic

Chapter 9

about and appreciative of my own health and the blessings that I do have, because nurses see people going through life's hardest stuff. The average person does not see the kind of suffering that we do as nurses unless it is in the media or they know someone personally. But we see suffering every day. Maybe it has made me a little more jaded, but it has grounded me and allowed me to practice gratitude more fully. Every time I work out, I am so thankful for my own body and for what I have because I am able to move and run, and so many people can't do that."

—*AK, NICU nurse and pediatric nurse practitioner, eleven years of experience*

"I am thankful for the patients on my floor. Ninety percent are going to get out. Some revisit us, but from the point they enter the hospital, that's what gets me. They will have to take medications for the rest of their lives, they can't spend time in the sun, and a small fever could mean something really bad in their disease process after their transplant. It's a different outlook on life. It gets me thinking about how grateful I should feel that I am healthy, that I can care for these patients on the other side of it. It's another reminder just to be grateful, but at times, it can be overwhelming. The thought of how grateful you could or should be can get to the point where the gratefulness becomes too much and becomes a negative. It makes me feel like I should be doing more. I'm living. I'm alive, but what am I doing with my life? What more can I do for the sick? I have to remind myself that I am already doing what I can. Remembering that is how I stay me."

—*DY, bone marrow transplant oncology nurse, nine months of experience*

When circumstances are at their worst—and nurses are affronted with those circumstances daily—we have to somehow be able to come to terms with the suffering that we are witnessing. Often, the only way that we can do that in this life is to be thankful for what we do have or for what we have left. There is something healing about this type of gratitude. For though we have witnessed cataclysmic horrors and our hearts break with helplessness, they can with time again be warmed and soothed through gratitude.

As we mentioned in Chapter Four, nurses are excellent providers of customer service. Anyone reading this who has ever worked in customer service will be familiar with what I am about to say. Nothing is more grating on the nerves or quick to harden the heart than someone—a customer, a client, a patient, whoever—who is ungrateful. In nursing, people are ungrateful a lot of the time. We get yelled at, cussed at, kicked at, spat at, inappropriately hit on, you name it, on an unfortunately frequent basis. One nurse had this to say on the topic:

"I would say that I have a new respect for nurses because before you become one, you have no idea. People always say, 'The schedule is so good,' or 'The pay is so good,' but we have to work way harder for our money than the doctors do, than anyone else does. Nurses are hustling. Be nice to your nurses. That's my final thought."

—*JF, PICC line insertion nurse, six years of experience*

But the patients that do earnestly thank us? They stay with us. For if nothing hardens the heart like an ungrateful person, then likewise, nothing softens the heart like a truly appreciative one. Many nurses attributed the thanks that they received from patients as the answer to the question, "What is a good memory that you have from your first year (or beyond) in your nursing journey?"

"I had this patient for two days in a row. I really liked him, and he really liked me, and it was so nice having someone vocalize how appreciative they are of you. He would tell me, 'I am really critical about customer service, but you really do things in a professional and kind manner.' It was nice hearing someone share that with me. He came back months later and said, 'It is so good to see you!' I

Chapter 9

think moments like that, times when I am able to actually build good rapport with patients, that are special."

—OR, *medical oncology nurse, eleven months of experience*

"Recently, I had a patient who came back who had a really large treatment course and had to be hospitalized. I see her outpatient now, and when she came back, she looked a lot better. She brought us all flowers, and she brought me a beautiful arrangement and told me that I had made a huge difference in her life. It was cool because I got to be there with her during the really hard times, too. She was in a ton of pain, was really emotional, and had severe skin issues. She was pretty much having all the bad side effects of radiation chemo. I was telling her that she would be ok and was able to help coach her through the worst part. I was able to help her when she was at her worst, saw her get better, and now she is fine."

—GH, *radiation oncology nurse, four years of experience*

"I had a patient when I was brand new who needed a child-size lung transplant because she had pulmonary fibrosis. She ended up passing away. I remember the family coming back up from the ICU, and they brought us chocolates. I later found out that the patient had a list of people that she liked working with, and I was on that list. That made me feel really good. I worked with her for months, so the fact that they took the time to come back and thank us was really special."

—JB, *direct observation and stroke nurse, four years of experience*

Ultimately, gratitude is an imperative daily practice, the goal of which is not to minimize the pain but to find the daily joy hidden within it. When one sees hell on Earth as nurses do, sometimes that is the only thing that you are capable of doing. One nurse stressed the importance of thankfulness as such:

NEW

"Honestly, I am burnt out already, and I haven't really come back from that, but to prevent it from getting worse, I am trying to choose to be thankful. There's always something to be thankful for, and it could be a small thing. It could be one five-second interaction with a patient where they smile and say thank you. [...] I am trying to change my perspective, but honestly, I have reached the limit of being able to change my perspective on my own. Any perspective change that is happening is based on the Holy Spirit, but being thankful in times of trials and tribulations comes with practice."

—RL, *medical-surgical sepsis nurse, three months of experience*

2. Facilitate kindness.

Often in life, it is through kindness that we can find joy. In an interview with Lady Gaga conducted by Oprah Winfrey for an issue of *Elle Magazine*, Oprah asks Lady Gaga the question, "What do you believe life is asking of us?"

The artist responds, "I believe life is asking of us to accept the challenge. Accept the challenge of kindness. It's hard in a world the way that we are; we have a very, very grave history. We're in trouble, and we have been before. But I think life asks us amid these challenges, this hatred, this tragedy, this famine, this war, this cruelty: can you be kind and can you survive?"

Kindness, too, is what can keep our hearts soft, but kindness is something that we must show to both ourselves and the world alike. To stay golden is to stay kind, and this kindness must be extended to our own hearts as well as to the hearts of others. I wrote the following excerpt on the topic of self-kindness at some point during my first year as a nurse.

*****

Chapter 9

As I write this, it is currently a Wednesday night. I am all snug at home. I have my twinkle lights on, a candle burning, some tea made, and a movie playing in the background. But where is my mind right now? Is it relaxing with my body, happy to be at home? No, it is not. Tonight, my brain has decided to fixate on stressing over my next shift, which is not until Friday.

I don't know about you, but I am tired of missing out on the joy in life because I am so preoccupied with whatever is happening inside my head. If I spend my whole first year as a new nurse only dwelling on the anxieties that I have about work, I am going to miss an entire year's worth of joy. That's a lot of joy to miss out on. But getting mad at myself for being anxious only makes things worse. So instead of getting upset at myself for being such a wreck, I have to remind myself a thousand times a day to take it one day at a time.

In the past, when I was struggling with depression and anxiety the most, I was the one-day-at-a-time champion. It would take all of my energy just to get from day to day. A lot of times, my days did not go as planned. I wouldn't get all my stuff done. I'd be late to things. I'd take too long of a nap. I'd cancel plans with friends because I didn't have the energy to go out. I could have beat myself up for all that. I could have been mad at myself for feeling weak, for procrastinating, for being sad, for literally anything. But I decided to cheer myself on instead.

Here is the first thing that I learned about one-day-at-a-time living. You have to be gentle with yourself. If you are going to be healthy at all, in any area of your life, you have to be kind to yourself every single day.

*****

It is hard to perpetuate kindness in the world if we are not also inwardly kind to ourselves. The self-hatred and negative thinking that comes with anxiety is one of the quickest ways to turn our soft hearts into stone. Therefore, the first imperative part of finding joy is to facilitate kindness within ourselves.

The second imperative part of facilitating kindness is being outwardly kind to others. It all comes back to the golden rule of treating others how we ourselves want to be treated. The golden rule itself is in fact one of the biggest ways that we can *stay golden*. Kindness not only softens our hearts, but it also softens the hearts of those around us. This allows the gold to gleam brighter and the sun to permeate the cloud-streaked skies that come with pain. We can demonstrate outward kindness through multiple avenues such as advocating for and standing up for the needs of another or through simply taking a moment to connect with someone in a small way. However we go about it, it is imperative that we don't forget to be kind.

On the topic of perpetuating kindness out into the world, nurses said the following:

"It is easy for us to get bored with what we do. Maybe it is the ten-thousandth time that we have done what we are doing, but it is the first time for that patient. Nursing can get repetitive. For us, that person is just another appendectomy patient, but for them, it is the first time that they are going through this, and I want to be the one who is there to hold their hand. It is a good reminder that what I am experiencing is not what they are experiencing. We have to treat every situation like it is brand new."

—EP, *medical-surgical oncology nurse, one year of experience*

"There have been a couple times where I have successfully advocated for patients. There was this twenty-seven-year-old who ended up passing away who needed a paracentesis just to relieve his pain. They usually only do emergency ones on the weekends, but I advocated for my patient because he was pretty much on hospice at this point and was in so much pain. So, I kept pushing for him. We ended up getting one of the ICU doctors to come see

Chapter 9

him, and they took seven liters of fluid out of his body. I felt so helpless. I kept thinking, *There has to be something I can do!* It was such a good moment being able to make him more comfortable."

—NM, *cardiovascular nurse, ten months of experience*

"The thing that made me the happiest was when I would have time to sit with the patients or give them a back rub or help them shampoo their hair. I really enjoyed getting to do something that let them know that I really was in a caring profession. We are taught to do that, but there is a lot more to healing and caring than just hanging an IV bag. Those times that I was able to connect with the patient or their family in a more meaningful way were the best memories."

—LS, *university health nurse practitioner, thirty years of experience*

But kindness isn't just something that liberates the heart when given—it is also something that permeates our souls when received. One of the beautiful things about nursing is that when we have the opportunity to work with a patient who extends kindness to us, our hearts are not just softened, they are changed.

"I remember in school I was struggling and getting C minuses. My grades were rough, I was having family drama, and I was so stressed out. We were on a cardiac floor for clinicals, and I ended up venting about everything to a heart attack patient. He had become stabilized, had a CABG, and was now recovering, and I just said, 'I am trying to do the best that I can for you. Can I get you any snacks or anything before I leave for the day?' The patient stopped me from rushing around and said, 'Remember that it is not what is up in here,' and he pointed to his head, 'it is what is in here,' and he pointed to his heart. That really helped me push through my anxiety and remind myself that as long as my heart was in the right place, I would be able to deliver good care. It was funny because the professors would always say, 'Don't ever vent to your patients,' but it really helped me. Sometimes the patients like it when we open up to them because it reminds them that we are human, too."

—*JS, medical-surgical renal telemetry nurse, three years of experience*

"Not that long ago, I had a patient who was imminent, so I only saw him a few times. His wife had been on hospice for a while, and I had seen her when I was precepting. She was even trying to set me up with her grandson. It was so sweet. She ended up passing in June, and then I started seeing her husband as a patient in September. It was broken heart syndrome, really, because when I saw the wife in June, the husband was totally active, still working, out in the backyard painting the shed. But after she passed, he became imminent with a terminal diagnosis. It was a really cool experience, though. I was there for three hours with him and his family. He was alert and talking, but he was doing the death rattle, breathing fast, all that stuff. The daughter and the son were there, too. I had scratched my car on a yellow pole six months before but hadn't done anything about it. The son noticed and asked, 'How long are you going to be here?' I thought he was asking so he could go and get some of his own work done while he knew I would be taking care of his dad. While I was in with the dad, the son goes out and waxes and cleans the yellow paint off the side of my car. It really touched me because it was so thoughtful.

"He said, 'You have been caring for my dad so well that I wanted to give you something back.' And I thought, *Oh my gosh you are going through a tragedy! You don't have to do anything for me!* But it showed me that what I was doing really mattered.

"Then, when I went to say goodbye to the patient, he told me, 'You could be my daughter.' I felt like that is why I wanted to be a nurse. The patients care, and I felt like what I was doing really did matter. A lot of time, nurses don't get to feel that way. He ended up passing the next morning, and the daughter texted me and told me about it. She took time out of her own grieving process to let me

Chapter 9

know and to thank me for my help. It was such a special time and a total reminder that yes, this work is hard, but it matters. People will take that time because they truly appreciate our work, even when it is tough. It was a reminder that we take care of the family just as much as we take care of the patient. That was really special."

—*LS, hospice nurse, two years of experience*

3. Seek beauty.

Everyone will leave you one day, whether it be by death, choice, or circumstance. The weight of that harsh yet truthful sentence would have once crushed me. But now? All it does is make me want to claim my time with the people that I have in my life right now the best that I can. Beyond that, it makes me want to claim my entire time on Earth *well*. As we discussed in Chapter Five, we are finite. There is no way that we can change that. But what we can change is how we live and love daily. Even though nothing gold can truly stay, we can choose to take a moment to allow ourselves to behold the golden parts of life that are right in front of us.

Maybe the gold will fade in a matter of days or a matter of minutes, but in the present, we can allow joy's golden splendor to empower us to feel content one day at a time, no matter the circumstance, even if it is just for a moment. Again, I am not spurring us to jump into the arms of hedonism. If I were, I would be telling everyone to, "Buy gold now," like one of those old infomercials. But ultimately, that kind of golden gluttony is not what sustains us.

I am not entirely sure at what point during my first year as a nurse I wrote the following segment, but I held onto it because I felt like it was one of the first times that I was truly able to understand how seeking beauty plays a significant role in finding joy.

*****

NEW

Here is another thing that I learned about living life one day at a time. In order to keep the anxieties of the next day at bay, we have to focus on finding the joy that the day we are presently in has to offer.

I lost my grandmother just a few weeks before I embarked on my first year as a nurse. The whole summer after I graduated college was a wild whirlwind of hospital trips, nights spent in sleeping bags on the floor of her house, family meetings, visits from the hospice nurse, and trying to cram for the NCLEX. It was absolute chaos.

Then, the following December, I was in the fourth month of my first year as a nurse, and we held the funeral service for her. It was small, just family, and I had brought a tiny African violet plant to put on her grave. It gets cold at night where the burial was held, so that poor plant didn't stand a chance of surviving, but that wasn't the point. The point was that that little plant was beautiful, and it would have made my grandmother smile even if it was only going to be beautiful for one day.

Beautiful for one day. Sometimes we cannot fathom what the next day will bring, but we sure can find some sort of joy in the day that we are living. Sometimes, I will have an unprecedentedly good shift. A nurse will bring churros for the staff. I'll get to be in the same section of the unit as my friends. I'll get to work with an aid who I know has my back. I'll get to give report to a really kind nurse. Maybe the night was far from perfect, but there were small pieces of joy hidden within it.

Then, other times, I will have an abysmally bad shift. I have to admit a complicated patient. My report is bad, and I am told so. I get a talking-to from one of the doctors. I am late on giving a ton of medications. There aren't any snacks in the break room. But you know what? It is just one shift. One day. As for what the next shift will hold? That is all for tomorrow. Today, you have to make it through the shift that's right in front of you.

Chapter 9

*****

If we seek little moments of beauty in our daily lives, then we will also be able to find little moments of joy. It doesn't matter how small those moments are—when we take the time to find them, we will find that those moments are actually what help keep us human. You may have noticed that I slid the word "small" in there just now. That was not without reason. Do you know what these moments of beauty and joy often take the shape of? These moments often take the shape of *small love*.

That's right, we were not going to mention one of the most painful parts of life, which is loss, without again mentioning that which makes life beautiful. If joy allows us the freedom to find beauty, *small love* is the way that we can cultivate that beauty within our own hearts. It is what allows us to perpetuate beauty into the rest of the world. While *small love* is simply small when it comes to an individual, it becomes large love when it is put into practice by a people. When we allow pain to point us to community, when we rejoice with one another, when we mourn with one another—that is when we can take the small amount of beauty that we each carry and perpetuate it on a larger scale into a dark and hurting world.

When asked the question, "What is a good memory that you have from your first year or beyond in your nursing journey?" nurses were able to give many beautiful answers to this question. They showed how golden flecks of beauty, joy, and *small love* can be found even amidst the darkest of circumstances.

"My favorite memory was when I had a patient who was a DNR. She was on palliative care, and I ended up talking to her for a long time about how her relationship with her daughter is one in which they don't really talk. Her cell phone was broken, so I helped her call her daughter on the room phone, and I left her alone for a couple of hours. They talked for a long time, and when she was done on the phone, she told me that that was the first time that she had talked to her daughter in three years. She told me that she hadn't had the courage to call her or to even dial the number. My helping her make that call gave her the courage to speak with her daughter. We have no idea what is going on in our patients' personal lives, so I felt so glad to be able to do that for her. I left and definitely cried happy tears after she thanked me."

—PM, *medical-surgical float pool nurse, two months of experience*

"Sometimes patients will be really sick but will be in a good mood or smiling or will give me a hug. One time, I was starting an IV on an old man, and all of a sudden, he burst out into song, and we ended up singing together. Once I was transporting a patient, and we sang together down the hallway. When you get to laugh or joke with a patient, it makes your whole day."

—MA, *emergency department nurse, ten months of experience*

"Whenever we give a bone marrow transplant, we sing the patient 'Happy Birthday.' We wear hats and give them cake. We call it 'Day Zero,' because it is a rebirth for them. When we do a transplant, the patient gets a new blood type. Their blood type changes because it is a rebirth of their entire immune and blood system. It is a new start for them."

—AI, *bone marrow transplant oncology nurse, two years of experience*

"I really loved my home health visits and getting to go into the patient's homes and take care of them in that setting. [...] I got to follow a lot of oncology kids in the home setting. One guy lived in a very small apartment, and he had a pet bird, and I am deathly afraid of birds, so when he opened the door with a huge white bird on his shoulder, I was like, 'There is no way I can come in your house with that bird out!' And he thought that that was hilarious. Getting to have that personal interaction with the kids and getting to meet their vulnerable families and provide some hopeful pieces of comfort and support are good memories."

—RV, *director of university nursing, twenty-one years of experience*

Chapter 9

> "Some of my favorite moments and memories are celebrating birthdays with my long-term patients, when the family brings in a cake or something. It is nice to take a moment away from being a nurse to celebrate a person."
>
> —HH, *surgical-telemetry step-down nurse, nine months of experience*

4. Focus on *what's now* instead of on *what's next*.

Focusing on what's next can either be a matter of anticipating that something better is coming, or it can be a matter of anticipating that something worse is coming. Either way, it is undeniably a matter of anticipation. When we get caught up in the whirlwind of anticipation in our minds, we tend to harden our own hearts. When we believe that what's next is going to be *worse* than what's now, we frantically calcify and wall off our own hearts in anxious preparation.

Conversely, when we believe that what's next is going to be *better* than what's now, we still end up calcifying our hearts to the present, but instead of building a fortress to protect ourselves, we construct a temple in order to worship our future fantasies.

Either way, our hearts, which are supposed to be soft to *what's now*, get hardened to the present because we are too busy either worrying over or romanticizing what is to come. Whenever we attempt to take control of the future, the softness of our hearts is replaced by the stones of the idolatry of tomorrow, and we are robbed of the golden joy of today.

Therefore, when we get ready to start carving and stacking stones to build either fortresses or temples around our hearts, we have to stop ourselves. In Chapter Seven we discussed the idol of the future *what if*, but those *what ifs* may never even come to pass. Then what was all of our striving for? What was all of our obsessive anxiety or infatuation for? Nothing. All we have done is robbed ourselves of the beauty that lies in the present.

NEW

We are so quick to build our own structures as if we can protect ourselves from the unknown ebbing tides of this life. But the truth is? We can't. We cannot possibly ever build a fortress to keep all the pain out of our hearts, nor can we possibly ever build a temple to keep all of our happiness in. But when we choose to find joy in the present, we are able to stop striving in our hasty building for a moment and are able to see the golden joy that the present day has to offer. In vain we build, and in vain we wither. In joy we rest, and in joy we thrive. Do not worship at the altar of *what if.*

While we have talked about what it means to stay gold and to seek gold, in the next chapter we will discuss what it means to hold onto that which is golden when the hardships of the world try to pull the gold and the sunshine away from us. If we are to go back to referring to our hearts as gardens, then we know that one hardship that gardens are susceptible to is *fire.*

Chapter Ten:
The Burn of Burnout

Fire not only burns through and ravages gardens, but it also melts down gold. Maybe it is the Southern Californian in me talking, but fire is not something to be messed around with. In fact, the county in which I grew up made it illegal for us to even have sparklers. To this day, when I am at an event where there are sparklers, I go into a panic. My internal dialogue is, "This is how we all die. I'm going to catch the person next to me on fire, and that's going to be it for all of us."

But aside from my own apprehensions about fire, it truly is something that has to be handled with caution. No one is exempt from making mistakes, and similarly, no one is exempt from becoming burnt out. When flames erupt, they do not discriminate when it comes to what they engulf. No matter how strong and resilient we consider ourselves to be, we are not immune to burnout. There are, however, things that we can do to help douse the flames and to soothe the scorching that burnout leaves behind.

As for myself, I got burnt out about one month into my first year as a nurse. You might be wondering how burnout occurred so quickly within me. *Isn't it something that takes place over a longer period of time?* you might be thinking. Well, yes. Burnout can be a slow burn, but it can also be a quick ignite. For me, it was a sudden spark that turned into a very large and long-lasting predicament. Burnout happened so quickly within me because I was doing everything that we have talked about previously in this book *incorrectly*. All of the lessons and topics that we have discussed thus far stem from my own mind and heart having been set ablaze and my having to grow back from that.

I wasn't the only one who found myself quickly being affected by this sort of fatigue, however. Another nurse described what burnout can look like for new nurses as such:

"It was like I was driving a car up a steep hill, running my headlights while the dashboard was already burnt out. You have to take a break before you can go back into things. The learning curve is so steep at first that it really is like driving a car because you are working so fast, so hard, so soon, that burning out happens more quickly when you are new. I wish that I had been warned of that, because in your first year, you will burn out more than you think and sooner than you think because you haven't learned how to drive more steadily like the older nurses do."

—EP, *medical-surgical oncology nurse, one year of experience*

A second nurse had this to say in response to the questions, "What did you wish someone had told you before you started? What do you wish was talked about more?"

"Just how draining it can be. It is morally and ethically draining. In school, they present you with a lot of theories and skills, but that is only twenty-five percent of it. Then, at work you have to talk to families, talk people off cliffs, and you get yelled at and cursed at. It is hard when you have a patient for three days and they are cussing at you. I wish someone told me to go job-shadow someone even before nursing school, because once you are in it, it's like, 'I spent all this money on school,' and then you begin to think, 'Oh man, I just don't know.'"

—TC, *critical care nurse, eleven months of experience*

In response to the questions, "How is nursing different from what you expected? How is it the same? Overall did you feel prepared?" a third nurse said the following:

Chapter 10

"I feel unstable right now, so how do I provide emotionally strong care to my patients if I don't feel emotionally strong myself? There are all those tropes that people tell you in school. For instance, 'You can't pour from an empty cup.' I get that they say those things to try and help you, but since those things are so over-said, there is no way for you to prepare yourself for what it means to actually feel empty. You do what you can by fighting for your own time physically, but you can't fully do that if you are already emotionally drained. I can't go to church very often. Sleep is good, but it doesn't prepare me to emotionally care well. That has been hard in a way that I wasn't ready for."

—BF, *progressive cardiac nurse, three months of experience*

It is imperative that we learn how to address our own fatigue, because if we don't, we will burn up *quickly*. Preventing burnout in our own lives is simply that. It is a learned skill, but often it isn't one that we can even endeavor to learn until we are already starting to feel the heat of the flames. As we discussed in the last two chapters, as resilient human beings we can most remarkably regrow but that doesn't mean that we want to actively seek out that which will set us on fire.

During fire season, people where I am from know what to do to mitigate fire risks: cut branches away from electrical lines, mow away dried vegetation, don't park a car that has been running with a hot engine over patches of dried grass, and no sparklers or unsanctioned fireworks. These are things that the community knows to do because we have seen fire time and time again. Similarly, where I am from, we can almost tell when a fire is coming. It is just a matter of where and when. Usually, the air is dry, the wind is warm, the grass is golden, and no one can remember the last time it rained.

The same can be said about feeling burnout within ourselves. As individuals, we have to learn how to recognize our own signs and symptoms of burnout. Three nurses explained this idea as such:

NEW

"Knowing what my own signs are for being at my breaking point has been really helpful for me. I know that if I am getting overly emotional or if I am having a hard time coping, then I need to take time for myself and do some self-care things. That way I can go back and give of myself at work. Nursing is not something that you can just give half of yourself to. If you are going to be at work, you have to be fully there. There was a point where I took a leave of absence because I was going through some personal stuff at home, hard stuff had come up at work, and I really needed to finish my dissertation. Most of the time I felt burnt out was when I had emotionally taxing things happen in my personal life. Then, showing up to an emotionally taxing job, it doesn't give you any time for yourself because you are so emotionally drained. When you are crying in the medication room, that is a sign that you need to take a step back!"

—*BS, internal medicine hospitalist nurse practitioner, eight years of experience*

"I feel like I have had to learn what burnout is. I definitely have experienced it. In some instances, I left the job that was causing it. That doesn't have to happen right away or in every circumstance, but it was recognizing that things weren't getting better and that I needed to do something different. I have done a lot of work around self-care. I have gotten to know myself well, including what is good for me and what is hard for me, where I thrive and where I do not thrive, and where I work well and where I don't work well. Learning about myself has been huge. I am a very burn-the-candle-at-both-ends type of person. I like to be busy. When I look back at school I think, 'How did I do all those things?' But now I know that I can't do all that stuff at once like I used to. I have learned what is healthy and what it means to practice self-care. For me, I need places that are naturally beautiful—to go on a hike, be in fall leaves—those are the kinds of things that bring me life and put things back into perspective."

—*KS, community health nurse, eight years of experience*

Chapter 10

"You will always feel burnout if you are taking care of others but not yourself. You have to be your number-one priority, especially if that means taking care of your spiritual health. But if you don't take the time to take care of your mental, emotional, and spiritual health, you will burn out. In society, we are so focused on being go, go, go, but really, we don't need to be. When you are feeling burnt out, you have to ask yourself, 'Why?' and then be ok with whatever the answer is. [...] There is always still going to be burnout because you deal with other people, but you have to find something that takes care of you, too."

—*LS, hospice nurse, two years of experience*

At my university, we had an anatomy professor who was known for her wide spectrum of antidotes. She would often say, "It tends to kill you." Do you know why this statement is relevant? Because it's true about burnout and fatigue. It tends to kill you *if you let it*. In order to not let it, we have to actively fight it. To actively fight it, we have to take care of ourselves holistically. Let's unpack this.

Nurses are supposed to be champions for holistic care. We try our very best to promote the physical, emotional, spiritual, and mental health of all of our patients. But as most people in caring professions do, we forget or don't have the time to care for ourselves in those same ways. How often do we use the airplane analogy in regard to self-care? Or should I say the airplane *reality*, because when you board a plane and the flight attendants give the safety demonstration they always urge you, in case of emergency, to put your own oxygen mask on before helping other people put on theirs.

Nurses are often terrible at this. We will run around helping others put their masks on while we ourselves are gasping for air. But in all actuality, we are going to be of no use to anyone if we ourselves are dead. If we let one area of any of the four points of holistic care erode and slip away in our lives, the rest are quick to follow.

NEW

We have talked about ways to tend to the different aspects of our holistic health previously. Now we are going to discuss the singular overarching theme that ties them all together. This is also the sole entity that allows us to protect ourselves from the flames of the burnout fire. While we often aim to achieve a healthy and balanced holistic life practice, we will never be able to be successful in that endeavor unless we actively practice the one thing that unites each of the four facets of holistic health.

Each of these components may seem starkly unrelated to the untrained eye, but the more we study each principle, the more we can come to realize that they are all interdependent on one another in creating a complete sense of well-being. None is more important than the next, but there is one power that allows for the unification of each of the four segments of our holistic selves. That one comprehensive entity is *rest*.

I didn't even begin to comprehend the practice of rest until one month after my first year as a nurse had concluded. In the past, I have been guilty of living life at a supersonic speed. I often would sacrifice sleep and self-care at the altars of achievement and adventure. That being the case, I never learned how to rest. I never learned how to slow down. Then, during my first year as a nurse, I once again failed to rest. This time I paid heavily for it, because I burnt out quickly right in the beginning and then had to struggle to survive with my own charred remains for the rest of the year.

Here is how *not* resting accumulated for me in an excerpt I wrote during my eleventh month as a new nurse.

*****

Well, today I took myself to urgent care. I am not trying to be dramatic, but it is what it is. And what it is, is this: I am not in the best place right now. What makes things more discouraging is that as I write this, I have exactly twenty-one shifts left until I reach my year mark. But somehow, with only that short amount of time left to go, I have managed to make myself so anxious that

Chapter 10

I now am presenting with persistent headaches, nausea, decreased appetite, and—here is the kicker—radiating left sided chest pain with palpitations.

I knew going into urgent care that they were just going to tell me that I was stressed out—and that is exactly what happened—but to appease the non-nurses in my life, I took myself in. They checked my vitals, ran a twelve-lead EKG on me, told me not to drink so much caffeine, prescribed me some pain medication, and sent me on my way.

While the nurse hooked me up to the EKG monitor, we got talking and I told her that I, too, was a nurse. She told me that she loved how diverse nursing was and how it was great and how I just needed to find the right fit. That was nice of her, but all the while I was thinking to myself, *What am I doing? What am I even doing? I am stressed out to the point where I have an EKG stuck to my chest.* If I were thirty years older, I legitimately would have given myself a heart attack.

I have given this job my all, my whole heart. I have felt knocked down and beaten by it, but I have still gone back to work again and again. I have learned resilience. I have *lived* resilience, but the resilience that I have learned has somehow not made the job any easier. So, there I was at the actual end of my rope, half-naked at an urgent care, hoping that there was something just enough wrong with me so that I could justify taking a break.

This is not a good position to be in. I know I let my burnout get too far. As someone who loves to declare themselves a mental health warrior, I felt disappointed in myself for allowing things to get so out of hand. I had to have a talk with myself on the way home. Why did I let myself get so burnt out? I got burnt out back in month two, but what did I do about it back then? I suppose I could have gone on a vacation, but then what? I would have just had to come back at the end of it, so I opted to power through the year. Against my own advice, I found myself time and time again trying to white knuckle through things. And for what? Certainly not so I could wind up in urgent care in my eleventh month.

The anxiety has gotten that much worse because I added the weight of having to be resilient on top of everything else. I was so focused on making myself get back up that I never took a moment to take a break in between the falling down and the ascent. I fell and rose over and over, but that cycle, without resting, is an extremely tiring process. I am no stranger to getting close to my breaking point, but with the onset of the chest pain, it is safe to say that my breaking point is coming up fast and that this time, if I'm not careful, I'll be going over the edge.

So, what did I do? I took a mental health day. Let me tell you, I don't like to call off because I feel like it means I am letting down my team. Then I realized that I am really going to let down my team if I drop dead.

*****

Things could have been worse. I remember the nurse practitioner who assessed me chuckling when I told him that I was a night-shift nurse. He said something along the lines of, "That would do it," in answer to why my anxiety was so high. He knew. I mean he *knew*. He even laughed when he told me to lay off the caffeine, which was a little rude, but it made me laugh, too.

After reading this, you might be thinking to yourself that what I just said about resilience might discredit the entirety of Chapter Eight, but I assure you, it does not. Resilience is still vitally important, but we have to remember that resiliency without rest is not sustainable.

During the course of my first year as a nurse, I was incredibly resilient for showing up to work despite my own trepidations, but at the end of the day, I still became burnt out. Why? I got burnt out because I never rested. I strived, I toiled, and I white-knuckled

Chapter 10

it against my own advice, trying to hold fast to the idol of making it to the end of the year.

There it is again, that word *idol*. Each time I fantasized about reaching my one-year goal and idolized the outcome, I wasn't living life one day at a time—I was holding onto the *idea* of a future joy. By doing so, I missed a lot of the daily joy that was right in front of me. What's more is that doing so burnt me out. I wasn't practicing true resilience by allowing the process to develop me—I was attempting to white-knuckle it. I was operating off of that false definition of resiliency in which we strive to strive perfectly.

The truth is, burnout could very well be the sixth vital sign for us as human beings. Just so we are all on the same page, nurses monitor the following five vital signs for each patient throughout every shift: blood pressure, heart rate, respiratory rate, temperature, and pain level. But we need to go one step further by adding burnout to that list of assessments. Go ahead, nurses and non-nurses alike, assess yourself right now by asking yourself the question, "Am I burnt out?"

If we add that to our list as the sixth vital sign, we allow ourselves to move from the realm of the solely physical into the realm of holistic care. We need to ask ourselves that same question every day. Actually, we need to be asking ourselves two questions: "Am I burnt out?" and, "What am I doing to rest and take care of myself?"

Maybe you like to consider yourself as a fierce person. That is exactly how I like to think of myself. One of my favorite quotes is, "Sharks are born swimming." I am unsure as to the original origin of this saying, but the first time I personally heard it was in the movie *Tower Heist* (2011). I am partial to this quote because it empowers us to be tough, tenacious, and brave. But unfortunately, we cannot be all of those things all of the time. We cannot fight all of the time. If we want to fight *well*, we need to rest *well*.

Often, in nursing, we are told that we will either sink or swim. And sharks? *They are born swimming.* But more often than not, even

NEW

though we may like to consider ourselves sharks, we flounder and barely keep ourselves afloat when we first find ourselves in new situations. Unlike sharks, it takes us time to learn how to swim gracefully and efficiently. In fact, when we are new, sometimes we sink, and someone has to dive into our mess and rescue us. Someday we will learn how to swim well, but until then? We just try to not drown.

Two nurses had this to say on the topic of drowning:

"There is just so much I am still learning. What is important to know is that even good nurses get overwhelmed. During my last shift, I felt like I was drowning. I felt like I wasn't progressing much, and my preceptor highlighted to me that other nurses were having a hard time on the floor that day, too, because we were short-staffed. Know that you will have days like that, days when you feel like you are drowning, and that that isn't necessarily your fault. Other outside things happen. They are out of your control, but they still play a factor. I think as a new grad, when you go in, you feel like you are going to save the world, like you can do it all. My preceptor gave me a healthy view of how things just happen, and you have to learn to work with it."

—*KJ, orthopedics nurse, one month of experience*

"When someone dies, you are going to want time to be quiet and reflect, but sometimes you literally don't have the time to do that because you have to take care of your other patients. You need to find something else to do outside of work or tell your charge nurse to help give you a ten minute break. You always feel like you are drowning; some days you just drown slower. Even if you have a slow day, you still feel like, 'Wait, what am I doing?' […] Don't feel alone in drowning. Know that the other nurses were drowning once, too."

—*KH, medical oncology nurse, eleven months of experience*

Chapter 10

Nurses have to reconcile this grizzly reality of death within ourselves, and we have to do it quickly, otherwise we will sink. We will drown. Then we will burn up, burn out, and be useless to both our patients and ourselves. One nurse brought the following to my attention, which greatly reshaped the way that I began to think about the importance of caring for one's self:

"I would stay in bed and sleep a lot. I wasn't really taking care of myself. Now I am getting better and am going out and doing things. It is just really consuming having to learn all these new things. That was hard. I was able to talk to one of my nursing friends about it, and she would force me to go out and do things. She reminded me that the things nurses do and see are not normal and that I can't take care of others if I don't take care of myself. People don't know that you see death all the time, so you have to go out and take care of yourself."
—MO, *pediatric cardiac intensive care nurse, one year of experience*

Why is resting important specifically to nurses? Because we see death all the time. Allow me to take a short, but important, digression for a moment. Nurses, please listen. What we see is not normal. We see things that many people do not see in their entire lives, and we see those things twelve hours a day, three days a week. Our lives are heavy. Have you ever been told that nurses are angels? Maybe you've read it on a coffee mug or something. As we have discussed, nurses get to bring love into dark situations. We get to bring a piece of the light of heaven into actual hellish circumstances. Maybe that's what makes having to see the depths of humanity's sorrow more bearable. When we walk into that dark sorrow, we get to bring into it the light of humanity's joy, which is love.

But the truth is, we aren't angels. Although we get to bear that title, in reality, we are Earthly humans delving into hell again and again, and we do not walk away from our travels to hell and back unscathed. Therefore, as nurses we need to rest.

NEW

As for you non-nurses, fear not, for you are not exempt from this discussion. For I have a question that pertains to you, too. That question is, "Why is resting important to all human beings?" Because we see *life* all the time. We fight to live, not die, and that fight is exceptionally difficult.

As for how this all relates to burnout? Well, the thing about burns is that they hurt. The process of burnout—whether it be a slow burn or a quick ignite—is painful because it turns us from human beings trying to live life well into husks, into shells, into *nothing*. We will all burn ourselves out— regardless of profession or life stage—if we do not rest.

Two nurses said this on the specific topic of how we can best address burnout within our own selves:

"The first step to fighting burnout is discovering what gives life to you as a person, as an individual, because it is not the same for everybody. For me, the two things that give me life are traveling and working with nursing students. Seeing the look of joy and discovery in the nursing students' eyes as they worked in our clinic was a continually fresh reminder of what an amazing place it really is. It helped me realize how cool my job really is. Not everyone likes teaching or having a shadow, so that might not work for everyone, but it worked for me."

—PE, *labor and delivery nurse, ten years of experience*

"Finding things that calm me down personally and help me be more me and more centered has been important. Then, that makes me be able to be there for my family and my patients more, to be present and not distracted. Being a good nurse and a whole person really makes sense in our career. You have to have that holistic look for yourself."

—CR, *medical-surgical respiratory nurse, sixteen years of experience*

Chapter 10

According to the interviews that I conducted, eleven nurses reported wanting to quit nursing completely. Do you want to know something? Of those nurses, none actually did. Many people made changes by switching specialties and exploring other options within the nursing world, but of the fifty interviews I conducted, only three of the twenty-five experienced nurses denied feeling burnout. Likewise, only six of the twenty-five new nurses reported not having felt burnt out, followed by the operative word *yet*. Otherwise, a total of forty-one nurses reported significant struggles with burnout at some point in their career.

So, how did forty-one out of fifty nurses address the burnout that they were feeling? How did they all stay in such a demanding profession? How did those eleven nurses end up not walking away? Well, they rested. In fact, the importance of self-care was stressed by eighteen of the nurses that I interviewed.

At work, we often experience burnout from giving one-hundred percent. Outside of work, we can help heal that burnout by living one-hundred percent. While we are all the same in that we all need to rest, we all differ in how we can each best personally rest. As we mentioned at the start of the chapter, the secret to living life well is to rest well.

Nurses are some of the most remarkable people you will ever meet. They are also the most adventurous. Many nurses are travelers. From short overnight camping trips to global cruises, a common theme for them was to get far away from the hospital. I remember one night around 4:00 a.m., one of my coworkers and most beloved friends said something along the lines of, "I hope I am able to give report quickly and get out of here fast." When I asked her why, she casually replied, "I have a flight to catch at 10:00 a.m. I'm going to Japan."

But it isn't just trips that help nurses get away from the hospital setting. Many mentioned hiking, going to the beach, and just getting out in nature. Other nurses identified specific hobbies such

NEW

as dancing, triathlon running, playing golf, crocheting, reading, journaling, yoga, and even beekeeping as restful de-stressors.

One nurse surmised the topic of rest and self-care better than I ever could by sharing the following with me:

> "Work hard, play hard. You have to work to prevent compassion fatigue. Take a trip with your girlfriends, go skiing, go camping, and be sure to plan your life out beforehand. I also do monthly massages and facials. I get a mani-pedi every two weeks. I get my hair done once a month. A lot of self-care. I take bubble baths. We are caretakers, so we have to take care of ourselves. 'Do what you love with who you love,' that is my motto. There's life outside of nursing. You can't forget that. Get rest. Take care of your body. Take care of your whole being so you can take care of others. Compassion fatigue is a real thing. [...] Do the things that you loved before you became a nurse. Be kind to yourself. Work hard, play hard. I could keep going!"
>
> —TH, *professor of nursing and burn ICU nurse, twenty-five years of experience*

This may sound extravagant to you, but truly, to fight against hell—which nurses have to do on the regular—we have to fight *like* hell. To power up and recharge for the next fight, we need to rest like hell and live our outside lives like hell, too. What that looks like is keeping ourselves holistically healthy. It can be in big, less frequent ways like traveling or in small, daily ways like taking a moment for yourself to sit down and breathe.

Two nurses expressed that very idea:

> "Taking time for yourself really helps. Not just taking days off, which does help, but even just at work taking a minute to yourself to be alone and have coffee helps. You have to take care of yourself and be aware of your feelings. Give yourself a pep talk, have a soda in the break room, send a text to someone—you have to take a little bit of time for yourself. It really helps."
>
> —MA, *emergency department nurse, ten months of experience*

Chapter 10

"Burnout is a tough thing. The best way to fight it is to take care of yourself. Get sleep at night, take your breaks during work, get away from the floor during your break, take vacations, get a circle of strong friends or coworkers who will support one another. It is a horrible thing to be burnt out, so make sure you get away. [...] Look forward to having something to do, like, 'When I get off work, I have this fun thing to do.' When you are getting burnt out, it is time to take yourself out of the situation. Then, when you are on vacation or taking a break, think about the pros and cons of where you work. Do the positives outweigh the negatives? Do you need to come up with more coping mechanisms? It is tough, especially when you are new to do that. "
—*SP, associate dean of collegiate nursing, twenty-nine years of experience*

This is where the critical need for rest addresses the idea of caring for ourselves holistically, because it is rest that provides us the space to take care of ourselves mentally, emotionally, spiritually, and physically. If we do not rest, if we do not take the time to step into the space of caring for ourselves, then we are gathering up the kindling that will eventually be used to burn us alive at our own personal stakes.

When we white-knuckle, toil, and strive, we don't just stop at gathering firewood, either. When we fail to rest, we not only go out looking for the sticks, but we pile them up, tie ourselves onto the stake, ignite the flames, and act as active participants in our own fiery demises. Then, we watch ourselves burn.

Why do we do that? Why do we continue to toil, knowing that we are adding fuel to the burnout fire? Well, as one of the nurses we cited at the beginning of this chapter said, as a society we are go, go, go. Perhaps we think that if we take a moment to rest then we are failing to build. Build what? you might be wondering. Well, anything—our careers, our bank accounts, our families, our futures, our dreams. Perhaps we are terrified to rest because we are so afraid of being passive, because if we are passive, then we are not actively building that which we are striving for. But truly, resting is not a passive action.

Rest is intentional and active, but in a way that if done wisely is filling rather than draining. Rest is not weakness. It is what allows us to rebuild our strength. It is also that which allows us the capacity to evaluate what is going on within ourselves and how our own personal, holistic health can be addressed and made stronger. As we said early on in this chapter, when one area of our holistic health erodes, the others are quick to follow. Therefore, it is imperative for us to take inventory of our own minds, souls, and well-beings and to rest at the appropriate times.

One new nurse reiterated this very notion by stating the following:

"You cannot be defensive about burnout—you need to be offensive."

—*CH, emergency department nurse, ten months of experience*

As for how one can be offensively fighting burnout, two nurses addressed the necessity of holistic self-care by stating the following:

"It circles back to community and counseling. Both of those things have been really beneficial for me. The times that I have been ready to quit, it was because I wasn't in a great space overall. It's important to have people in your life who you can ask questions of, questions like, 'What is going on in other areas of your life? What is your community like right now? Where are you finding joy?' It is during the times that I feel more isolated and stressed that I think, I can't do this anymore, but when I am in a good space and doing things I love, then nursing and my negative experiences become much smaller.

"We have to have community, family, friends, and things we love to do in order to have a healthy life. We have to find ways to

Chapter 10

rest, and by rest, I mean find ways to recharge, which does not only mean sleep and Netflix. Rest can mean going on a hike, watching a sunset, or drinking a delicious cup of coffee with a friend. Those are the things that have kept me from quitting. It's also really helpful to continue to evaluate what I really want with my life in order to keep things in perspective. Where do I want to be in life? And in nursing?"

—KS, *community health nurse, eight years of experience*

"You have to have time to relax and get away and not think about your patients or nursing. It is so easy to get burnt out. You don't realize how quickly it happens. I haven't even worked as a nurse for a year. You really just have to find time for what you like to do. The signs I see in myself of burnout is when I start dreading work or I really don't want to go in. I have to ask myself if I am burnt out or if I am too tired. That thought is the main sign for me. One thing I want to do is to Sabbath and to do it well, to rest intentionally—not just to watch TV, but to spend time with the Lord, to spend time in nature. Set aside a day where you don't do anything other than rest intentionally. That is something that I am working towards."

—AH, *medical-surgical respiratory nurse, ten months of experience*

In truth, I didn't start learning about how to rest until one month after my first year as a nurse was up. Then, things began to change when I went on a spiritual retreat shortly thereafter. Leading up to it, my therapist was excited for me and said something to the extent of, "I hope it is a restful time for you." In my head, I was already thinking to myself, *What? I don't want to rest! I want to have fun!* Ironically, the theme of the retreat itself turned out to be... *rest*.

The word that I did not know how to define and the practice that I ignorantly did not want to participate in became front and center in my life for three days straight. There was no escaping from having to rest this time. I had no idea that I had such an aversion

NEW

to it, but I figured that if everyone else was resting, I could at least give it a try. In the end, I didn't just try resting and then move on. Instead, I realized something that completely changed the way that I care for myself from a holistic perspective.

About six months prior to going on this retreat, I had an idea for a poem brewing in my head. The line that I kept repeating to myself at the time was, "Being free doesn't mean being wild." But that was it. I knew that there was going to be more to that sentiment, a Part Two, if you will, but for the life of me, I couldn't come up with anything. Then, on the first night of the retreat, six months later, the second part came to me: *being free doesn't mean being wild. Sometimes, it means being still.*

I recognized, then and there, that I had been living my life wildly. I had been wildly trying to hold onto my own sanity that whole first year as a nurse. I had been trying to buy my own freedom with my own wild striving. It broke my heart to realize that I had no idea how to stop, even after my first year as a nurse was over.

Here is the reality. We cannot have freedom without stillness. If we avoid being still in fear that the act of stillness might bring pain with it, then we hold ourselves captive to our own idyllic versions of freedom. It is *stillness* that frees us to reflect on pain in a way that allows us to better understand and appreciate joy.

We become indebted to so much in this life: our jobs, our relationships, our futures. None of these are necessarily bad things in and of themselves, but when they overwhelm, when they consume, when we cannot take a break and rest in fear of losing them, then we have forsaken our own freedom. The only solution to remedy that error is to rest, but when our burnout feels like it will last forever, it is hard to remember the reality that burnout rarely actually lasts forever.

Three nurses spoke on the finitude of burnout as such:

Chapter 10

"You need to remind yourself that this doesn't have to be for forever. This is just a chapter or season in my life, and God never wastes anything."

—*NM, cardiovascular nurse, ten months of experience*

"I reframe by realizing that I am here in this moment for a reason. It doesn't matter for how long I am going to be there for or even if I am leaving soon—I am there for that moment. I am meant to be there. Even if I don't like it, I still have a purpose for being there for that shift, and I am going to do a damn good job. You can't let those feelings take away from your job. But it is so important to identify that you are feeling that way and to work against it. It is ok to realize that this isn't the spot for you and there is hope that you aren't going to be there forever. I think that takes the pressure off and helps you be more present. It is ok to find freedom in that mindset. The good thing is that there are so many areas in nursing you can go into, so it is ok to feel that way."

—*JW, high risk labor and delivery nurse, ten months of experience*

"When you are burnt out, know that the season that you are in doesn't have to be forever. I would think to myself, 'Is this just going to be my life from now on? Am I going to work twelve-hour shift after shift until I retire?' But no, life is always changing. It is dynamic. Keep talking to people and stay positive. Other job opportunities will come your way, especially with nursing because it is so broad. There will always be other opportunities, especially if you keep working hard. You won't always feel burnt out."

—*AK, NICU nurse and pediatric nurse practitioner, eleven years of experience*

Burnout is only finite if we choose to put an end to it. We can only put an end to it by promoting rest in our lives. Sometimes that rest is taking a vacation or a break. Sometimes it is finding another job. Sometimes it is just taking a small moment for ourselves. But at the end of the day, if burnout isn't addressed, it will completely overtake us.

NEW

But we are not without hope. For though gold melts as it is heated, it can be reshaped. Even while it is in its liquid state, it still holds onto its glittering beauty. Heat may hurt, but beauty can still be found both amidst it and after it.

When a wildfire happens, the plant matter that is reduced to ash fertilizes the soil so that new plants can grow more robustly than before. Therefore, even burnout can hold merit if we let it, for it can bring times of refinement and learning with it. Just because we feel burnt out now doesn't mean that we will always be burnt out in the future. Just because parts of our lives might feel ugly doesn't mean that they won't be made beautiful in time. But in order to stop the burnout from progressing from the realm of refining to devastating, we need to:

1. "Make our pain our power."
2. Reclaim our time.

Both of these topics are ones that we have discussed previously in this book. But how can we do this? We can accomplish both of these things by resting and only by resting. The best way we can claim our time is by making peace with it. As we said in Chapter One: when we make peace with time, we make peace with ourselves.

It is resting between dances that allows the dancer to be able to continue dancing. It is resting between tears that allows the mourner to find comfort. As we have discussed, being able to turn mourning into dancing is what empowers us to be able to live life well, but that too takes rest. It all takes rest, and we are lying to ourselves if we think that it doesn't. If we want flowers to regrow in the garden of our hearts where the fire once was, then that also takes rest.

When we take a moment to rest, we take a moment to remember our own humanity. When we run ourselves into the ground, forgetting to take a break from the personal wars that we wage in an effort to obtain our own goals, we forget that we are in

Chapter 10

fact alive to begin with. It is rest that allows us to reclaim our time and personhood. We are more than the scrubs that we wear. We are more than the jobs that we perform and the titles that we hold. We are more than the new, uncomfortable circumstances that we find ourselves to be in. But we have to slow ourselves down and rest in order to remember that.

Author Ray Bradbury illustrates this idea beautifully in his book *Dandelion Wine*. This book chronicles the summer of a young boy named Douglas and pulls the reader into a time of sunshine and childhood where rest is tangible and life abounds. The main character Douglas has this realization:

"The grass whispered under his body. He put his arm down, feeling the sheath of fuzz on it, and, far away, below, his toes creaking in his shoes. The wind sighed over his shelled ears. The world slipped bright over the glassy round of his eyeballs like images sparked in a crystal sphere. Flowers were suns and fiery spots of sky strewn through the woodland. Birds flickered like skipped stones across the vast inverted pond of heaven. His breath raked over his teeth, going in ice, coming out fire. Insects shocked the air with electric clearness. Ten thousand individual hairs grew a millionth of an inch on his head. He heard the twin hearts beating in each ear, the third heart beating in his throat, the two hearts throbbing his wrists, the real heart pounding his chest. The million pores on his body opened. I'm really alive! he thought. I never knew it before, or if I did I don't remember!"

Maybe it is age that jades us to the miraculous fact that we are alive, or maybe it is hurt and hard happenstance. Either way, we somehow manage to forget the beauty of our own humanity and the miraculous fact that we are alive to begin with. Just as this character took a moment to breathe, to listen, to feel, and to rest, so should we. If we do not, we won't just burn out, but we will lose our own centers. We will lose sight of the fact that we are alive.

NEW

Now as we have said, being alive is no easy feat, but when we rest, we take a moment to reclaim our time on this Earth. With rest, we don't just reclaim our time—we reclaim ourselves.

So my friends, as we tumble towards the end of this book, let's take a moment to rest together. We have all been running towards our own personal finish lines as we have simultaneously been creeping up on the finish line of this narrative. Maybe that finish line for you is completing your first year as a new nurse. Maybe it is finishing your first year in another career field. Or maybe it is just trying to remember your own humanity in whatever new situation that you find yourself to be in. Whatever the case may be, if you want to finish your own personal race well, you are going to need to take a minute to rest before you run that last home stretch.

In the next and final chapter of this book, we are going to talk about what it means to finish something, to graduate from being new and step into simply being human. The gardens of our hearts have been planted, pruned, burned, and have regrown. Now it is time to rest and watch them flourish.

Chapter Eleven:
The Moment You Know You're Going to Make It and the Moment You Know You're Not
(In the Way That You Thought You Would)

We have held the pain of mourning. We have danced in celebration with joy. Now it is time to bring them both together. In the real world, life isn't just one or the other. To quote surgeon, researcher, and writer Dr. Atul Gawande and his book *Being Mortal: Medicine and What Matters in the End*:

"In the end, people don't view their life as merely the average of all its moments—which, after all, is mostly nothing much plus some sleep. For human beings, life is meaningful because it is a story. A story has a sense of a whole, and its arc is determined by the significant moments, the ones where something happens. Measurements of people's minute-by-minute levels of pleasure and pain miss this fundamental aspect of human existence. A seemingly happy life may be empty. A seemingly difficult life may be devoted to a great cause. We have purposes larger than ourselves."

How we get into our deathbeds at the twilight of our lives is largely determined by how we got out of our beds to face life all the mornings that we were alive. Therefore, our time spent on Earth transitions from living one day at a time well to *one life lived well*. We are neither solely mourners nor are we solely dancers nor are we the average of the two. The only reason we separated pain and joy from one another at all was so that we could learn to better

NEW

understand each of them. But truly, at the end of one's life, pain and joy do not stand apart. We are an *aggregate* of our experiences, a collection of our own stories with our hearts and minds serving as the libraries in which those chronicles are shelved.

But unlike individual books, our lives are not limited to one simple prologue and one conclusive epilogue. Throughout the narrative of our entire lifetime, each of us will live out a million different stories. Many of those stories will be interwoven, some beautifully, some messily. Some will have clear-cut endings, and others will never provide us with any sort of solid conclusion.

On the topic of prologues, William Shakespeare wrote in his play *The Tempest,* "What's past is prologue." Conversely, on the topic of epilogues, singer-songwriter Natasha Bedingfield wrote in her song "Unwritten," "The rest is still unwritten."

Though centuries apart, between the sentiments penned by these two artists, the totality of our lives as human beings on this Earth is captured. Our pasts continually serve to set us up for our futures, and our futures stretch out in front of us as blank canvases of the unknown waiting to be painted on. It is the *present* that marries these vastly different tenets of time together. It is how we choose in the here and the now to use our pasts to create something beautiful in the future. As for all the time in between our pasts and futures? Between each of our own personal prologues and epilogues? That is the aggregate which we call life.

When I set out to write this chapter, the painting that I intended on creating for us was one in which we could clearly see what is to be expected when we transition from being new, to just being human. When the countdown to the end of our first year is up, our season of being new is over, and we have reached the once seemingly impossible, life after that becomes just another day.

I originally had this chapter outlined to address what I like to call the tidy ending and the messy ending, and I thought I could simply leave endings at that—chalked up in totality to one of those two options. But as I contemplated these two ideas further, I began

Chapter 11

to realize that many of the endings that we have in life stay with us. Whether they be clean or disastrous, each of our endings uniquely contribute to our next beginning.

For now, before we discuss endings and epilogues, let's start by discussing the aggregate, the arching portions of the narratives of our lives. To take this conversation deeper, we will be exploring a series of three questions that I posed to each of the nurses that I interviewed. To the twenty-five new nurses, I posed the question, "How has your perception of yourself changed?"

This was the final question that I asked each of the new nurses. Incidentally, this was also the question that I enjoyed asking the most as well. There is something beautiful about getting to witness someone rise from that which was previously tumultuous. In multiple interviews, the responses to this question brought tears to my eyes, because in reality, after you have been a nurse, whether it be for one month or one year, you will never be the same.

Then, to parallel that question, I asked each of the twenty-five experienced nurses, "How do you feel your first year as a nurse shaped you into who you are today?"

We mentioned never being the same in the wake of loss in Chapter Eight, but now we will discuss it in the wake of growth. In the life of a nurse, there is a tremendous amount of exponential growth that stems and blooms out of both the times of pain and joy. It is important to remember that growth is miraculous no matter what it sprouts from.

The question I then asked all fifty nurses, new and experienced alike, was, "When was the moment that you knew you were going to make it?"

While these three questions may appear to be very diverse in nature, they are all linked together by growth. As to why the answers to these questions will be clustered together? It is because the answers to each contribute to the aggregate.

In my head, the stories of nurses who finished their one-year race in a whirlwind of colorful, celebratory confetti would represent the tidy ending, whilst the nurses who finished their one-year race dragging themselves, battered and bruised, across the ground would represent the messy ending. The latter ending, while still an ending, was one that left the runner exhausted and overwhelmed. At least, that is what I thought this chapter would be formed by.

But truly, how the end of a nurse's first year appears does not matter nearly as much as what that nurse decides to do with the lessons learned from its conclusion. So, in the end, whether the goals that we set for ourselves are obtained in the presence of victorious confetti or in the presence of gritty mud, the only thing that really matters is how we choose to build off of the growth that we developed during the last race and transition it into the next race that we run.

In reality, those are not the only two possible conclusions for how races can end. Sometimes we don't finish the original race that we set out to run or thought that we had to run. Sometimes we have to forfeit the race altogether. That is where wisdom comes into the equation, for a wise runner knows their body, knows when they are at risk for injury, and knows when to exit the race. In fact, five of the experienced nurses I spoke with left their first nursing jobs before they hit that one-year mark. But do you know what? They still went on to be extremely successful nurses in other areas of the nursing world.

Those three possible conclusions—finishing the race messily, finishing it tidily, or not finishing the original race we set out to run at all—come into play in the very title of this chapter: "The Moment You Know You're Going to Make It, and the Moment You Know You're Not (In the Way That You Thought You Would)."

I want to highlight in earnest that when it comes to transitioning out of the realm of being new and into the realm of regular life, approaching that finish line looks strikingly different for everyone. While we have journeyed together, we might not necessarily conclude together, and we most certainly won't finish

Chapter 11

in the same way. Beyond that, the way in which we finish will most likely end up being a surprise to each of us because the future is always unknown.

One new nurse said this:

"I feel like a million bucks wearing blue scrubs. I feel so proud to call myself a nurse. When I meet someone, I pray that they ask me what I do so I can tell them I am a nurse and then I can talk about it. I love learning all the time, and I love being challenged. I feel happy and proud to be a nurse. As a nursing student, you feel like the bottom of the barrel. No one cares about your being there, no one takes you seriously. But people trust you and look to you when you are the nurse. They listen to what you are saying. People rely on me more, and that makes me feel more confident in my abilities. I feel like nurses can do anything. Now that I am a nurse, it's like I can do anything. It wasn't always like that, but we have such a huge role, and it is so exciting and fun for me to be able to step into that role with people."

—KH, *medical oncology nurse, eleven months of experience*

Meanwhile, a second new nurse gave the following answer:

"It is ok if you hate your job. It is ok if you go into it and you just hate it. I haven't passed that one-year mark to know what it looks like on the other side of the door, but realistically, I feel far from it. One shift at a time, am I right? All I hear is that you just need to stick it out. It'll get better. It'll be fine. But what if it's not? What if I don't make it? What if there is a better job for me out there than this? I don't like this job at all, but people all tell me the same thing. Everything revolves around work, and I see people who have been doing it for years, and they just don't have the character or the heart in it. We need to be real about that, too. [...] I think it has confirmed that maybe I just have a low threshold for dealing with certain types of stress and pressure with deadlines and stuff. Some people thrive in that kind of environment. I don't know how and why, but I don't, and that's ok. It doesn't make me weak or mean that I am a worse nurse. We all have different skill sets, and this just isn't mine. We are all strong in different ways, and that's ok."

—RL, *medical-surgical sepsis nurse, three months of experience*

Perhaps the first statement was more on the confetti end of the spectrum and the second lays more in the realm of mud, but both of these responses to being new are equally valid. In truth, all of the twenty-three other interviews that I conducted with the new nurses lay somewhere in between those two extremes. I celebrated with the first nurse, and I mourned with the second. They are two contrasting reactions, but two equally important realities of what being new can truly be like. What does link these two opposite reactions, however, is this idea that one of the experienced nurses shared with me:

"Most of us are bumpy the first year. For me, it was all about learning how to accept yourself as who you are and not as what you should be. What you go through is a process of realizing what works for you and accepting your own strengths and weaknesses and not comparing yourself to other nurses. That was what I realized my first year. I don't have to be this specific type of nurse or person. God created us as who we are meant to be. Did I fully realize this all in one year? No! It takes years to really be ok with where you are. […]

"The biggest thing on my heart for new nurses is that there is more than just hospital nursing out there. One shoe doesn't fit everyone. The nursing programs teach everything around hospital nursing, and I know that is where most of the jobs are, but I had about eight friends who either dropped out or were kicked out of school because they were just not that hospital kind of person. It is so important for nurses to know that there are other options out

Chapter 11

there. One of my most tender-hearted friends who failed out the first time went into doing private nursing where she works one-on-one with patients, and she was the only one I knew who did that. That just goes to show that there is no one type of nursing.

"For people like me who are emotional, there are other places for you. So many friends of mine were so depressed when they failed out. By the end of my program, seventy-five percent had either failed or dropped out because they didn't want to have to go into the hospital. It was so sad because they went into nursing wanting to help others with compassionate hearts. My biggest thing is to cherish who you are. God has a place for everyone, and he knows who is hurting, which patient is hurting, and he knows how to use you specifically to talk to them. Don't compare yourself to others, and know that there is a place for every personality. If you really want to keep nursing, don't feel like you need to be a certain type of nurse. We don't all need to be cookie-cutter people, fitting one type of nursing. You have to find your niche."

—HG, *hospice nurse, ten years of experience*

Cherish who you are. While we can grow anywhere, to best cherish who we are, we need to find where it is that we can best bloom. This, too, was a lesson that another experienced nurse shared:

"When you keep everything inside and don't talk to someone about the difficulties that you are experiencing, that is when things become too stressful. It is always ok—and this is what I would tell my students—to find an area that you feel is not for you. I just had a student that I was mentoring, the last one that I worked with and became friends with, who wasn't sure if she should be in nursing. I honestly did not encourage her to stay in nursing because she had a deep desire to go into missions and she was having a hard time with all that nurses had to deal with. She was very talented in other areas. She had a strong desire to teach English as a second language in a foreign country on missions. […] She ended up feeling very relieved to go back to a Bible college and into the mission field.

"I would say that if one finds that they don't really fit in with the nursing picture, that is ok. I have been able to talk a lot of students through that process, and I think that is where my counseling degree came in handy. It is ok to not keep doing what you're doing if it is stifling. There are many areas in nursing that one can work, so maybe it is just about finding another area.

"I never wanted students to feel like they were failures, even if they were not doing well in school. Maybe they were just in the wrong area. Maybe they were just having problems because that wasn't where they were supposed to be. Maybe the Lord has something else for them. Maybe they want to stick with it and see what happens. But if not, that is ok. Not everyone has to be a nurse. And that first year is hard. If one is having a lot of problems, first look for another area, take a little time off, research it more, and then pray about it. Sometimes we need the Lord to help us find out where we need to be."

—*WB, hospice nurse, thirty years of experience*

I tried desperately to fit myself into that cookie-cutter mold because I genuinely thought that that is what I should do. Beyond that, I beat myself up for not being able to fit it. It took interview after interview with nurse after nurse for me to begin to realize that all of what I was feeling was ok. My writing this book essentially stemmed from my own needing help, needing advice, needing support, and needing wisdom in making sense of everything that I had gone through during my first year as a nurse. So, yes, I admit maybe I started this book with slightly selfish motives, but I assure you that finishing this book truly is for *you*. To quote the great Elton John and Bernie Taupin's "Your Song," "I know it's not much, but it's the best I can do. My gift is my song, and this one's for you."

While I may not have even a fraction of the answers to life, sharing my own experiences and the hard-earned wisdom of fifty

Chapter 11

of the bravest people that I know so that no one has to go through being new alone is in fact the very best that I can do. That is how I turned my own mourning into dancing. Writing is how I personally decided to take what was painful for me and turn it into something beautiful in order to perpetuate joy, light, and love out into the world. It is what allowed me to keep going in the moments that I most desperately wanted to stop. In the midst of my first year as a nurse, I found encouragement in the words of another new nurse:

"Just keep going, keep at it. Even though it is hard and frustrating, it is rewarding, too, even if you get your butt kicked that day. [...] It is admirable to keep going—it builds character. I kept a little card they gave me in school that said, 'Keep going, ask for help, you are never alone.' We are all in this together. We are never alone. We don't have to be enough—we just have to keep going."

—*MA, emergency department nurse, ten months of experience*

This nurse was completely and profoundly correct when she said that we don't have to be enough, because we are never alone, not in nursing and not in life. In life, we all are unified in six things:

1. We *all* hope.
2. We *all* doubt.
3. We *all* need to be reminded of who we are.
4. We *all* find ourselves in times of sinking and mourning.
5. We *all* find ourselves in times of rising and dancing.
6. We *all* need to reframe our ambitions, name our fears, and make changes that will ultimately keep us healthy and truly alive as opposed to just surviving.

We started this book together trying to navigate what it means to become and stay healthy human beings in the midst of new situations. To do that we became hikers, wedding guests, gardeners, concert attendees, astronomers, weightlifters, runners, dancers, and mourners. But at the end of it all, we simply sat down and took a moment to just be *people*.

Regardless of what we wear to work—scrubs or no scrubs—we have to remember that we were humans before we were professionals. Beyond that, we were humans before we were anything else. But to be holistically healthy humans? We need to keep in mind the six points that were presented above. Let's discuss them in further detail, not just with the stories of nurses, but with the lived experiences of other *humans*.

1. We all hope.

"Overall, I realized that I can do this. It has really built my self confidence that I can communicate with doctors, do scary things, and think critically. It has built my confidence in my own skills and abilities. Even though there are days when I think negatively and harp on myself, I do see qualities in myself that make me think that I will be a good nurse. It is a weird state of feeling humbled, like I am the worst nurse on the unit, but I also feel the confidence that I can do it. It has been a mixture so far for sure, but a positive experience over all."

—*SK, pediatric critical care nurse, two months of experience*

"It is awesome when I get to introduce myself as a nurse. I am so proud, not in a cocky way, but in an I-love-this way. I remember the first time I got to do that. It was amazing, because it is a dream of mine that has been realized. I didn't get into my clinical program right away, but God used that. His plan is good. I had my own mini journey. This dream in me was placed a long time ago, and now I get to live it. I am so thankful, because it is what I hoped it would be. I know it will be hard, but I love getting to help people and getting to see that my best efforts do help them get better."

—*KJ, orthopedics nurse, one month of experience*

Chapter 11

2. We all doubt.

"I thought that I knew myself a lot better than I actually did. I prided myself in knowing who I was and what I like and what I don't like. I used to think I was Type A, that I was a perfectionist, but now actually being in the thick of something, I know that that is not me at all because I don't fit that mold. I don't feel like I fit the mold of a typical nurse. I still am really hard on myself. I don't think that highly of myself, and that has been hard in nursing because I feel dumb. Making mistakes is hard. I wish I could be in something where I could be more expressive and I don't have the weight of responsibility on me. When I am not meeting that expectation, it feels like I am not being the best nurse.

"Nursing is such a glorified job, but I feel like I am not helping anyone. People tell me that what I do is so amazing, but I don't feel the meaning or the depth of what I am doing. I think it is because it feels impersonal to me right now. Maybe I would like ICU more. I want to provide more intimate, long-term care for my patients. My floor is so busy, and we only get the patients for one shift, and sometimes not even the whole shift, because our turnover is so high or they are going for procedures and aren't on the unit. It is hard not being able to get to know them better.

"Like I said, if you had talked to me before this, you would probably think, 'Wow she knows exactly what she is thinking and feeling,' but now I am questioning myself. What am I thinking? What am I feeling? So, I don't feel certain of myself right now."

—BF, *progressive cardiac nurse, three months of experience*

"It has shown me that I am harder on myself than I need to be. Having self-destructive cycles doesn't help anyone. It is ok that I don't feel like I am there yet. It is a prayer of intention. God is ok with my praying for the things that I want to become. The reality is maybe I am not there yet, but he will help me become the person and the nurse that he wants me to be. It is a lot of self-realization.

NEW

[...] I feel like I can do it. It won't be easy or a walk in the park, but I can do it. For the longest time, I felt like I wasn't a strong student, so how can I be a strong nurse? But now I can see that as an individual, I really can do my best and be the best nurse that only I can be. We were defined all through school by the grades that we got, but now we are defined by the care that we give. It is hard to get your mind around that. People care that you care well about people."

—PM, *medical-surgical float pool nurse, two months of experience*

3. We all need to be reminded of who we are.

"I would tell new nurses that honestly, no matter how hard it gets, you will get there. You will become the nurse that you want to be. You will get there. Maybe not in your timing, but in God's timing you will. You will have to go through hard times, but in those times is when you learn how to be a nurse. No one starts out being great at something, and you will have to work hard to get there. I would say to surround yourself with people who will stand around you and beside you to remind you of why you are doing this in the first place, because it is so easy to lose sight of that when things get hard.

"I would feel like I would lose myself when I thought about work. I felt not that smart, but people would remind me of who I really was, that I am smart, I am confident. They would remind me of who I was before all the hard stuff. I am that person. I was just getting lost in my own thoughts of what I am. But they would remind me of the truth of who I was. Don't let the nurse that you think you are say those things to you. [...]

"I definitely feel like it is awesome that I have overcome all that I have had to go through to get to the point where I can say that I am a nurse. I take care of really sick kids. It is crazy to have gone from not feeling like I could do it to taking care of one-to-one critical patients who are intubated in one year. I have grown

Chapter 11

so much, and to see myself taking care of open-heart patients has shown me that I persevered. I faced challenges, I met them, and overcame them. That is who you are. All of these experiences help shape us into who God wants us to be. Yes, you will go through hard things, but it makes you the nurse you were supposed to be. In God's timing, it is so much better. Because I have gone through those things, I feel more competent than I was before. Now I am a nurse that has something to say."

—MO, *pediatric cardiac intensive care nurse, one year of experience*

"Nursing is not going to look the same for everyone. You don't have to start in bedside. You didn't fail just because you are not in the hospital. Nurses are needed in so many different areas, especially within communities that are underserved or overlooked. Just because I don't wear scrubs to work doesn't mean that I am not making the most of my nursing career. It just means that it doesn't look exactly like what I thought it would when I was in nursing school.

"Nursing is your profession, but it is not your identity. It is ok to not do nursing after nursing school. It's not the end of the world. They seem to forget to tell you that in school. I wonder how many people graduate from nursing school, get their license, and stop being nurses? Why is there no research on that? I know so many people who majored in business and don't work in business-related areas. [...] I have always realized that I don't fit the bedside role, and because I didn't fit that bedside-person mold, I used to feel inferior and ashamed of the work that I was doing. But I know now that it is just different, and I am at peace with that. I really love the person that I am becoming."

—DH, *registered nurse consultant, seven months of experience*

4. We all find ourselves in times of sinking and mourning.

"Being new again in a new specialty is disconcerting. You go from a place of being comfortable and competent, and all of a sudden you are not competent again. It is hard. Be ready for that. It is hard to be the one who doesn't know everything again. It is disconcerting, and you have to step back and recognize that you don't have to know everything right away. It is challenging, but I think that it is worth it. You can't let that challenge stop you from pursuing a new opportunity that could be your happy place. You don't know until you try it, and the good thing about nursing is that you can still be a nurse but be a nurse in an area that is completely different."

—*LC, operating room nurse, thirty-seven years of experience*

"My pride took a hit, but it was a necessary hit. I have been graciously humbled by God. Not just humbled as a nurse but humbled in what God is trying to tell me that I need as a person. I realized I had a lot of pride in my life and heart about certain relationships and my ability in other areas. I took a lot of things for granted. While that has been really hard, I am grateful for it. I am still in the middle of working through and recognizing some of those things, but it has changed my perspective in that I don't think as highly of myself, but in a good way, not a self-deprecating way. I can see more clearly in who I am in comparison to God, and I see how much I need him. I have become much more honest with myself.

"It has been such a good thing to become more acquainted with my limits and how to fail. I sometimes think about something someone in school wrote, 'I have the courage to fail well.' That stuck out to me. Before I wanted to avoid failing, but now I know that I will fail. My prayer is, 'How can I fail in a way that is honoring and humbling?' His power is in my weakness. It's how I can point to him and honor him. I know that as a human, I can't do anything apart from him, and when we acknowledge that about ourselves is when we really can succeed. I've been a Christian for how long and I am just now realizing this? But now I have realized it in a genuine way."

Chapter 11

—OR, medical oncology nurse, eleven months of experience

5. We all find ourselves in times of rising and dancing.

"It has shown me how capable I truly am. Going into this, I figured that I wasn't going to struggle. I didn't know it was going to be so hard. Furthermore, I didn't realize how much my failures were going to affect me and how that was going to affect every aspect of my life. It caused me to really doubt myself, and I didn't foresee that. But like I said, I have seen myself rise to the occasion in ways that I didn't think possible. I have seen myself take on tricky situations, patients, and doctors that normally would terrify me. Even though I still don't know what I am doing, it has grown my confidence in that my patients and coworkers like me. I haven't killed anyone. I am so much stronger than I realized. I have made it this far because of my resilience, motivation, and determination, which are all areas that I thought I was once weak in. It translates into my daily life and gives me more backbone and has given me the drive to pursue things that I might not have pursued to begin with. I feel like if I can do this, I literally can do anything. When it comes down to it, I feel like whatever comes next I can handle it."

—JW, high-risk labor and delivery nurse, ten months of experience

"I have realized that I can handle more than I thought I was capable of. In school, I didn't feel like I was capable of much, but now, after handling and dealing with patients, their families, and codes, I have realized that I can handle a lot. I can do it today, next week, and the next week. I have realized that I am also not as strong as I thought I was, but in a positive sense. Because of that I've been able to grow more humble."

—CH, transitional care nurse, five months of experience

"Reflecting back on everything that I have put myself through mentally and physically, it helps me be proud of my hard work. I still don't know everything, and I'm not always confident, but I am so proud of my endurance. When I tell people I am a nurse, I am proud of how much I have put into this to get the results that I have gotten. Other people tell me, 'I could never do that.' I am proud of the work I do and the sacrifices that I have made to get to where I am."

—HW, *medical-surgical stroke and diabetes nurse, six months of experience*

"Overall, my perception of myself is that I am consistently growing and learning, and that is who I want to be. It is not who I am to let fear hold me back. Now I know what it means to overcome fear and be on the other side of that. That is not to say that I won't feel afraid again but that I feel more equipped to handle it. Now I love what I do. I never even saw myself doing pediatrics, but somehow God has opened doors, and I'm not just surviving but thriving. Once I was just hanging on, but now I love what I do, and I can enjoy it rather than just being stressed out."

—MO, *pediatric cardiac intensive care nurse, one year of experience*

6. We all need to reframe our ambitions, name our fears, and make changes that will ultimately keep us healthy and truly alive as opposed to just surviving.

"Don't feel like you are stuck because you are not. I would say to keep your options open."

—TC, *critical care nurse, eleven months of experience*

"We spent so much time in school with a goal to be a nurse, and now that I am one, I have to ask myself, 'Now what is my goal?' That is a little sad to me because now my dreams are gone in a way, but it is because I met them. Now I need to find a new dream, but until, then I am just trying to be a better nurse, travel, pick up new hobbies. It is completely ok to not know if you want to move up specialties or go back to school. I kind of wish someone had told

Chapter 11

me that reaching your dream would kind of mean losing it, but that is ok. Now I can just enjoy life every day."
—*MA, emergency department nurse, ten months of experience*

"I would recommend that you have a short-term goal of what you want your life and career to look like but to also have long term goals as well. [...] Always have goals to try and reach, but at the same time, being flexible for when those goals don't align with God's plan for your life is just as important. I think that is how I have been able to stay sane for all these years: I have goals, but I won't be bent out of shape if that goal hasn't been met because God is in control of my life and will lead me down the path that he wants me to take. You always have to have a new goal. Once you have obtained a goal—and I personally have achieved my long-term goal—you begin to think, 'What is my next goal?' Intertwined in that is preparing a way for them as well."
—*CS, professor of nursing and nurse house supervisor, twenty-five years of experience*

"Nursing is an emotional career. That isn't true for everybody, but it does have its ups and downs. I think everything in life does, but in nursing, it is especially true because you are dealing with people and their lives. I think that you experience emotions in nursing more than you do in the average job. You can always learn something from every job. Whether you love it or hate it or you are there for a long time or a short time, you can always learn. But with that, you don't have to stay at a job that sucks the life out of you. Don't leave at the first sign of challenge by any means, but don't stay just for the sake of staying or for the pride in thinking that you need to do that one thing.

"There are so many different ways to be a nurse. You don't have to stay in the hospital. There are so many avenues and different roles in the community. A lot of times, people who don't like their first job think that they don't like nursing in general, but I would caution against that. Hospital nursing is not the place for everyone. Learn and grow, but also be willing to try things that are different. As you do that in your career and personal life, you will have a better understanding of what is good for you. Find a place that you love. Find what excites you. Ask yourself, 'What kind of population do I enjoy working with?' For me, I want to spend my career focused on those who are marginalized and often seen as the outsiders. Everyone has a place, or several places, where they can thrive. Look for the kinds of positions where you can thrive and learn from all the ones where you don't."

—*KS, community health nurse, eight years of experience*

"One of my biggest takeaways is that you need to take care of yourself. Self-care needs to be a priority. If you don't take care of yourself mentally or physically, you aren't going to be able to take care of other people. It is not sustainable. Just because you can work doesn't mean you always should, whether that is working in general or in a field that isn't the right fit for you. Encouraging people to advocate for themselves as well, doing hard things, challenging yourself, being outside of your comfort zone— it is all ok, but if it is taking too much out of you mentally or physically or taking away from your mental health, don't do it. Life is too important and too short. Find something you feel alive doing. If it is hard and scary that is ok, but if there is joy in the midst of it, it's worth it.

"I really feel for people who struggled with depression their first year. Don't stay there if you don't have to. It's a hard balance because maybe you need to push past it, but don't drive yourself to an unhealthy space where you become sick or suicidal. For me, I pushed myself to work as long as I could physically, but not just because I could. I didn't want to work myself into the ground and make myself so sick that it puts all the other things I want in the future in jeopardy. Don't work that specific job if it is going to run you into the ground."

—*AB, women's oncology breast clinic nurse, four years of experience*

Chapter 11

"Allow yourself to be happy. I think that there is something to be said about putting your time in and getting used to being a nurse, but it took me a long time to realize that I was unhappy. Once I did, I was able to step away from it and do something that would be better for me overall. I don't know where I got this perception, but I thought that I had to be a hospital nurse on the same unit for two full years. Looking back, I was putting so much pressure on myself. I don't know where I got that from. Don't put so much pressure on yourself. [...] It is ok to admit if it is too much. You need to recognize where you are at with your own health. It is ok to admit to yourself that you can't do it all. You don't have to settle."

—*LS, hospice nurse, two years of experience*

So far we have discussed the first two types of endings: the tidy ending and the messy ending. Now it is time to talk about the third ending: the moment-that-you-know-you're-not-going-to-make-it-in-the-way-that-you-thought-you-would ending. The not-finishing-the-original-race-that-you-had-set-out-to-run ending. Let's discuss this type of ending in the lens of my personal nursing journey. This is a story of two parts.

Part One: The Messy Ending

The first part of my own nursing narrative falls into the category of the messy ending. I *did* complete my one-year race. I finished it covered in dirt, but I completed it all the same. I worked exactly one year and one shift as a registered nurse and then *I walked away*.

That's right. I left my job with nothing lined up and with every intention of quite possibly never returning to nursing. When I told people what I was doing, they were surprised to say the least. In fact, you are probably surprised by what I just told you. Beyond that, you might be incredibly angry with me right about now. I mean I would be angry if I read an entire book about how to be

NEW

new and then found out at the end of it all that the moment the author wasn't technically new anymore she quit her job.

But as we just discussed in Chapter One, this isn't a book about how to be a new nurse or new professional well, it is about how to be a holistically healthy human being in the midst of new situations, and in order to be a healthy human being, I knew that I had to leave. It was a hard decision for me at first, especially when I thought about how I might be letting you, my reader, down. I came to realize, however, that I needed to practice what I was preaching. Staying in a job that was crushing me just to prove that I could make it as an experienced nurse? That was not the message that I wanted to send.

The message that I did want to ultimately send can be summed up by the final line of the movie *My Best Friend's Wedding*, which is, "Maybe there won't be marriage, maybe there won't be sex, but by God, there will be dancing." We may not get everything that we hoped for in life. Maybe our dreams will fall short. Maybe our hard work won't pay off. Maybe being new will prove to be too much. The truth simply is that we don't know.

But instead of walking off into the unknown completely blind, we can know that ultimately, with all that we discussed in this book, dancing and beauty will somehow stem from our own lives if we let it. As we have discussed, that is how we can claim our time on Earth well.

My choice was greatly affirmed when an experienced nurse said the following to me in an interview about one month after I had left my job. Little did this nurse know, but he was giving this advice directly to me.

"To give advice to another nurse: quitting doesn't always mean giving up. It means changing your values as a person. We need to make changes that support our values as people and as nurses."

—JS, *medical-surgical renal telemetry nurse, three years of experience*

Chapter 11

My whole first year, I felt like a gambler betting on the uncertain because I tried time and time again to bet on my career in attempts to answer the question, "Will I make it as a nurse, or will I not?" The one question that all new nurses want to have answered is one that I mentioned earlier on in this chapter, and it is one I asked all the nurses I interviewed. That question is, "When was the moment that you knew you were going to make it?"

Synonymous questions could be, "When did it start to hurt less? When did it start to feel like you knew what you were doing? When did it start to get better?" Most commonly, outside of my research and in my personal life as a nurse, a lot of people told me around months eight or nine. Inside of my research, results varied anywhere from the first shift they completed on their own without a preceptor to up to two years and everything in between. For many, it was an aggregate of moments or a sense of competency not attributed to a singular occurrence at all.

As for myself, it was at the end of my eighth month when I knew I was going to make it. I had seen myself grow. I had seen myself improve. I had seen myself become a decent and safe nurse. *That was the moment when I knew I was going to make it.*

Then, at the end of my ninth month, I saw that while I could make it as a nurse on my floor, I didn't want to. *That was the moment when I knew that I wasn't.* Well, at least I wasn't going to make it in the way that I thought I would. All too suddenly, I found myself confronted by the infamous, *Now what?* What was I going to do once I reached the end of my one year? Other people were genuinely concerned for me, but for once, in the face of the extreme wilderness of the unknown, I wasn't concerned for me. As my first year as a nurse ended, I found myself emerging braver than I could have ever imagined. But it was uniquely nursing that empowered me to stand up for myself and fight for myself.

I spent the entirety of that year fighting to get to the point where I knew that if I chose not to fight anymore, it wouldn't mean that I was giving up. Instead, I knew that if I made it to my one-year mark, surmounted what I once thought was insurmountable, and then decided not to fight anymore, I wouldn't be quitting. I would be moving on. I would be making a choice that would empower me to live well and get healthy. I earned the right to make a good decision.

After an adventure like nursing, you will never be the same. After nursing, you will always be a little bit more of a sojourner in the regular world. You don't leave the front lines of caring for others in the context of life and death without a few battle scars. But some scars profoundly remind us of lessons that should never be forgotten. Beyond that, some scars are there precisely to remind us of what we need to share with others so that what we've learned during our times of struggle will not be wasted.

Learning how to be a nurse is what ultimately taught me how to be a human. It is what taught me how to mourn, dance, claim my time, and live life well. Those are lessons that I want to be reminded of often. Those are lessons that we all need to be reminded of often. Nurse or not. New or not.

That is where I was originally going to end the book, but then...

Part Two: The Didn't-Make-It-To-The-Finish-Line Ending

When I wrote the original ending of this book, I was hoping to conclude with my own messy ending, an ending in which I finished the race, even though I was caked in dirt and debris. But the truth is, that isn't where my journey as a nurse stopped. As I mentioned above, that was only Part One.

While I described my messy ending to you in this final chapter, I had originally intended to follow up with an epilogue in which I was going to tell you that I finally got my confetti ending. I was going to tell you that I left the world of nursing for a time, wrote a book, emerged stronger than before, and went into my dream job of emergency nursing, all of which I did do.

Chapter 11

I reached my goal of making it to my one-year mark at my first nursing job, and I then took time off to finish this book. After three months of unemployment, I completed the first draft. One week later, I started as a nurse at an emergency department. I got hired for part-time nights, at a hospital in my direct local community that I had been hoping to work at for quite some time. I genuinely thought it was going to be confetti—hard, scary, and overwhelming—but confetti nonetheless. So I took the position, then I found myself walking right back out of the job a short time later. Had I been wrong to *take* the job? Had I been wrong to *leave* the job? With complete certainty, I can tell you *no* in answer to both of those questions.

We talked about the first two types of endings, the messy and the tidy, the mud and the confetti, but what about the third type of ending? The ending in which the racer never finishes the race at all? Well, this is that ending.

We mentioned this type of ending previously in the context of a racer forfeiting a race because they risk injury, but if we left it at that we would be casting this concept in a slightly negative pallor. Are racers who have to stop mid-race to avoid injury happy about it? Probably not, especially if they have trained tirelessly to run that particular race. More likely than not they are probably extremely disappointed. But since life isn't a race, this metaphor can only be taken so far. My emergency experience is what led me to truly contemplate this third type of ending. It got me thinking, *Is it possible to quit something well? Is it possible to stop well? What about fail? Is it possible to do that well, too?*

One of the nurses that we noted earlier on in this chapter, supplied us with the following notion:

"I have the courage to fail well."
—OR, *medical oncology nurse, eleven months of experience*

If we can learn how to live *well*, dance *well*, mourn *well*, and do

NEW

everything else in between well, then yes, we can most certainly learn how to fail *well*, too. In order to do so, however, we need to redefine what it means to fail.

This is where the ending to my own personal nursing journey comes in. For now, at least as I write this, it appears to be that my career as a traditional nurse is over. But once a nurse, always a nurse. The things we see, the patients we cared for, the people we worked with—they stay with us. After being a nurse, you will always be a sojourner in the regular world.

I don't know if I really like to use the word fail in this situation, but at the end of the day? I didn't necessarily succeed either, at least not in the conventional way. Maybe the career I was planning on went up in smoke, *again*. Maybe my practically guaranteed worldly success was reduced to a cinder, *again*. But do you know what didn't disintegrate into ash this time? Or waste away in the heat of the flames? My mind. My heart. My person.

To me, walking away from all of this with my personal being intact and stronger than before—maybe even wiser, too—is a greater victory than if I had been traditionally successful. I failed. But I did it well. Quitter did not become my name. Failure did not become a weight that I carried. But I was only able to fail well because I was able to reframe my ambitions and name my fears.

We mentioned these two lessons earlier in this chapter, but only in part, which is why they bear repeating in the lens of this third type of ending. For with this ending, the kind where we have to exit the race before we finish, is where we have to do this in full. It is because I had to do this in full that I was able to learn what it truly means to fail well.

I didn't do this alone, however. If I had, this scenario would have ended in true failure, the kind that hurts and diminishes. But this healthy type of failure, a kind that empowers, teaches, and grows, was accomplished in large part because of the leadership team that I was surrounded by. How? They met me with a combination of honesty and grace.

Chapter 11

Towards the end of my emergency job, when I sat down with the leadership team to talk about how I was progressing, they first asked me how I felt everything was going. I had been working with preceptors for the short amount of time that I was there. I had progressed, true, but I still had an inordinate amount of work ahead of me if I was ever going to become independent. We had already extended my orientation time once, and they were kindly obliging to extend it again if needed, but both they and I felt similarly in the following ways: I told them that I could see this reaching one of two conclusions, with me sitting right in the middle of a fifty-fifty split.

The first way I saw things going was that if I continued to precept for longer, really worked for it, studied in my free time, etc., then maybe, just maybe, I would be able to practice as an autonomous ED nurse. But even then, that was a maybe. To work in that setting, your brain has to function in a very unique capacity of rapid critical thinking under chaotic circumstances, which albeit is not my strongest of suits.

That brings us to the second option. Maybe at the end of the day, it just wasn't the right specialty for me. I would've had to rewire my brain to become successful in this department. Not only that, but I would've had to rewire myself. I had done that before to become a nurse in the first place, but would I be able to do it again to become this type of nurse? And if so, at what cost? That got me thinking, *Not every experience is something that we all need to have.*

Emergency department nursing had been my dream for seven years. I worked exceptionally hard for it, and I am extremely fortunate to be able to say that I achieved that dream and lived it out, even if it was only for a short amount of time. But the length of time you spend in the midst of your dream isn't as important as what you learn from it. This was an experience that I was fortunate to have had even for a moment, but I found that it really was just meant to be for a moment, and not the long term, when I realized that being an autonomous nurse in the ED was not an experience that I needed to have.

My momentary time in emergency is a time that I will always look back on well. Beyond that, I am exceptionally grateful for the men and women who I was able to work with during that time. They welcomed me in. I truly felt like we started and ended as family—no hard feelings, no cut ties, just a baby nurse being poured into and encouraged by more experienced nurses. That's a good team. That's good people.

After we discussed those two options, what they both would look like, we also discussed me. As a person and as a nurse, we laid it all out there. Honesty paired with grace. I was affirmed both as a person they genuinely liked and as a good nurse, but maybe I just wasn't the best person or nurse for that specific environment, and that was ok.

I felt beautifully humbled by the whole thing. They took a risk hiring me. They showed me favor by allowing me to train longer. They gave me freedom to decide what I wanted to do in regard to moving forward. Then in the end, they extended me the grace to be able to walk away.

But I was only able to fail well because I didn't have to make the decision alone. If I had gone to them on my own, quit on my own, I don't think I would have been able to fail well. I would have doubted myself and my decision, and I would have felt like I had given up, hadn't measured up, wasn't strong enough, what have you. I would have believed those lies about myself. But instead, together, we were able to uncover the truth in the situation by naming my fears and reframing my ambitions.

1. Naming my fears.

I was afraid to quit. I had never truly failed or quit something before. In my first nursing job, I made it to the one-year mark like I had set out to do. But this? Quitting before I even made it off precepting?

Chapter 11

Quitting before I became an autonomous emergency nurse? Was I only wanting to quit before that point because I was scared? No. As I said, we were able to discuss that this specialty might just not be right for me. That feedback was invaluable, because they were able to speak the truth over me, the fear free truth, that this simply is not a job for everyone. In my case? After their observations of myself and my performance, that could very well be the way things were going to go. And that was ok. Not every experience is something that we all need to have.

2. Reframing my ambitions.

When I was asked what it was that I really wanted to do, I knew almost immediately. I had been giving my one-hundred percent the whole time I was there, but I realized that this was neither what I wanted to give my one-hundred percent to nor *could* give my one-hundred percent to in the long run.

If we force ourselves to rise and lift a weight that we were never meant to carry in the first place, if we white-knuckle and toil, it will ultimately do us more damage than good. Maybe we pushed through and finished that particular race, but if we injure ourselves to the point where we can't ever run again, then what was the point of it all? I didn't want that for myself. If it meant giving up something that was once a dream of mine to stay healthy, so be it. Dreams change, people change, I *changed*. It was time for me to reframe my ambitions.

Therefore, I ultimately decided to quit traditional hospital nursing, *again*. An emergency department nurse was the only type of nurse that I had ever wanted to be, and then I realized that it was not going to be a sustainable option for me. I was the wrong fit, and I knew it, but I only was able to come to that conclusion by trying it.

Often, we tend to think of suffering and mourning as more noble than dancing. But truly, in life, they are equally important. Sometimes we are called to suffer, to hang on for dear life, and to wait it out. But other times we are able to find spaces and margins in life in which we flourish and thrive.

As an experienced nurse said this:

"Be true to yourself, know what you want, and then do that. There is nothing wrong with doing what you love."
—JB, *direct observation and stroke nurse, four years of experience*

Some races are harder than others. Some are easier on the joints. Additionally, some racecourses change as we run them. Sometimes we change as we run the race. There is nothing wrong with finding joy and beauty in what we do as long as we continue to allow beauty to perpetuate from it.

The team at this emergency department helped me to not only achieve and live out my dream— they also helped me let it go. They helped me let go of the idea of finishing a race that, ultimately, I was only supposed to run for a short time. I finished a lap or two, but in order to not sustain injury, I had to stop before I crossed that particular finish line.

One of the nurses who we quoted earlier stated the following:

"It is admirable to keep going. It builds character."
—MA, *emergency department nurse, ten months of experience*

That is true. Pushing through the difficult often does build character. Sometimes that type of growth is good for us and necessary for our overall development. But what is just as important is how we use the character that we have built in the past to make healthier decisions in the future. Therefore, it is just as admirable to know when to walk away as it is to keep going. Being able to make that distinction? It takes a tremendous amount of self-awareness.

So I did fail this time around. I didn't finish this race in a way that the world would deem as successful or in a way that I myself intended or imagined. But I did finish it in a way that freed me and

Chapter 11

will allow me to run the next race and the next by pulling myself out of this one. This brings us to the last area of life which we can endeavor to live well in-*the unknown*.

It is the unknown that serves as the hazy and murky middle, the in the meantime of each of the many stories of our lives. The unknown is where we spend the majority of our time on Earth. After the excitement of new beginnings, before the resolution of conclusions, the unknown is seemingly boundless, and the waiting it brings with it can seem endless.

We find ourselves searching for its horizon, itching for its answers, in an attempt to see how our past selves and current selves will grow into the future, but the unknown is one mystery that we will never be able to fully comprehend. This begs the question, "If it is in the unknown and the waiting where we spend the most of our time, then how do we claim that time well?" To tackle the unknown, we need to first be aware of the following sentiment: the thing about growth is... *it's not linear.*

In conjunction with this idea, Dr. Judy Boychuk Duchscher states the following in her book *From Surviving to Thriving: Navigating the First Year of Professional Nursing Practice:*

"The challenge with painstaking growth is that if we don't grow from it in one situation, 'life' will introduce it again... and again... until we learn whatever lesson it is trying to teach you. You have a lifetime of work ahead—don't rush through your experiences."

As we mentioned earlier, each of our endings uniquely contributes to our next beginning. The only thing is that we don't know how or when that will be made true. Sometimes we may feel like we have grown exponentially. Sometimes we may feel like we have shrunk. Sometimes it is one step forward and two steps back. Sometimes it is moving forward at a rapid pace. Sometimes it is changing the way that we take steps all together. We won't ever preemptively know how the ways in which we have grown will affect our futures; it is often only when we look back that we will be able to see how things have been made beautiful in time.

Therefore, after all of this, we part ways stepping into our own personal areas of the unknown. But, truly, it is the unknown that shapes and grows us the most. While that growth isn't necessarily linear, or even what we expected in the first place, if we give our own personal growth time, we will be able to find peace within the foggy mist of the seemingly endless unknown.

In my tenth month as a nurse, when I initially decided that I would be leaving my first nursing job at the end of my first year with nothing lined up, I realized that I was going to have to face the unknown head-on. To process all of it, I wrote the following poem entitled *Of Trees and Clouds:*

*****

Of Trees and Clouds.

If you want to talk of trees and clouds I am well acquainted
Because clouds and trees are on my mind so profusely it's like they're painted
But as for the forest and the sky I am a stranger
For the clouds and trees loom so thickly I can't see what lies ahead, making my shortsightedness a danger
I can't see the forest for the trees or the sky for the clouds
No matter how high I try to climb, no matter how many times I've vowed
Is it because of my youth, my ignorance, or because I'm too proud?
Is that why I feel lost in my thoughts? Because they ring in a pitch so unbearably loud?
My own voice tells me that the trees are too tall and too many to count
And that the clouds are too dense to see through or surmount
Somehow it's worse to know that the forest and the sky are out there, but that I just can't see them
Because my eyes are acting as fools trying to look at paintings in a darkened museum
Where I'm looking at the art but my mind can't perceive it
Where I hope in my head, but my heart still feels unlit

Chapter 11

Awake! Awake! I cry to my mind
Don't let those thoughts lock you away in a treacherous bind
Don't just look, but see, I beg of my eyes
Don't atrophy, but think, I beg of my mind, don't fade away in the presence of lies
My eyes are cluttered with trees, my mind is shrouded by clouds, and my heart is filled with foxes
Trees which block, clouds which hide, and foxes which overturn the plans I've made, toppling them out of their tidy boxes
It feels like a mess, the inner workings of my heart
And as for the future and choices that I have to make, I have no idea where to start
Will I ever be able to see the forest or the sky?
Or must I wait for the foxes rooting around in my heart to die?
But when I feel my mind's unrest take me to a place where I feel death's hug
I look to the rock from which I was hewn and to the quarry from which I was dug
I remember that trees burn down, clouds evaporate, and foxes run away
In the end stones are the only things that stay
And that is what I am made of, strength and stone
I just have to remember that I don't have to do this alone
For on our own we cannot move forests, wage war against storms, or trap all the world's foxes
But together we can help one another tear down whatever it is that blocks us
From whatever blocks us from our minds and truly seeing
From whatever blocks us from our lives and truly being
And little by little though it will take work and time
The perils of shortsightedness will loosen from our minds
And we will be able to see the forest beyond the trees and the sky beyond the clouds.

*****

In reality, we tend to view the unknown in two ways: as a vicious monster that is chasing us in the night, bringing chaos into our lives once it catches us, or as a heroic champion of ultimate adventure and fulfiller of hopes and dreams.

But, in reality, it is neither. The unknown, quite like time, is not a bipartisan entity. It is neither promising the coming of the bad nor the ushering in of the good. Both of those things may come with the unknown, but the unknown in and of itself doesn't bring good or bad, it simply *is*.

While we cannot control the unknown, we most certainly can choose how we rise to greet it. As for the best way to approach it, we just need to be ready. Ready to mourn. Ready to dance. Ready to do both simultaneously and rest in between. It is when we are ready for the unknown that we allow it to truly grow us; no matter what that growth looks like, no matter what the unknown brings with it.

One nurse alluded to the abstract of the unknown with the following response to the ever increasingly important question, "When was the moment that you knew you were going to make it?"

"I don't think that moment has come for me yet. I see the light at the end of the tunnel, but it is very distant, and I don't know what that light means yet. I have little moments where I feel like I might be ok, but there is no resounding feeling like I am going to be ok. It is up and down right now."
—BF, *progressive cardiac nurse, three months of experience*

We may not know what that light means yet. We may not know what it will bring or when it will come, but making peace with those elements of the unknown and being ok with not knowing is what makes even the frightening aspects of the unknown beautiful.

Dr. Ichak Kalderon Adizes, founder of the Adizes Institute Worldwide, wrote the following in his autobiography *In Search of Love* on the topic of learning:

"Even today, after writing twenty-some books and lecturing in over fifty countries, I feel ignorant. There is so much more to learn, so much more to know, and so much more to tell. There is

Chapter 11

no light at the end of the tunnel. There is no end. Instead I have learned to enjoy being in the tunnel itself."

When it comes to learning, growing, and the unknown, there is no finish line. While certain chapters of the stories of our lives have conclusions—lights that we can look forward to, and mountains that we can surmount—these three integral pieces of life never truly conclude. Therefore, we have to make peace with being in the tunnel of time by recognizing that as we walk *in* it, everything will eventually be made beautiful by our journey *through* it.

As two experienced nurses eloquently put it:

"Nursing in general is such a journey. You are never going to arrive. There is no perfect job. It is going to have its highs and lows, whether that is a day or a season. But it is also just a beautiful way to grow as an individual and as a professional, as well as a way to connect with people. For me, that is the heart of it: connection. I used to think it was about me helping others all the time, but it really is a two-way street. I learn from my patients all the time! If we choose to do so, we can learn from our patients and our communities and the mistakes that we make. There will always be challenges, but we can turn those into adventures. There are highs and lows, for sure, but it is beautiful.

"Nursing is so applicable, regardless of when and how you use your nursing skills. Things that you learn are not wasted, even if it ends up looking different than you expected. Whether it is with one person or with a community, you can ask yourself, 'How can I bring change?' For me, doing community and public health work, it isn't only about working with an individual. I often ask, 'How do we empower a person, or a community, to change?' 'How do we empower people to choose health?' Even if it is something small, like helping people to wash their hands more and, therefore, cutting down on the spread of disease.

NEW

"For me, nursing is about connection and empowerment. I love community health because I get to be with people out in the real world and figure out how to make things work. It involves the same assessment skills, but they are just applied differently. 'Why are people not receiving care? Is it transportation issues? Illiteracy?' It always starts with assessment. Once you get around to evaluating what has been done, you get to learn from what worked well and what didn't. One-on-one work really matters, but for me it is also about how to bring change to communities and how to enable that change to continue and to grow."

—*KS, community health nurse, eight years of experience*

"What I have learned is that my identity is not in my career. No matter what failures I face at work, no matter what praise I get, my identity is in the Lord. No matter what happens in my career, whether I advance as a nurse, quit, or become a mom, my identity is in Jesus, and that is who I am. That is my foundation. God's calling for me is stronger than the calling of nursing. I am thankful that I am a nurse for this season, but if that isn't forever—if he has other things in store for me—I am excited about that too. Nothing is ever wasted. Every minute, every moment of our lives has purpose to it, and all of our experiences have purpose, and we can learn something from everyone."

—*AI, bone marrow transplant oncology nurse, two years of experience*

It is ok not to know, because *'He has made everything beautiful in its time.'* When we know how to plant and grow our own roses in the midst of any and all circumstances, it does not matter if the next unknown season of our lives appears to be barren or blooming, or if the tunnel of time surrounding us appears to be brightly illuminated or darkly foreboding. For when we can get roses to flourish within ourselves, there is no place their beauty can't reach. Therefore, the unknown—whether adorned with effervescent success, shrouded in cataclysmic failure, crusted

Chapter 11

in mud, or glittered with confetti—is always an adventure. And, beyond that, it is always an opportunity for us to grow, whatever befalls.

What it all comes down to is this wise observation that my mom made after reading my *Of Trees and Clouds* poem. Her insight, which perfectly addresses and encapsulates the unknown, life, being new, all of it, was this: "There is no straight shortcut through a forest. Nor an easy approach to the clouds. The trick is to not get lost."

As for what it takes to be ready for navigating the unknown, it is the same as what it takes to be ready for being new. While being new only lasts for a time, the unknown will always stretch out before us. If we can navigate the first without getting lost, then we can successfully traverse the second. We just have to be open to it.

So, my dear readers, my dear *family*, now that we know how to plant and tend to the roses that grow from our own holistically healthy lives, thorns and all, it is time for us to go forth into the world and perpetuate their beauty. It is time for us to go forth, claim our time, and live our lives well.

Epilogue:

I walked out of the hospital for the last time on the morning of February 29th, 2020. I bet you can tell me what happened two weeks later. I didn't want to mention COVID in this book because the devastation and trauma that the disease has brought is something that we are still actively battling as I write this. There are still too many unanswered questions, lives too recently lost, and brokenness that is still too fresh for any sort of conclusion to be reached. When people ask me about it, I am quite frankly at a loss for words. All I can think to myself is, *we do what we can*. Beyond that? I don't know, just like everyone else.

But what I do know is this: as we have discussed, trauma takes time to process and to heal from, and even then, after we have healed, we will never be the same. When I was fifteen, I lost my father. This is a story for another time, one I hope to tell you in full, another day, in another book. But I wanted to mention it now, because we will all go through loss at one point or another and we will all find ourselves asking, *now what?* Life as we know it is over. *Now what?*

When I was first going through that loss, the best advice I got was from the mother of a girl I had gone to elementary school with, who had lost her husband a few years prior. She told me that things would get better with time, but that they would always be weird, and that both of those things were ok. This advice might sound familiar to you, because it is what largely inspired both Chapters Six and Eight. But, that leaves us asking the same question that we have been asking ourselves for the entirety of this book—what are we supposed to do in the meantime?

Epilogue

I personally did not lose anyone to COVID. When quarantine came, I was privileged to be living in a safe space, with enough resources to be able to provide for myself. I had privilege upon privilege upon privilege. Therefore, I have no claim to knowing the full extent of the uncertainty, pain, and grief that came with quarantine. That being the case, I knew that it was up to me to do something positive with my privilege instead of hoard it to myself. So, what I decided to do in the meantime, as the world descended into chaos, was become a disaster response nurse.

Prior to my first field deployment, I was nervous; not because of the possibility of catching the disease, but because of the apprehensions that I personally had toward nursing. But, thinking about all my nursing brothers and sisters who were going to work day after day, battling death in ways that they never had before, allowed me to put aside both my own personal fears as well as the survivor's guilt that I had felt for leaving in the first place. Instead, it was love for them, my family, that triumphed over the feelings of fear and shame. Love for them spurred me to do what I swore to myself I would never do again, which was return to nursing.

This time, however, things were different. Unbeknownst to me, it quickly became one of the most incredible things that I have ever done in my life. During that deployment, things that I had once considered to be ugly became beautiful. On the first night I was there, one of the team members said something along the lines of, "We aren't happy that there is a need, but we are happy to help those who are in need."

Nurses are never happy that there is death and disease in the world, but when we get to walk alongside people during those vulnerable times, that is when the beauty comes in. That is something that I never fully understood until I was deployed. After interviewing nurse after nurse, after working alongside nurses, after watching my friends from nursing school become these amazing bad ass practitioners, I still did not understand why anyone loved nursing as much as they did. Being a nurse terrified me more than anything else in the world. People told me that I just had to find my niche, but, for the life of me, I never thought that I would. I had walked out of Emergency thinking that I was going to be the exception to the rule. I thought that, not only did I not have a niche, I wasn't meant to be a nurse *at all*.

But then, on that deployment, I began to see what the other nurses saw. I began to feel what the other nurses felt. The fears, trepidations, burdens, and weight of it all dissipated into joy. One of the doctors, who I can only describe as pure sunshine, told me, "I've listened to you talk with your patients. You are so good at what you do. This is your calling." And, for the first time in two years filled with pain and doubt, I believed it. For the first time, I thought to myself, *I am a nurse and I love it. I am a nurse and it is an honor.* I am not happy that there is pain. But it is my joy to help those who are in pain.

On my way home from deployment, I couldn't stop crying. I have cried a thousand and one times over nursing, but this time the tears were different. This time I wept, and I mean *wept*, tears of both joy and humility. All I could think was, *who am I to get to do this? Who am I to get to be with and serve people in such a capacity?* Being able to live life with people when they are at their weakest, to love them when they are at their darkest, is the greatest privilege that I have ever known. Now I know what it means to be a nurse.

In nursing, our practice begins with the science of obstetrics, the specialty of caring for those in the midst of childbirth, and ends with hospice, the specialty of caring for those who are in the midst of passing away. We start with birth and end with death, but our jobs are not limited to the realms of those two opposites. Instead, our job is to help others make sense of what lies in the middle. As for what lies in the middle, I can only explain it as such:

In Chapter Five, we described music as being the science of the soul. Let's take a moment to expand on that idea. Our sense of hearing develops while we are in utero before we come into the world. It is also the last of our senses to leave us before we

Epilogue

go out. There is a time to be born and a time to die. What lies in between those two polarities is life itself, and life is a time to sing; to sing songs of joy, to sing songs of lament, to sing songs about everything all at once.

The beautiful thing about nursing is that we get to ensure people's lives begin and end with music. We sing in the delivery room. We sing at the hospice bed. We sing as the chemo infuses. We sing as the anesthesia hits. We sing as the ambulances arrive. We sing as the patients wave goodbye as they get into their cars. Sometimes we sing with our actions. Sometimes we sing actual songs with our faces pressed to those of our patients, cheek to cheek, even if that means that the plastic coverings of our face shields brush up against their ears. In the past, nursing has often been described as an art. But that begs the question, "The art of what?"

After delivering babies with my own two hands, after preparing bodies to be taken to the morgue, I can tell you that there is still so much mystery surrounding both birth and death. Scientists will always endeavor to find answers to the questions surrounding where we go and where we come from, but it is the unique sector of science that is nursing that allows us to ask, "What about *now*? What about *here*? How do we make the life that we have in the present be as beautiful as possible?" Therefore, *nursing is the art of helping others be human.*

I had to wait months between leaving the hospital and going on my first deployment. I spent those months in quarantine predominantly alone. I had the privilege—and I do acknowledge it as privilege—to sit and unpack the ramifications of what it means to be both a nurse and a human. To be a nurse and not practice, to be a nurse and be scared of disease, to be a nurse and, when people ask me for the answers, find that I have none.

The biggest thing that I realized was that although I left the hospital, I never really left the hospital. The sick will always surround us. I don't just mean the physically sick, but the mentally, emotionally, and spiritually sick as well. The person checking your groceries? Sick. The family member on the phone with you? Sick. The person staring back at you when you brush your teeth in the mirror? Sick.

We often don't think of ourselves as fragile until some sort of disaster befalls us. With COVID, suddenly disease and death loomed at everyone's door. Everyone had to reevaluate life as they knew it, not just the patients being admitted to the hospital and not just the nurses taking care of them. We all had to confront ourselves and ask, "Am I well? Am I actually healthy? Am I going to survive this? What was that life that I had been living prior to lockdown? What is it now? And what will it one day be?" Therefore, *nursing is the art of helping ourselves be human.*

As Ecclesiastes scholar Iain Provan once wrote, "Death must teach us things that no one else can." It is through death that I have learned about life, and it is through nursing that I have been allowed to become such a student. And I have learned. My God, have I learned. All the wisdom that I uncovered, though nothing new under the sun, is exactly what we have talked about throughout the course of this book.

My conclusion is this: Nursing *is* the art of being human. It is just as important to take care of ourselves as it is for nurses to take care of their patients. We must do so with gentleness, with kindness, with love, and even with song. That way, when we don't have all the answers, we can be ok with the unknown because we know how to treat ourselves. We can make sense of the in between because we know how to allow for beauty and roses to grow in any terrain, no matter how rocky or forsaken the soil seems to be. And when we can't? Or when we forget how to? We know that we can ask others for help along the way.

Whatever time you find yourself to be in as you read this, whether you are in a time of mourning or in a time of dancing or in a mixture of both, know that I, and the fifty other nurses who

Epilogue

allowed their hearts and lives to be shared within the pages of this book, stand with you. You are not alone.

As I said in the beginning;

Together we live, together we fight
Whether it be within the shadow of darkness or beneath the gleam of the light
So, from the first cry of life, to the last sigh of death, who will journey with you no matter what life pulls from the folds of its purse?

I will, because I am your nurse.

Acknowledgments:

To the nurses who inspired and contributed to this book,

    When I first started the journey of writing this I was scared and lost, but because of you I was able to find my way again. You didn't just build me up as a nurse, you built me up as a person. I will cherish your heartfelt wisdom indefinitely. You influenced me more than you know and I hope that the stories you shared will continue to encourage new nurses for years to come.

To the nurses and health care team that I served alongside my first year as a nurse,

    Thank you for helping me carry the weight, for helping me rise, and for helping me become who I am today. I struggled a lot that first year, but knowing that I had you to stand beside me each shift, gave me the courage to come to work. I originally wrote the poem at the beginning of this book for you for Nurses' Week 2019 and it bared repeating because you are the bravest people that I have ever met.

To the nurses and healthcare teams I have worked with since completing this book,

    Thank you for bringing so much healing to my life. You have taught me to love nursing and have helped make something once so painful, so beautiful and alive with joy.

To my nursing students,

    Thank you for allowing me to learn and grow alongside you. It was an honor to get to walk with you on your nursing journeys. I mean it when I say that we are lucky to have you join us.

To all the nurses and healthcare workers reading this,

    You are my family. Thank you for bringing light into a dark and hurting world. I know it isn't without cost. I am humbled every day to be part of such a profoundly powerful community. I hope I can make you proud.

With love,
T.

NEW

References:

Chapter One:

1) *A Process of Becoming: The Stages of New Graduate Professional Role Transition*
Written By: Dr. Judy Boychuk Duchscher
Journal: Journal of Continuing Education in Nursing
Volume: 39, Number: 10
Pages Referenced: Pages 441-450
Publication Date: October 1st, 2008
Electronically Retrieved: May 16th, 2019
Retrieved From: EBSCO Information Services

2) *The Explosive Origins of the Nobel Prize*
Written By: Juan José Sánchez Arreseigor
Magazine: National Geographic History
Publication Date: October 5th, 2017
Electronically Retrieved: September 26th, 2019
Retrieved From: National Geographic (Online)

Chapter Two:

1) *Healing the Healer: A Caring Science Approach to Moral Distress in New Graduate Nurses*
Written By: Jacqueline van Wijlen, MN, RN, NP
Journal: International Journal for Human Caring
Volume: 21, Issue:1
Pages Referenced: Pages 15-19
Publication Date: January 1st, 2017
Electronically Retrieved: June 18th, 2019
Retrieved From: EBSCO Information Services

2) *Grey's Anatomy*
Season 1, Episode 1: *A Hard Day's Night*
Episode Written By: Shonda Rhimes
Directed By: Peter Horton
Created By: Shonda Rhimes
Produced By: Betsy Beers, Tammy Ann Casper, Rob Corn, Mark Gordon, Peter Horton, Ann Kindberg, Debra Lovatelli,

Tenley Torres Force

Ben Neumann, James D. Parriott, Shonda Rhimes, Gabriella G. Stanton, Krista Vernoff, Harry Werksman
Original Air Date: March 27th, 2005
Original Network: American Broadcasting Company
Production Companies: The Mark Gordon Company, Touchstone Television
Distributed By: American Broadcasting Company
Note: The original line from the pilot episode was, "It's a beautiful night to save lives," but is repeated as, "It's a beautiful day to save lives," throughout the course of the show.

3) *The Brothers Karamazov*
Written By: Fyodor Dostoevsky
Translated By: Constance Garnett
Published By: The Macmillan Company, New York City, NY
Publication Year: 1922
Pages Referenced: Page 55
Electronically Retrieved: October 2nd, 2019
Retrieved From: Google Books

4) *Love Actually*
Screenplay Written By: Richard Curtis
Directed By: Richard Curtis
Produced By: Tim Bevan, Liza Chasin, Eric Fellner, Debra Hayward, Duncan Kenworthy, Chris Thompson
Theatrical Release (United States): November 14th, 2003
Production Companies: Universal Pictures, Studio Canal, Working Title Films, DNA Films
Distributed By: Universal Pictures

Chapter Three:
1) *Reality Shock: Why Nurses Leave Nursing*
Written By: Marlene Kramer
Published By: C.V. Mosby Company, St. Louis, MO
Publication Year: 1974
Pages Referenced: Pages vii-viii & 3-4

2) *From Surviving to Thriving: Navigating the First Year of Professional Nursing Practice*
Written By: Dr. Judy Boychuk Duchscher

NEW

Published By: Nursing the Future, Saskatoon, Canada
Publication Year: 2012
Pages Referenced: Pages 2, 14, & 19

3) *The Brothers Karamazov*
Written By: Fyodor Dostoevsky
Translated By: Constance Garnett
Published By: The Macmillan Company, New York City, NY
Publication Year: 1922
Pages Referenced: Page 55
Electronically Retrieved: October 2nd, 2019
Retrieved From: Google Books

4) *I Never Promised You A Rose Garden*
Written By: Joanne Greenberg (1964- under the name Hannah Green)
Publication Edition: 2009
Published By: Henry Holt and Company, LLC, New York City, NY
Pages Referenced: Pages 107-108

5) Book Description For: *I Never Promised You A Rose Garden*
As Described On: Amazon.com
Written By: Joanne Greenberg (1964- under the name Hannah Green)
Publication Edition: 2008
Published By: St. Martin's Publishing Group, New York City, NY
Electronically Retrieved: September 25th, 2019
Retrieved From: Amazon.com

Chapter Four:
1) *Avatar the Last Airbender*
Season 2, Episode 9: *Bitter Work*
Episode Written By: Aaron Ehasz, Elizabeth Welch Ehasz, Tim Hedrick, and John O'Bryan
Directed By: Ethan Spaulding
Created By: Michael Dante DiMartino and Bryan Konietzko
Produced By: Eric Coleman, Michael Dante DiMartino, Aaron Ehasz, Bryan Konietzko, Alexander Westerman, Miken Wong

Tenley Torres Force

Original Air Date: June 2nd, 2006
Production Company: Nickelodeon Animation Studios
Distributed By: ViacomCBS Domestic Media Networks

2) *Mere Christianity*
Written By: C.S. Lewis (1952)
Edition: A Revised and Amplified Edition, 2001
Published By: Harper Collins, New York City, NY
Pages Referenced: Pages 121 & 128

3) *10 Things I Hate About You*
Screenplay Written By: Karen McCullah and Kristen Smith
Directed By: Gil Junger
Produced By: Jeffery Chernov, Jody Hedien, Seth Jaret, Andrew Lazar, Greg Silverman
Theatrical Release (United States): March 31st, 1999
Production Companies: Touchstone Pictures, Mad Chance, Jaret Entertainment
Distributed By: Buena Vista Pictures

4) *Reality Shock: Why Nurses Leave Nursing*
Written By: Marlene Kramer
Published By: C.V. Mosby Company, St. Louis, MO
Publication Year: 1974
Pages Referenced: Page 230

5) *"Music is the Space Between the Notes."*
Quote By: Claude Debussy
Cited By: Jonathan G. Koomey in *Turning Numbers into Knowledge: Mastering the Art of Problem Solving*
Published By: Analytics Press, El Dorado Hills, CA
Publication Year: 2001
Pages Referenced: Page 96
*Note: This quote is most often attributed to Debussy, but also has been attributed to Motzart, making its true origin difficult to ascertain. In addition, variations of this same quote have been attributed to others as well.

Chapter Five:
1) *Vapor (A Meditation)*

NEW

Performed By: The Liturgists
Written By: Michael and Lisa Gungor
Album: Vapor, Track: 1
Produced By: The Liturgists
Released: March 1st, 2014
Published By: The Liturgists, 2014
Electronically Retrieved: October 28th, 2019
Retrieved From: Spotify

2) *A Theory of Harmony*
Written By: Ernst Levy
Edited By: Siegmund Levarie
Published By: State University of New York Press, Albany, NY
Publication Year: 1985
Pages Referenced: Page 59

3) *The Old Astronomer*
Poem From: *Twilight Hours, A Legacy of Verse*
Written By: Sarah Williams
Published By: Strahan & Co Publishers, London, England
Publication Year: 1868
Pages Referenced: Page 69
Electronically Retrieved On: October 30th, 2019
Retrieved From: The Internet Archive

4) *Why Do Clouds Float When They Have Tons of Water in Them?*
Written By: Douglas Wesley (1999)
Journal: Scientific American- Sustainability
Online Publication Date: June 10th, 2002
Electronically Retrieved On: March 15th, 2019
Retrieved From: Scientific American (Online)

5) *The Gifts of Imperfection*
Written By: Brené Brown
Published By: Hazelden Publishing, Center City, MN
Publication Year: 2010
Pages Referenced: Page 70

6) *I Have Made Mistakes*

Tenley Torres Force

Performed By: The Oh Hellos
Lyrics Written By: Tyler and Maggie Heath
Album: Through the Deep, Dark Valley, Track: 9
Produced By: The Oh Hellos
Released: October 30th, 2012
Published By: The Oh Hellos, 2015
Electronically Retrieved On: November 2nd, 2019
Retrieved From: Spotify

Chapter Six:

1) *2019 Women's Weightlifting Championship*
Video Title: *2019 IWF World Championships- Women's Group 71kg Group A*
Uploaded By: Weightlifting.Archive
Footage From: The Olympic Channel
Publication Date: September 23rd, 2019
Electronically Retrieved On: November 6th, 2019
Retrieved From: Youtube.com

2) *Where Prayer Becomes Real*
Written By: Kyle Strobel and John Coe
Published By: Baker Books, Grand Rapids, Michigan
Publication Year: 2021
Pages Referenced: Page 57

3) *Howl's Moving Castle*
Screenplay Written By: Hayao Miyazaki
Adapted from the Novel By: Diana Wynne Jones
Directed By: Hayao Miyazaki
Produced By: Rick Dempsey, Tomohiko Ishii, John Lasseter, Ned Lott, Hayao Miyazaki, Toshio Suzuki
Theatrical Release Date (United States): June 17th, 2005
Production Companies: Buena Vista Home Entertainment, DENTSU Music and Entertainment, Mitsubishi, Nippon Television Network (NTV), Studio Ghibli, Tohokushinsha Film Corporation (TFC), Tokuma Shoten, d-rights
Distributed By: Buena Vista Pictures

Chapter Seven:

1) *Star Wars Episode III: Revenge of the Sith*

NEW

Screenplay Written By: George Lucas
Directed By: George Lucas
Produced By: George Lucas, Rick McCallum
Theatrical Release Date (United States): May 19th, 2005
Production Companies: Lucasfilm, Mestiere Cinema, Pandora Films, Santa International Film Productions Co. Ltd., CTV Services
Distributed By: Twentieth Century Fox

2) *Ever Yours: The Essential Letters*
Written By: Vincent Van Gogh
Edited By: Leo Jansen, Hans Luijten, Nienke Bakker
Published By: Yale University Press, New Haven, CT
Publication Year: 2014
Pages Referenced: Page 711

Chapter Eight:
1) *"Resilient"*
Definition By: Merriam-Webster's Dictionary
Electronically Retrieved: November 14th, 2019
Retrieved From: Merriam-Webster's Dictionary (Online)

2) *17th Annual Trauma/ Critical Care Symposium*
Symposium Host: Cottage Trauma Center, Santa Barbara Cottage Hospital
Presentation Title: *Prehospital Fire & Mudslide Response- 1-9 Debris Flow*
Presented By: Kevin Taylor, Division Chief of the Montecito Fire Department
Symposium Date: July 13th, 2018

3) *The Two Towers*
Written By: J.R.R. Tolkien (1954)
Publication Edition: Del Rey Edition, 2000
Published By: Ballantine Books, New York City, NY
Pages Referenced: Page 102

4) *Trauma and Addiction: Crash Course Psychology #31*
Video Title: *Trauma and Addiction: Crash Course Psychology #31*
Uploaded By: CrashCourse

Tenley Torres Force

Presented By: Hank Green
Written By: Kathleen Yale
Directed By: Nick Jenkins
Publication Date: September 22nd, 2014
Electronically Retrieved On: November 20th, 2019
Retrieved From: Youtube.com

Chapter Nine:
1) *The Outsiders*
Written By: S.E. Hinton (1967)
Publication Edition: Speak Platinum Edition, 2006
Published By: The Penguin Group, New York City, NY
Pages Referenced: Page 148

2) *Nothing Gold Can Stay*
Written By: Robert Frost
Published By: The Yale Review, New Haven, CT
Publication Year: 1923
Electronically Retrieved: November 23rd, 2019
Retrieved From: The Poetry Foundation

3) *In Lady Gaga's Haus, All Are Welcome*
Interview With: Lady Gaga
Interview Conducted By: Oprah Winfrey
Article Written By: Oprah Winfrey
Magazine: Elle
Publication Date: November 6th, 2019
Electronically Retrieved: November 20th, 2019
Retrieved From: Elle Magazine (Online)

Chapter Ten:
1) *Tower Heist*
Screenplay Written By: Ted Griffin, Jeff Nathanson, and Solomon J. LeFlore
Story By: Adam Cooper, Bill Collage, Ted Griffin, Eric Ehrenhaus
Directed By: Brett Ratner
Produced By: Bill Carraro, Brain Grazer, Karen Kehela Sherwood, Eddie Murphy, Kim Roth
Theatrical Release Date (United States): November 4th, 2011
Production Companies: Universal Pictures, Imagine

NEW

Entertainment, Relativity Media, Rat Entertainment
Distributed By: Universal Pictures

2) *Dandelion Wine*
Written By: Ray Bradbury (1957)
Publication Edition: The Grand Master Editions, 1985
Published By: Bantam Books, New York City, NY
Pages Referenced: Pages 9-10

Chapter Eleven:
1) *Being Mortal*
Written By: Dr. Atul Gawande
Published By: Metropolitan Books, New York City, NY
Publication Date: 2014
Pages Referenced: Page 238

2) *The Tempest*
Written By: William Shakespeare (1611)
Edited By: Frederick James Furnivall
Published By: Duffield & Company, New York City, NY
Publication Year: 1909
Pages Referenced: Page 26
Electronically Retrieved: December 30th, 2019
Retrieved From: Google Books

3) *Unwritten*
Performed By: Natasha Bedingfield (2004)
Lyrics Written By: Danielle Brisebois, Natasha Bedingfield, Wayne Rodrigues
Album: Unwritten, Track: 4
Produced By: Danielle Brisebois, Wayne Rodrigues
Released: November 29th, 2004
Published By: Sony Music Entertainment UK Limited
Electronically Retrieved On: December 30th, 2019
Retrieved From: Spotify

4) *Your Song*
Performed By: Elton John (1970)
Lyrics Written By: Elton John and Bernie Taupin

Tenley Torres Force

Album: Elton John (Deluxe Edition), Track: 1
Produced By: Gus Dudgeon
Deluxe Edition Released: 2008
Published By: Mercury Records Limited
Electronically Retrieved On: December 30th, 2019
Retrieved From: Spotify

5) *My Best Friend's Wedding*
Screenplay Written By: Ronald Bass
Directed By: P.J. Hogan
Produced By: Ronald Bass, Patricia Cullen, Bill Johnson, Gil Netter, Patricia Whitcher, Jerry Zucker
Theatrical Release Date (United States): June 20th, 1997
Production Companies: TriStar Pictures, Zucker Brothers Productions, Predawn Productions
Distributed By: TriStar Pictures

6) *From Surviving to Thriving: Navigating the First Year of Professional Nursing Practice*
Written By: Dr. Judy Boychuk Duchscher
Published By: Nursing the Future, Saskatoon, Canada
Publication Year: 2012
Pages Referenced: Page 140

7) *In Search of Love*
Written By: Dr. Ichak Kalderon Adizes
Published By: Adizes Institute Publications, Carpinteria, CA
Publication Year: 2019
Pages Referenced: Page 225

Epilogue:
1) *The NIV Application Commentary: Ecclesiastes, Song of Songs*
Written By: Iain Provan
Published By: Zondervan Academic, Grand Rapids, MI
Publication Year: 2001
Pages Referenced: Page 148

All scripture quotations, unless otherwise indicated are taken from The Holy Bible New International Version, NIV. Copyright 1973,1978, 1984, 2011 by Biblica Inc.

Glossary:

To allow for better clarity and insight into the medical terminology and nursing language used throughout this narrative, this code links to a complete glossary of terms on my author website for your convenience.

You can also find it here: https://www.tenleyforce.com/glossary

Tenley Torres Force

Author's Bio:

Tenley Force,
RN, BSN, MA

Tenley Force is a writer, disaster response nurse, and seminary graduate, who was born and raised in Southern California. It is her passion to explore what it means to truly be human under the pressures of death and inadequacy, in order to better equip others to live holistically healthy lives.

In addition to serving as a disaster response nurse both domestically and internationally, she has practiced in a variety of settings including medical-surgical respiratory, emergency (briefly), COVID response, school nursing at the university level, and as an adjunct nursing clinical instructor.